# RAINY DAY ECONOMICS

## DESIGNING A SYSTEM THAT THRIVES IN THE WORST OF TIMES

**Written by**
**Joseph Thomas Plummer**

Edited by
Jeff Raderstrong

Foreword by
Jesús M. de la Garza

*For our pale blue dot and our humanity.*

# Foreword by Jesús M. de la Garza

When Joe asked me to write the foreword to this book, I immediately thought of how I first learned about rainy day funds from my mother when I was in elementary school. She used an empty powdered chocolate milk container, modifying it with a cap that had a slit, welded at a nearby garage shop. My daily school allowance was 25 cents for a snack during recess. She encouraged me to save 10 cents daily in my homemade piggy bank before leaving for school. Once the piggy bank was full, we would go to the bank to deposit the savings into a real account, intended for unexpected school supplies. This practice of saving for a rainy day, though on a much larger scale now, has been a cornerstone of my financial planning ever since.

What constitutes a rainy day event? Some rainy days are "Black Swans", which are rare, high impact, and hard-to-foresee events. Other rainy days are more common and easier for us to plan for. The purpose of a rainy day fund is simply to make us more resilient in difficult times.

Resilience is the capacity to withstand and recover from difficulties. Michel Bruneau's 4R Resilience Framework outlines four main characteristics of resilience: robustness, redundancy, resourcefulness, and rapidity. Robustness and redundancy relate to the ability to withstand an adverse event, while resourcefulness and rapidity pertain to the ability to recover from such an event.

Rainy Day Economics is a framework for building societal resilience to prepare for and recover from various types of events. The U.S. Coast Guard motto, "Semper Paratus," which translates to "Always Ready," epitomizes the values of the Rainy Day Economics framework. The framework advocates for a long-term view, focusing on critical societal issues, such as addressing man-made and natural catastrophes like lead in drinking water and Category 5+ hurricanes.

This book articulates a vision of the future where we are all able to thrive together in the face of adversity. Instead of being unprepared for the rainy days in a perpetual state of reaction, the book recommends we focus on five pillars – design, sustainability, human-centered capitalism, resilience, and the arts. As you'll soon read, Joe has a unique set of experiences and education that inform this new vision.

I first met Joe in Fall of 2007 when he enrolled in my Construction Management class at Virginia Tech. Since then, I have witnessed him time and again taking the road less traveled by to try to make the world a better place. His three masters degrees are clear evidence of his thirst for absorbing knowledge and his ability to navigate interrelated, complex subject matter. Joe would tell you that he is a constant work in progress, but I believe this book is a signal that he is hitting his stride and that we can expect a lot more from him in the coming years.

*Jesús M. de la Garza*

# Table of Contents

# Part 1:
# The Foundations
# of Rainy Day Economics

# Chapter 0

## STARTING FROM GROUND ZERO
### September 11, 2001

*"Al Qaeda didn't shout 'Death to Tribeca'. They attacked
America, and these men and women and their response to it
is what brought our country back."*

*– Jon Stewart testifying in front of Congress in 2019*

---

On the morning of September 11th, 2001, I was at Westfield High School in Chantilly, Virginia, just three miles South of Dulles International Airport in the suburbs of Washington, D.C. It was my freshman year in Mr. Anderson's World History class when I first heard the news. Mr. Anderson was one of the more engaging and fun teachers at Westfield. He would play along when we imitated Agent Smith from *The Matrix*, a film which had been released a couple years earlier. We'd annunciate in our best Hugo Weaving voices: "Mr. Anderson," and he would respond with a quote or reference from the movie. While I already knew I wanted to be an architect, Mr. Anderson taught in a way that fostered an early interest in social sciences. I didn't know it or appreciate it at the time, but a lot of the world history lessons in Mr. Anderson's class were related to economics.

Mr. Anderson was giving a typically well-structured lesson that morning, when there was a knock at the classroom door. A woman that I didn't recognize, one of the administrators I think, was going around to every classroom. She looked distraught and serious. She told Mr. Anderson something, and he responded in disbelief. He walked to the front of the class and attempted to give a short explanation that something had happened or was happening, and then moments later he turned on the TV and put on the news. By this time, both of the Towers had been hit as well as the Pentagon.

I grew up in a community of public servants, many of them supporting the Department of Defense and the Intelligence Community. This meant that many of the kids in my school were the sons and daughters of people that served those agencies. My father, a former U.S. Marine Corps Captain, worked nearby for a defense contractor that had hundreds of people at various government agency sites, including a few at the Pentagon that day. Many of our neighbors served government agencies, some of them in leadership roles. On September 11th, it was as if our community was activated. I imagine it was similar for many communities near or on military bases.

One of my classmates left the classroom crying, because her father worked at the Pentagon. It wasn't long before we were all sent home early, but there was a short period of time when all of the planes hadn't been grounded yet. We were uncomfortably close to Dulles International Airport where one of the already crashed planes had taken off from less than 2 or 3 hours earlier, with many planes now circling above us preparing to land or fly into another building, and we were not far from a plethora of other potential targets in Northern Virginia.

The reports would later say that Flight 93 – which crashed in rural Pennsylvania – was likely going to target The White House or The Capitol, but what came to mind for many in Northern Virginia were the dozens of other government agency buildings spread throughout the region. They definitely weren't targeting a field in Pennsylvania though or any rural locations in the American Heartland for that matter. They were targeting what made the United States so powerful and influential in the international community, namely our military, intelligence, financial, and trade institutions.

## A Starting Point for Rainy Day Economics

I'm writing this book in the months immediately following the 2024 Presidential election in the United States. This particular election was without a doubt the ugliest in my lifetime. If I think back to the first time I voted in a Presidential election, in 2008, the rhetoric then between the two Presidential candidates was generally civil. Senator John McCain and then Senator Barack Obama both seemed to have respect for each other and each other's followers.

This respect was witnessed in a powerful and unexpected way on October 10th, 2008, when Senator John McCain was responding to questions in a Town Hall event, and multiple times he refuted his own supporters as they were describing Senator Barack Obama as a terrorist.

*"I have to tell you. He is a decent person and a person that you do not have to be scared as President of the United States."*

*"He's a decent family man, citizen that I just happen to have disagreements with on fundamental issues, and that's what this campaign is all about."*

*- Senator John McCain talking about his opponent Senator Barack Obama (without being prompted to say something nice).*

That was over 16 years ago. The 2024 Presidential election was different. There was no "John McCain moment" where either major party leader in a genuine unscripted way effectively reigned in their more extreme supporters or rose above the mudslinging. But according to many political experts, that didn't matter. What mattered most in the 2024 election was the economy. Maybe that has always been the case, but this time around, it rang more true to me than ever. And so I started writing this book.

Rainy Day Economics is about designing an economy that thrives in the worst of times. I'm going to take you on a short journey through about 25 years of my life, searching for learning moments from what I call rainy days. Rainy days, in this book, are referring to all types of disasters, tragedies, and economic hardships. This term, "rainy days", is a shorthand and a catchall and of course doesn't do justice to the enormous and complex reality of these events and the impacts that they have on so many people. The term allows us to classify and group the worst of times and develop a body of knowledge and a societal architecture to address associated challenges. Over the course of the next 16 chapters, I am going to talk about a wide array of rainy days in rough chronological order, from terrorist attacks and massacres to natural disasters and health-related events. I'll talk about the rainy days experienced by individuals, families, communities, cities, and countries. I'll unpack some of the challenges we face as we design and redesign our economics for rainy days. And, I'll talk about some of our institutions that are tasked with making our society more resilient.

To help serve the conversation and also to reveal my own biases and perspectives, I am going to tell some personal stories of mine and also discuss parts of my educational and career path. I'll also tell some stories of others I've met over the years. I'll weave in events from recent history that many will be familiar with, and I'll also make some references to popular music, movies and other cultural aspects of our society, which will hopefully make some of the ideas in this book more relatable and digestible. This form of research and writing is most closely aligned to autoethnography, which is an approach that describes and systematically analyzes (graphy) personal experience (auto) in order to understand cultural experience (ethno). This book is not a rigorous scientific inquiry, and it is also not intended to be a traditional memoir. Rather, it is a personal exploration of economics that I am sharing with the world in the hopes that it might serve a societal conversation.

Rainy Day Economics, as I've defined it, has five key pillars, which you will see illuminated in different ways from chapter to chapter. The five pillars of Rainy Day Economics are as follows:

1. **Design:** As William McDonough once said, "Design is the first signal of human intention." Place-based architecture, civil engineering, and urban planning inform intentionally designed systems.

2. **Sustainability:** Long-term thinking and strategic foresight are essential in order for society to thrive. Three common frames are utilized – environmental, social, and financial.

3. **Human-centered Capitalism:** The underlying operating system of our economy must serve humanity. Humans are more important than money, and therefore success is measured by improvements to quality of life (Yang).

4. **Resilience:** We strive to reduce probability of failure, consequences of failure, and time to restoration, and we assess resiliency using the 4Rs – robustness, redundancy, resourcefulness, and rapidity (Bruneau).

5. **The Arts:** As we see time and again, creative expression in all forms is vital to individuals, communities, and the country when trying to understand and navigate difficult times.

It is my hope that this Rainy Day Economics framework will advance our societal architecture, the systems we design, build, and iterate on together to improve quality of life for everyone, especially in the worst of times. Furthermore, I am going to try to make the case that government at all levels, but especially the federal level, is a force for good in the United States.

Rainy Day Economics will hopefully engage a broad coalition of humans interested in improving our society's economics, but my intent is to first engage those that are open to ideas, the people that from time to time change the way they vote, and also those that at times choose to disengage from the conversation. The independent, frustrated, flip-flopping, change-seekers are the people that I think have the most power to influence the direction of our society.

Rainy Day Economics may turn out to be an ideal primer for young economics students in the distant future. And, as you'll read in the chapters ahead, the education of an economist is and always will be, in my opinion, ripe for new iterations, permutations, and evolutions. The education of economists is becoming increasingly influenced by place-based conversations and learnings. Like architects, economists are responsible for understanding the place in which they are practicing economics.

Imagine you are designing a house for you and your family or a community center for your neighborhood. Your house and neighborhood exists in a place that has unique characteristics and a community with many people that have opinions and perspectives, some similar to your own and some different. This is simply a book of design ideas for our economy informed by personal stories. You don't have to like or agree with every design element of the house you live in or the community center where your kids go to play. Likewise, you don't have to agree with every designed system in the economy. You also don't have to participate in the design of your house, your community center, or our economy. But the design of our economy, like our democracy, thrives when we all participate in the process.

As you're reading this book, pretend you are a master architect that just had an intern submit an initial design. Critique the ideas. Write your thoughts and feedback in the margins. Replace entire chapters with your own stories. Iterate in whatever way you feel compelled to iterate. This book is not a treatise, and you are not a cog in a machine. You are an intelligent human with an active and creative mind, and you've lived an interesting life with hardships of your own that are valid that can inform this conversation. As Robin Williams proclaimed in the movie *Dead Poets Society*, *"No matter what anyone tells you, words and ideas can change the world."* This book is intended to be a conversation starter and you are meant to contribute verses and ideas and stories to inform our society's economics so that everyone can thrive.

As we delve into different rainy day stories, think about how you relate to the places, the people, the communities, and the institutions that make each story unique. This first story is about the September 11th terrorist attacks in 2001. It is important to remember that the terrorists attacked the United States of America, and not just New York City and Washington, D.C.

## *Hijacking an Economy*

When I started writing this book in the days and weeks following the 2024 Presidential election, I wasn't sure where to begin. And then I heard the famous song by Bastille called "Pompeii." The song poses the question *"Where do we begin? The rubble or our sins?"* It quickly became obvious that I had to start from Ground Zero. The September 11th terrorist attacks exemplify how rainy days can hijack an economy if we aren't intentional about how we design our societal systems. The impact of the September 11th terrorist attack can still be felt today and the ripple effects have not yet subsided even now more than two decades later. The terrorists didn't just hijack planes on September 11th. By executing a successful attack at such a large scale, they also successfully hijacked our economy. The impact was not just the death and destruction on that day. We have to account for everything that has happened since that day because of the attacks.

This includes all of the health impacts to the first responders that were at Ground Zero searching for survivors and cleaning up debris after the two towers fell. This includes the cost of the wars in the Middle East, both the upfront cost and the cost to support veterans when they came home. This includes the national debt that we incurred to pay for those wars in the Middle East. Accounting for all of the direct and indirect costs associated with a terrorist attack is essential in order to design a system where terrorists aren't able to continue to erode the quality of life in America so many years after they executed their attack on us.

To give us a sense for how effective the 9/11 terrorist attack was at hijacking our economy, it is useful to look at federal deficit spending in the United States. The last fiscal year where the federal government had a surplus was the one immediately preceding the September 11th attack. For those that don't know, the federal government's fiscal year goes from October 1st to September 30th. From October 1st, 2000 to September 30th, 2001, the federal government successfully operated under budget with a surplus to the tune of about $130 billion.

If the terrorists hadn't attacked us on September 11th, the federal government could have reduced the national debt for the first time since 1957. In 2001, the federal debt was in the neighborhood of $5.8 trillion. If we do some basic math, it tells us that paying down the national debt might've been feasible in a reasonable amount of time if we were to have sustained surpluses at a similar level to what was achieved in 2001. Contrast that to the national debt today, which simply cannot be paid down with modest budget surpluses.

The terrorist attack caused an initial shock to the economy, which slowed tax receipts, but the bigger impact to the economy was caused by a significant increase in federal government spending on homeland security and war in the Middle East. The creation and operation of the Department of Homeland Security alone added a trillion dollars in spending over the 20 years that followed the September 11th attack.

This book is about designing our economy with rainy days in mind. September 11th, 2001 is just the first of many rainy days that I'm referencing as case studies for this conversation. To generate some creative thinking on rainy day economics, I'm going to also suggest some design prompts throughout the course of this book to help us iterate on the system of systems that make up our economy.

> ***Rainy Day Economics Design Prompt 1:*** *Imagine for a moment that we knew the September 11th terrorist attack was going to happen exactly as it did, but we couldn't prevent it from happening. How might we design our economy such that we wouldn't have to utilize deficit spending in the aftermath to move forward?*

This design question is not an easy one to answer. Some, including myself, will argue that we shouldn't have gone to war after the September 11th terrorist attacks, at least not the way and at the scale that we did. And this would in some ways nullify the design question above, because if we didn't go to war, there may not have been any deficit in the years following 2001. Others will argue that we had to go to war, and there was no getting around it, and we had to go to war at the scale that we did in order to prevent another attack.

There are a number of political arguments that are attached to questions of fiscal spending in times of war. If the consensus of the day is pointing to war, then the design question above is paramount and must be answered. How do we defend ourselves from physical attacks, while not becoming susceptible to financial warfare where our enemies can bait us into continuous massive deficit spending? This is relevant to all rainy days, not just terrorist attacks. This is directly related to the 1st and 2nd pillars of Rainy Day Economics – design and sustainability.

For society to advance, it is useful to discuss merging some elements of fiscal and monetary policy. I'm not the first, and likely won't be the last, to suggest that fiscal and monetary policy should be combined, at least in some areas of our economic design. What's the difference between fiscal and monetary policy? Fiscal policy is what we do with our money. It is how we approach our budget and what we decide to budget for. Monetary policy is about how money exists and how much money exists at what value and velocity with what interest rates in our economic system.

There is such a thing as scarcity of money. In my opinion, 20+ years of deficits and a ballooning national debt is an indicator of scarcity of money. We as citizens can argue about what we should or shouldn't spend money on, but the reality is we've sent our elected officials to Washington, D.C. for over 20 years to decide what to fund together at the national level, and time and again the result has been deficits. So, that to me is an indicator that there is a desire of our republic, according to our aggregated elected representatives, to do more than the tax revenues of the last 20+ years would fund. The question that merges fiscal and monetary policy is *"how do we make it so that we can fund all of those budget line items that made it through the legislative and executive branch while also paying down the national debt in a reasonable amount of time?"* Naturally, it is an optimization problem that is solvable using straightforward computational modeling coupled with a fair and transparent Congressional budget process that is more closely aligned with annual tax revenue and rainy day funds.

As Robert Wright describes in his book, *One Nation Under Debt*, America's national debt has been engrained in our country's story, including our successes and our failures, since the beginning. One of the key relationships that Robert Wright highlights in his book is the relationship between wars and national debts, where throughout world history nations will take on massive debt to go to war, and as a result will later feel the impacts of that debt in significant ways. After reading even just a little bit about the major wars of the past few hundred years, it becomes apparent that nations might not go to war as often if they aren't able to finance them.

*"Instead of saving for a rainy day to come, most likely a war, governments wasted surplus income on frivolities — trinkets, pageants, 'splendid buildings… and other public ornaments.' During an emergency, like a major war, taxes inevitably proved too low and too slow to meet the need. Borrowing became a dire necessity."*

*- Robert Wright, One Nation Under Debt*

Robert Wright's book also illuminates the wisdom associated with the federal government taking on a healthy amount of debt when needed under some constraints. Our states have retained some of this wisdom over time. At the state level, we expect budgets to be balanced and to include rainy day funds for economic downturn and for natural disasters among other potential scenarios. But most states in America are able to take on debt under certain constraints.

The notion of creating and utilizing rainy day funds at the federal level seems like an obvious low-hanging fruit to navigate an uncertain future and also to mitigate the impacts of a ballooning national debt. We may need a reset moment, though, where we navigate quickly to zero or low national debt and implement a variety of customized national rainy day funds and endowments.

Our ability as a country to finance societal efforts by utilizing debt at times makes our ability to thrive possible, but debt can also be used to commit a country to war without confronting the difficult conversations with citizens that might be disgusted by the thought of sending young people into hellish conflicts. Debt enables citizens to become complacent and desensitized to war. In the United States, we don't often see the impacts of war in our daily lives, but first responders and soldiers carry with them the trauma of war long after an attack or battle or emergency response.

## The Long-term Impacts of the Terrorist Attack and the War

When firefighters, paramedics, and police officers in New York City responded to the attack on September 11th, they were exposed to toxic chemicals from the collapsed World Trade Center buildings. Residents and workers near the World Trade Center were also impacted. According to the Center for Disease Control, "An estimated 400,000 people were exposed to toxic contaminants, risk of physical injury, and physically and emotionally stressful conditions in the days, weeks, and months following the attacks." The first responders faced the most acute exposure at Ground Zero where they worked for days, weeks, and in some cases months to search for survivors, put out fires, and clear debris. These toxic chemicals included asbestos, lead, cadmium, polycyclic aromatic hydrocarbons (PAHs), and other hazardous substances. As time went on, the effects of that exposure have taken a toll on those first responders.

There are long-term impacts that extend years beyond what we might consider the inciting rainy day. If we are serious about designing a system where people can thrive in the worst of times, then we must consider the long-term ripple effects that continue for decades after a rainy day event. Unfortunately, in recent years, first responders and their advocates have been forced to go to Congress to beg for support as they navigate the health impacts of the September 11th attack. Jon Stewart's testimony to a House of Representatives Committee in June 2019 was a compelling reminder to Congress that they decide what gets funded and for how long at the federal level and it is their job to make sure what is important gets funded.

*"The official FDNY response time to 911 was five seconds. Five seconds.*

*That's how long it took for FDNY, for NYPD, for Port Authority, for EMS, to respond to an urgent need from the public. Five seconds. Hundreds died in an instant. Thousands more poured in to continue to fight for their brothers and sisters.*

*The breathing problems started almost immediately, and they were told they weren't sick, they were crazy. And then as the illnesses got worse and things became more apparent, 'Well, okay, you're sick, but it's not from the pile'. And then when the science became irrefutable 'Okay, it's the pile, but this is a New York issue. I don't know if we have the money.'*

*. . .*

*Mr. Johnson, you made a point earlier and it was one that we have heard over and over again in these halls. And I couldn't help but to answer to it, which was he said, 'look you know, you guys are obviously heroes and 9/11 was a big deal, but you know, we have a lot of stuff here to do and you know we got to make sure there's money for a variety of disasters, hurricanes, and tornadoes', but this wasn't a hurricane and this wasn't a tornado. And by the way, that's your job anyway! We can't fund these programs, you can.*

*Setting aside that no American in this country should face financial ruin because of a health issue, certainly 9/11 first responders shouldn't have to decide whether to live or to have a place to live.*

*. . .*

*And I am awfully tired of hearing that it's a 9/11 New York issue. Al Qaeda didn't shout 'Death to Tribeca'. They attacked America, and these men and women and their response to it is what brought our country back. It's what gave a reeling nation a solid foundation to stand back upon to remind us of why this country is great of why this country is worth fighting for, and you are ignoring them! And you can end it tomorrow.*

*Why this bill isn't unanimous consent and a standalone issue is beyond my comprehension. And I have yet to hear a reasonable explanation for why it'll get stuck in some transportation bill or some appropriations bill and get sent over to the Senate where a certain someone from the Senate will use it as a political football to get themselves maybe another new import tax on petroleum, because that's what happened to us in 2015, and we won't allow it to happen again."*

In 2002, economists at the Federal Reserve Bank of New York published a detailed account of just the short-term economic impact of the World Trade Center attacks. These costs included the loss of earnings, property damage, cleanup costs and the shock to the New York City economy. Their findings suggest that the attack on the World Trade Center cost somewhere between $33 billion and $36 billion. This of course didn't include any indirect impacts.

The wars and conflicts that followed September 11th have cost over $8 trillion according to the United States Treasury. It is conceivable that the country would have still been involved in some of the conflicts in some way even if the September 11th terrorist attacks hadn't happened. However, the scale of American warfare after 2001 was clearly enabled by a nation in mourning and a federal government that seemed to be willing to move (or blow up) mountains to find and kill the people responsible for the September 11th attacks.

According to the Watson Institute for International and Public Affairs at Brown University, over 15,000 U.S. military service members and U.S. contractors and over 400,000 non-U.S. civilians have died in the Middle East as a result of the post-911 wars. The impacts of these wars will be felt for many years. Did our leaders know that the prolonged conflicts would cause the United States to go into deeper national debt? Did they know the impact that the deficits and national debt would have on our public discourse? Did they know how many lives would be lost in those conflicts? These are difficult questions to answer. Focusing on sustainability, the second pillar of Rainy Day Economics, allows and encourages us to consider these long-term scenarios and impacts and prevent them or prepare for them.

# Chapter 1

## FIRST IN, LAST OUT
### August 29, 2005

*"Resilience is the immune system of our nation."*

*- Admiral Thad Allen, United States Coast Guard*

---

The summer of 2005 was the beginning of my higher education journey. I had been rejected from Virginia Tech's prestigious architecture program, but I was determined to become an architect. I was admitted to two other architecture programs out of state at Miami University in Oxford, Ohio and Northeastern University in Boston, Massachusetts, but my girlfriend at the time was admitted to Virginia Tech, and I wanted to make it work with her. I was also admitted to George Mason University's civil engineering program, and a long-distance relationship with my girlfriend was logistically easier if I went to an in-state school. Out-of-state tuition was also considerably more expensive, so the choice was easy.

I decided I would try to transfer to Virginia Tech's architecture program after my freshman year at George Mason University. I was going to do everything I could to make my Virginia Tech architecture school application competitive the following spring, even though I knew they only accepted five transfer students from outside the university every year.

I was a mediocre student in high school, spending more time running and playing ice hockey than studying. The summer after high school I worked residential construction and took an English Composition class at night. I figured English was my worst subject, so my strategy was to devote as much time and attention to solely that class for the months preceding my first fall semester in college. The strategy worked as I earned an A-minus, which surprised me a little bit given that I wasn't a good writer. To this day, I'm still trying to figure out how to write well.

That English Composition course set the tone for the next couple years of college for me. I knew I wasn't the smartest kid in any class, but I figured out a rhythm to studying that I never had in high school. I committed to a regular cadence of at least a few hours a day in spaces where I wouldn't be interrupted. When things didn't make sense, I would study more. I signed up for Fall semester courses attempting to challenge myself while not cratering my chances at performing well enough to transfer to Virginia Tech. The Fall course lineup was as follows:

ECON 103 – Microeconomic Principles
ENGL 201 – Reading and Writing About Literature
ENGR 107 – Introduction to Engineering
ENGR 183 – Engineering Computer Graphics
MATH 113 – Analytic Geometry and Calculus I

To be honest, I was a little bit intimidated by this course schedule. While I had already taken calculus in high school, it had been a struggle. I knew English would be a major time sink given the amount of reading, and the engineering classes, while engaging, were known to be challenging. The class I knew nothing about was Microeconomic Principles. I had never taken an economics course in high school, and I didn't really know anything about economics going into that semester. The required text for the economics course was Henry Hazlitt's *Economics in One Lesson*. Hazlitt's book undoubtedly shaped my worldview and my understanding and opinions about economics as I found myself constantly evaluating his ideas with a healthy mix of skepticism and curiosity.

*"The bad economist sees only what immediately strikes the eye; the good economist also looks beyond. The bad economist sees only the direct consequences of a proposed course; the good economist looks also at the longer and indirect consequences. The bad economist sees only what the effect of a given policy has been or will be on one particular group; the good economist inquires also what the effect of the policy will be on all groups."*

*- Henry Hazlitt, Economics in One Lesson*

As I was starting my first fall semester of college, I read and heard pieces of the initial news of Hurricane Katrina heading towards the Gulf Coast of Mississippi and New Orleans. I remember not thinking much of it at first, as there had been numerous tropical storms and hurricanes in my lifetime, and this just seemed like the normal news you get in advance of a major storm. On Monday August 29th at 11:30 am Eastern Time, I started my first economics course. At that exact same time, President George W. Bush declared emergency disasters in Louisiana, Mississippi, and Alabama. In the days, weeks, months, and years that followed, the massive impact of Hurricane Katrina and the scale of the government response slowly sank in.

I remember talking to my father in the days following when Katrina made landfall. I could hear it in his voice on the phone. When I asked him about what was going on, I remember him remarking simply, "It's bad. The levees broke." One of my friends from high school had joined the United States Coast Guard and was part of the response to and recovery from Hurricane Katrina. As I was listening to lectures on economics, calculus, and engineering, he was helping people through one of the worst times in their lives. The more I read about what was going on, the more I wanted to get out of the classroom and go do something to help.

The United States Coast Guard was the first in to provide significant organized response to the disaster. U.S. Coast Guard helicopters and boats rescued people from rooftops and flooded streets, and also provided information to the National Guard and the Federal Emergency Management Agency (FEMA). The U.S. Coast Guard rescued 33,544 people in the aftermath of Hurricane Katrina.

For all of the rainy days in this book, the "response" is referring to the immediate actions taken to rescue people and provide essential aid in the days and weeks following an event, and the "recovery" refers to the long-term process of rebuilding infrastructure and communities impacted by an event. Both response and recovery are part of the 4th pillar of Rainy Day Economics, which is resilience. There are four characteristics of resilience, which are 1) robustness, 2) redundancy, 3) resourcefulness, and 4) rapidity. All of these characteristics of resilience work together to reduce the probability of failure, the consequences of failure, and the time to restoration.

I didn't travel down to the Gulf Coast of Mississippi to help with the recovery until months later during a school break. The United Methodist Volunteers in Mission (UMVIM) organized opportunities for churches to send volunteer groups down to effected areas to help families rebuild homes. The church I had grown up in, Floris United Methodist, organized a few initial trips in the months following Hurricane Katrina, and one of them was specifically designed for college students on breaks from classes.

We caravanned down to Mississippi with a group of about 30 people. One of the leaders on the trip was from Mississippi, and he had already led a few volunteer groups immediately following the disaster. I remember him talking about the United Methodist's *"first in, last out"* mentality when responding to natural disasters. Driving into the effected area after the disaster was eerie. We could tell how high the water was in certain places by the markings on the trees. As we got closer to the coastline, there were empty concrete slabs where homes used to be and pockets of piled debris alongside the road even after months of cleanup efforts.

There was a building that housed all of the volunteers, and it was right on the Mississippi coast with a beautiful view of the Gulf of Mexico. A handful of the volunteers were runners, so a couple of the mornings or evenings on each trip would include a run along the road that paralleled the coastline. Our time during the day was spent rebuilding homes for people, which usually included basic framing, drywall, and painting. At night, we would all gather to eat dinner together and then play card and board games. By the end of each trip, we had only slightly advanced the completion of a few houses. There was no way that our volunteer efforts alone were going to get the Mississippi Gulf Coast communities back on their feet in a timely manner.

Over the course of my undergraduate education, I volunteered on five of those United Methodist mission trips to the Gulf Coast of Mississippi. That seemed to be the limit for most people, because people had to work. There are a few people I know that found a way to go down 2-3 weeks a year, but for most people that wasn't possible. Floris United Methodist Church is a particularly large congregation and was able to send a few groups of people down to the Gulf Coast of Mississippi every year for at least those first 4-5 years after Hurricane Katrina made landfall. But there was clearly a limit to the number of volunteers that would engage and the number of trips that would happen every year.

That limit was determined by a number of variables. How much time off from work could people get to go on these volunteer mission trips? Most people in the United States get 2-3 weeks of paid vacation that is accrued, so it is hard to predict how many people will have the time available. How much money did it cost to go on these trips? These volunteer trips weren't super expensive, but there were costs to volunteers. How many people were willing and able to volunteer in this way? Not everyone is cut out for heavy lifting or long days in the heat and humidity of Mississippi. How many people had other personal priorities taking up time in their lives?

There are countless life events that are prioritized over volunteering for a mission trip, as they should be. Caring for the young, sick, and elderly at home is a common reason for not volunteering.

Even if there were an unlimited supply of volunteers from faith communities across the United States, it wouldn't make sense to rely on them to facilitate an entire natural disaster recovery. It would just be too slow and inconsistent. And to be honest, the quality of homes built by volunteers committed for a week is generally going to be lower than homes built by people working consistently and specializing over weeks and months. The fact that we as a society rely so heavily on faith-based communities for natural disaster recovery is not wise or healthy. However, college students and young adults are ideal agents of recovery as they generally don't yet have young kids or elderly parents to care for, and they are generally more willing to commit their time to volunteering. Young adults are also generally less jaded, and they can upskill in a matter of weeks to build higher quality homes.

> ***Rainy Day Economics Design Prompt 2:*** *Design a system that engages thousands of volunteers when they are young adults to help communities recover from natural disasters and to strengthen communities that have experienced economic hardship.*

The reason why we need to design a system to engage thousands of volunteers on rainy days is because these events that we are talking about create regional emergencies that far exceed the capacity of a solely local or even state response and recovery. In the case of Hurricane Katrina, tens of thousands of military and government personnel were activated for the initial response. This is an important part of Rainy Day Economics, because the scale of most of the events necessitates help from outside the region, and not just on the day of the event. Understanding the scale of rainy days is important, because it allows us to design appropriately sized systems that will allow us to adequately navigate similar rainy days in the future.

*AmeriCorps and our nation's volunteer capacity*

The United States actually already has a system for engaging thousands of volunteers when they are young adults (and also old adults) to help communities recover from natural disasters and to strengthen communities that have experienced economic hardship. AmeriCorps was created over 30 years ago by the National and Community Service Trust Act of 1993. The beginning of the AmeriCorps VISTA program goes back even further to the 1960s, an idea originating from President John F. Kennedy and then created by the Economic Opportunity Act of 1964.

AmeriCorps members take the following pledge:

> *"I will get things done for America – to make our people safer, smarter, and healthier.*
> *I will bring Americans together to strengthen our communities.*
> *Faced with apathy, I will take action.*
> *Faced with conflict, I will seek common ground.*
> *Faced with adversity, I will persevere.*
> *I will carry this commitment with me this year and beyond.*
> *I am an AmeriCorps member, and I will get things done."*

In the years that followed Hurricane Katrina, AmeriCorps programs had over 100,000 participants that provided an estimated 7.7 million volunteer hours helping communities in the Gulf Coast region rebuild and recover. The result was over 15,000 homes repaired or rebuilt. AmeriCorps is the type of designed program that Rainy Day Economics seeks to inspire. The program adds to our society's capacity to respond and recover from natural disasters.

If you think about the time and number of people it takes to build one house, then you can start to grasp how much time it would take to recover from a natural disaster that destroys 100,000 homes. For example, if you know it takes 10 people a month to build one house, then you can calculate how many months it would take 1,000 people to build 100,000 homes. Simply divide 1,000 people by 10 (the number of people required to build one house per month), and we get 100 houses per month if we have 1,000 people. And so if we are able to build 100 houses per month with 1,000 people, then it will take 1,000 people 1,000 months to build 100,000 houses.

We can also flip the calculation to tell us how many people we would need if we wanted to rebuild 100,000 houses in 10 months. We'd simply divide 100,000 by 10 months to get 10,000 houses per month and then multiply that number by the number of people required per house (10) and the result is 100,000 people. I've used fake numbers here to articulate how to do a basic estimation. In reality, it takes a lot of time and resources to coordinate volunteers with the appropriate skillsets to build houses from scratch. However, we can reduce the time to build to a matter of weeks with less people per house if we utilize modular design and prefabrication. These types of solutions can effectively address and integrate all five pillars of Rainy Day Economics – design, sustainability, human-centered capitalism, resilience, and the arts.

## Designing and prototyping healthy post-disaster housing and green schools

There were a number of failures in the response to Hurricane Katrina, as well as in the recovery process in the years that followed. If you're interested in a set of deep historical accounts of the hurricane, *The Great Deluge* by Douglas Brinkley is the book to read. Douglas Brinkley captures the nightmarish series of events and some of the tragedies that happened during and after the hurricane due to government mismanagement.

Acknowledging the failures in our responses to rainy days will allow us to develop better systems, but if we ignore the failures, then they will be repeated in the future. Similarly, if we choose to eliminate government agencies when they make mistakes, then people impacted by rainy days will be worse off in the future.

In response to Hurricane Katrina, FEMA deployed over 20,000 travel trailers and mobile homes to provide shelter for people in the Gulf Coast region that had lost their homes. Studies would later find that thousands of those trailers and mobile homes that FEMA deployed emitted formaldehyde high enough to cause adverse health effects including coughing, chest tightness, nausea, and skin rashes. While there has been some investment in advancing post-disaster housing since Hurricane Katrina, there is still a lot of room for improvement.

> ***Rainy Day Economics Design Prompt 3:*** *Design a healthy, environmentally sustainable home that can be easily mass-produced for victims of natural disasters. Design a system to either store or manufacture thousands of these homes and deploy them within days of a disaster.*

Post-disaster green building is not only important for housing. Green building can help communities revitalize their built environments and create the conditions for a thriving local and regional economy post-disaster. Healthy schools are also particularly important for students, teachers, and parents to recover from disasters. After Hurricane Katrina, the City of New Orleans established the Recovery School District and developed a Master Plan that rebuilt or renovated 85 schools over 10 years. The schools were designed to be long lasting, resilient, energy-efficient, and high performing buildings at the center of communities. Green school designs prioritized day lighting, fresh air, and good acoustics, which are crucial building characteristics to foster student learning.

## *Design of Cities, the Army Corps of Engineers and why the levees matter*

During my second semester at George Mason University, I signed up for a course titled "Design of Cities" that was particularly relevant to what was happening in New Orleans in the months and years following Hurricane Katrina. The course was essentially a primer on urban planning. The other courses I took that semester were core general education courses.

ARTH 311 – Design of Cities

CHEM 211 – General Chemistry I

ECON 104 – Macroeconomic Principles

MATH 113 – Analytic Geometry and Calculus II

PHYS 160 – University Physics I

The Design of Cities course focused on the history of Washington, D.C.'s urban planning and some of the notable architecture in the city. The City of New Orleans and Washington, D.C. have some similarities. Both are built on, near, around and in the middle of wetlands. When people say they want to "drain the swamp" that is Washington, D.C., they are referring to the bureaucracy and corruption, but the saying originated from the notion that the city is built on undesirable wetlands. Both New Orleans and Washington, D.C. are laid out in grids with some major diagonal roads crossing the cities. Both cities have architecture and urban planning with significant French influence.

The City of New Orleans, however, has faced more difficult engineering challenges. Perhaps the most notable of which is keeping water from flooding the city during major storms. In metropolitan New Orleans, the average elevation is 1.8 meters below sea level. The city maintains dry conditions by utilizing a complicated system of levees, pumps, and upstream control structures on the Mississippi River. During the Hurricane Katrina disaster, the system of levees, pumps, and upstream control structures failed catastrophically. As a result of this system-wide infrastructure failure, 80% of the city was flooded to depths up to three meters.

The Army Corps of Engineers had used the previous storm of record from the past century to design for what they considered to be the most severe storm that could be considered reasonably characteristic of the region. The storm of record had winds of 101-111 miles per hour. Hurricane Katrina had winds of over 120 miles per hour. In total, there were over 160 miles of damaged levees and 50 breaches, which increased flooding by at least 300% according to the American Society of Civil Engineers. One engineering question that emerged was *what should be the design hurricane?* In other words, as engineers are designing levees and flood management systems, what are the wind speeds and water levels that they should design the structures to withstand?

There were countless civil engineering, city management, emergency preparedness, and design questions that came out of Hurricane Katrina. And, there were numerous system and organizational failures that can serve as learning moments for future leaders. Many of these failures and learning moments are documented in Douglas Brinkley's book *The Great Deluge*. During the evacuation of Greater New Orleans the day before Hurricane Katrina made landfall, cars were leaving at a rate of about 18,000 per hour, but there were over 110,000 residents that didn't own or have access to a car. The Superdome stadium was refuge to over 25,000 people, but during the storm parts of roof were ripped off by the extreme wind, and the surrounding area was flooded. Emergency generators at hospitals in the region failed and stranded hundreds of staff and patients without power for lighting, air conditioning, or medical equipment. The State of Texas housed over 220,000 evacuees from Louisiana in shelters and hotels, but there were still so many people stranded in the region. These are challenges that cities will continue to face with every major storm.

Evacuation, emergency power, healthcare, and shelter should all be top of mind for city managers, economists, engineers, and elected leaders.

## Learning abstract design, divergent thinking, and the value of iteration

In 2006, I was admitted to Virginia Tech's prestigious architecture school, and in order to stay on track, I was required to take a summer studio course – the *Qualifying Design Lab*. In that first design studio in 2006, we were given a prompt to design a cube with certain features and constraints. After a week of working on this, our class presented a pristine and unique portfolio of cubes to the professor on a long table in the main lobby of the architecture school building, Cowgill Hall. The cubes were made of everything from wood to metal to plastic. Our class had utilized the amazing facilities available to us, which included a wood shop, a metal shop, laser printers, and screen-printing rooms. By all accounts, these were finished products that we had all worked hard to complete by the deadline.

The professor looked at the cubes and pensively circled the table seemingly searching for something. He eventually broke the silence with a question.

> *"How many of you would be ok with me smashing your cubes with a baseball bat?"*

Complete silence. No raised hands. What was wrong with our cubes? Did we miss something in the prompt? The professor went on asking more questions.

> *"What if I told you these cubes were completely wrong, and that you needed to start over?"*

Half of the class had stayed up all night just to get the current cubes finished on time, and the idea of completely restarting seemed daunting. The professor then switched gears a little bit and asked the opposite question.

*"What if I told you these cubes are perfect, and that I need you to make a thousand more by the end of the semester?"*

Our class was sufficiently confused. Were our cubes good or bad? We knew there was no way we could finish making a thousand cubes by the end of the semester. The impossibility of the timeline indicated to us that it was clearly a hypothetical, so the room started to warm up. The lesson that day was about process.

None of us wanted our cubes smashed with a baseball bat, because we liked what we had made. We had invested time, money, and creativity to make those cubes. And, if they weren't what the professor was looking for, then we would've been sad that we didn't get it right. And, if the professor thought the cubes were perfect and really did want a thousand of them by the end of the semester, we all knew that we didn't have the time or the money to make that many that quickly. The professor explained that we were there to learn about process and about how to think and question and critique. Once we understood that, we were free to experiment, and we became more curious and more creative.

We spent the rest of the time that day critiquing cubes and asking why design decisions were made and how each student addressed the constraints of the prompt. At the end of the day, the professor gave us another prompt to design a new cube with different constraints and features. Our class was teeming with new ideas. The professor gave us permission and direction to not show up with singular finished cubes next time, but rather to show up with new approaches, ideas, experiments, questions, and struggles.

From that point on, our goal wasn't to get the right answer on the test of making a cool cube. Instead, our goals were to be curious and to ask good questions and to recognize tensions and contradictions and pain points and tripping points and to acknowledge the inspired work of others. These fundamental principles of design are essential to Rainy Day Economics. As we think about how to design our societal system of systems, we should strive to recognize tensions, contradictions, pain points, tripping points, and acknowledge the good work of others as we iterate towards a better and better-designed society where everyone contributes to the process.

## Timeless Societal Architecture

After making it through the Qualifying Design Lab over the summer, I was excited to progress into the 2nd year of architecture school, where the design prompts were less abstract. The buildings that housed the architecture and industrial design studios were overflowing with creativity going into the Fall semester in 2006. You could walk through the open floor plans and see hundreds of projects coming to life. Each student had their own desk, and the desks were not like the desks in a high school classroom. These desks were like doors that had been converted into working tables, on average maybe three feet deep by six feet wide, for designing and constructing models of buildings, products, and furniture.

Around the edges of each architecture studio sat the graduate students with projects that were much further along with elaborate drawings pinned to the walls. The professors' offices were often adorned with modern furniture and eye-catching examples of designs that they and their students had worked on in the past. The architecture library was a different kind of library. Not only was it filled with inspiring books, it also had modern furniture that was in some cases designed by students, and in other cases it was famously designed furniture by designers that we would eventually study in our classes.

That year was an immersive experience where every class we took related to the others, and we were in a constant state of hyper-stimulated inventiveness. When I spoke to non-design students, there was a sense that everything they were learning was theoretical. When I spoke to design students, everything was a step away from being drawn or prototyped or modeled or in some cases fully built. In fact, there were people in the architecture studios working on the post-disaster housing I mentioned earlier. There was also a team of older students competing in the U.S. Department of Energy's Solar Decathlon working to build a house powered entirely by solar energy. There were industrial design students that prototyped furniture that was still in use when we graduated. There were students that mastered how to design shoes and then went on to work for the biggest shoe companies in the world.

The second year architecture curriculum didn't have much room for electives. Most of our time was spent in the studio working on designing our first buildings. The time we spent in traditional classrooms was focused on the history of architecture and structures. My second year course load was as follows:

Fall 2006:

ARCH 2015 – Architecture II
ARCH 3115 – History of Architecture I
ESM 3704 – Basic Principles of Structures
MATH 1535 – Geometry and Mathematics of Design I
WOOD 1234 – Introduction to Wood Science and Forest Products

Spring 2007:

ARCH 2016 – Architecture II
ARCH 2034 – The Art of Building
ARCH 3116 – History of Architecture II

ARCH 4075 – Building Structures I
MATH 1536 – Geometry and Mathematics of Design II

Sometimes I wonder how many people we need to be working on societal problem sets and what kinds of professionals we need most. Architects, engineers, and designers must be at the top of the list, the creative, action-oriented professionals that have been trained to construct everything from the tiny components in the phones we use to communicate to the structures that keep our cities from flooding during a hurricane. Frank Gehry once said, *"Architecture should speak of its time and place, but yearn for timelessness."* What if the design of the systems that make up our societal architecture yearned for timelessness? What if the levees never fail again?

Design is the first pillar of Rainy Day Economics, because without design, we are simply in a constant state of guesswork and reaction. Everything in this book is going to tie to the five pillars of Rainy Day Economics, but design will always be the first and most important signal of our society's intentions to create better systems. The other four pillars of Rainy Day Economics – sustainability, human-centered capitalism, resilience, and the arts – all emerge after first adopting a design perspective and process.

# Chapter 2

## WHERE DO WE GO FROM HERE?
### April 16, 2007

*"No one deserves a tragedy."*

*– Nikki Giovanni*

---

It was an unusually cold night some amount of days before April 16th. My roommate and I hustled to get ready for an intramural softball game. A couple of the other guys were waiting for us out in front of our residence hall, West Ambler Johnston. We all piled into an old black Jeep Cherokee and drove over to the intramural fields across from Lane Stadium. We met the rest of our beloved intramural team on the field and began warming up in the brutal cold. Before the game, our team captain gave a rousing speech in an effort to get us to forget about the cold. It was a great speech that could've been placed in any film about the college experience. The essence of the speech was, "It's brutally cold, but we're still here!"

It was an epic game for the ages. At some point during the game, my roommate managed to wipe out on his way to first base and consequently messed his shoulder up pretty bad. We encouraged him to walk it off. Later that night, my roommate woke me up and asked me to take him to the hospital. We began our trek to pick up my car at "the cage", which was just a fenced-in parking lot at the edge of campus. This was my first trip to the Montgomery Regional Hospital, which was an easy 10-minute drive from campus. When we arrived at the Emergency Room, I remember being underwhelmed with the hospital's facility and staffing. I was comparing it to facilities in the DC area, which were of course bigger and better staffed. My roommate ended up being fine, just a gnarly sprain.

On April 16th, I woke up and got ready the way I always did for class. We lived on the third floor of West Ambler Johnston. When I got down stairs to the exit nearest D2 (the main dining center), there were police officers waiting checking ID's and writing down names. After I left the building, I let my roommate know that he should remember his ID. It was possible then to make it through a day without using your student ID to get in and out of buildings, so it wasn't unusual for people to forget their student ID.

I proceeded towards the Drillfield heading to my Building Structures class, which was in the Pamplin bridge classroom. I went around the far side of D2 (the main dining center) nearest War Memorial gym. My girlfriend lived in Main Campbell, which was on my route to class, so it was easy to stop by in the mornings sometimes. When I got to the Drillfield, I turned left towards the crosswalk in front of East Campbell.

Immediately after I turned, there was a series of noises across the Drillfield to the right of Burrus Hall near Patton Hall, one of the engineering buildings. I turned while still walking and almost ran into someone. The guy I almost ran into said, "Did you hear that? It sounded like a bunch of people screaming." I stopped briefly and looked with him, but then continued on. I started walking across the Drillfield watching the area in front of Patton Hall as I walked. I couldn't tell what was happening. I started hearing sirens getting louder as I reached the other side of the Drillfield. I was just reaching the crosswalk when a police car sped into the one-way Drillfield loop in the wrong direction and was heading straight for me. This was unusual even for an emergency. Cars, including emergency vehicles, only go one direction around the Drillfield. Under no circumstances had I ever seen an emergency vehicle drive that fast and in the wrong direction on the Drillfield loop. It just didn't ever happen. As it got closer, I noticed one of the front tires was flat. As it passed in front of me, I saw the front wheel was creating sparks. The police vehicle pulled up onto the curb to the right of Burrus Hall.

I stopped and looked over at the area in front of Patton and Burrus, and I still couldn't see what was going on. I was all about getting good grades and not being late back then. Walking over to see what was going on didn't cross my mind. I walked up to the Pamplin Bridge where my Building Structures class was to take place. When I got there, no one was in the classroom. I was early, but not that early. I began walking around the bridge and Pamplin Hall. I could see the Drillfield from the Pamplin Bridge. I walked around to the Pamplin Hall atrium passing a class on the left on the way there that was in session. There were many people in the atrium as there often were. I walked back to the bridge. I saw ambulances pass on the Drillfield going towards Patton Hall, again in the wrong direction and at high speed.

I heard the door to the class that was in session open. People from the hall were walking in to see the TV. The instructor had turned on the TV. I walked by and stepped in. I was immediately reminded of where I was on September 11th, 2001. The memory of my freshman year world history teacher Mr. Anderson at Westfield High School answering the door and walking to the TV to turn on the news. The class reactions were similar too. I heard screams in the Pamplin atrium. I walked out to the atrium, and no one was there. Someone said a SWAT team had just come through. I walked back to the bridge. I tried calling my girlfriend. I stood by the window on the bridge for a long time. I saw the Cadets posting up along the walkways outside telling people to get inside. The ambulances kept passing on the Drillfield. I walked back to the classroom where the TV was. The headline indicating a shooting at Virginia Tech, Norris Hall.

I walked back to the bridge. I remember thinking the other section of the Building Structures course had class in Norris or one of the buildings next to it. All second year architecture students were required to take the class. My phone was useless, as was everyone else's. No one else was on the bridge. I saw two of the Cadets talking and continuing to direct people indoors. I sat down in the bridge leaning up against the wall of my classroom. An older woman saw me and suggested I get inside a classroom. I stayed watching the ambulances go by on the Drillfield. I had a pretty good idea of what was going on at this point. The ambulances seemed endless. At some point, I was able to get in touch with my girlfriend. She had been getting calls from friends and family. We didn't have smart phones then. The first iPhone was actually released later that year.

It seemed like hours later, before we could leave the building. After getting out of the building, I went straight to my girlfriend. She had been able to check in with some people. I remember getting back to my room in West Ambler Johnston. Everyone that day had two tasks. The first was to answer the phone when possible and let people know that you were alive. The second task was to check in with everyone you knew at Virginia Tech. I remember being worried about everyone I had ever known or met at Virginia Tech. My high school, Westfield High School, had sent 30 to 50 students of each graduating class to Virginia Tech. "Are you ok?"… "Yes, are you ok?"… "Yes." There were so many short conversations that day that meant so much.

Walking out of West Ambler Johnston with my roommate, there were reporters and camera operators with lists of names asking everyone that was leaving the building if they knew any of the names listed. My roommate and I were completely silent and ignored the reporters. The reporters just wanted a reaction, a story that would increase their ratings.

On April 17th, which seemed like days later, Virginia Tech held a convocation ceremony at Cassell Coliseum. As my girlfriend and I were waiting in line outside, we ran into a friend from high school. Again, not many words exchanged. Phrases like "how are you doing?" had a lot more meaning, as did the short responses. A nice bus pulled up right next to us while we were in line. Some of the students in line were quietly asking who the people getting off the bus were. They all looked familiar, but I couldn't place them in my mind until Senator Mark Warner got off the bus, and then I looked again at the others and realized it was a bus full of our elected officials from Virginia. I think that was when I realized the world was watching. The entire federal legislative delegation of Virginia came to Blacksburg. President George W. Bush flew in from Andrews Air Force base with Governor Tim Kaine, who was on an economic development trip in Japan, but had rushed back to be with us.

Perhaps the most important moment during the convocation was right after Nikki Giovanni finished her poetic speech. I cannot begin to describe the kind of sadness I was feeling when she walked up to the microphone. It seemed as if there was nothing that anyone could say to make things ok. She began to speak to us, saying exactly what we needed to hear. The moment she finished her speech, I heard the loudest roar of emotion from the packed Cassell Coliseum, a level that I hadn't ever heard before in any stadium or arena and haven't heard since then. Lane Stadium is loud, but the roar of emotion that I heard that day was on another level. And then someone started the chant, "Let's go Hokies!"

*Nikki Giovanni's poetic speech, April 17, 2007*

*We are Virginia Tech.*
*We are sad today, and we will be sad for quite a while.*
*We are not moving on, we are embracing our mourning.*
*We are Virginia Tech.*
*We are strong enough to stand tall tearlessly, we are brave enough to bend to cry, and we are sad enough to know that we must laugh again.*

*We are Virginia Tech.*
*We do not understand this tragedy. We know we did nothing to deserve it,*
*but neither does a child in Africa dying of AIDS, neither do the invisible*
*children walking the night away to avoid being captured by the rogue army,*
*neither does the baby elephant watching his community being devastated for*
*ivory, neither does the Mexican child looking for fresh water, neither does the*
*Appalachian infant killed in the middle of the night in his crib in the home*
*his father built with his own hands, being run over by a boulder because the*
*land was destabilized. No one deserves a tragedy.*

*We are Virginia Tech.*
*The Hokie Nation embraces our own and reaches out with open hearts and*
*hands to those who offer their hearts and minds. We are strong, and brave,*
*and innocent, and unafraid. We are better than we think and not quite*
*what we want to be. We are alive to the imaginations and the possibilities.*
*We will continue to invent the future through our blood and tears and*
*through all our sadness.*

*We are the Hokies.*
*We will prevail.*
*We will prevail.*
*We will prevail.*

*We are Virginia Tech.*

We went home later that week. My girlfriend and I stopped at James Madison University on the way back to visit friends. It turned into a reunion of sorts. A bunch of us got together for lunch. The conversation seemed about normal when one of my best friends started to ask me if

I had seen any movies recently. He was going through movies that he'd seen recently or that he knew were in theaters and so he asked me, "Joe, did you see *The Shooter*." The other people at the table overheard this and were taken aback that he would ask such a question. I began to explain that I didn't, and my friend quickly realized what I, and the others at the table, thought he was asking. He was referring to a movie that had been released weeks earlier called, "The Shooter" starring Mark Wahlberg. My friend was just trying to distract me with conversation about the latest movie. That moment seemed to be a reflection of how much guns had permeated American culture.

When we came back to the Virginia Tech campus, there had been an outpouring of love to our community. Letters, videos, pictures, posters, sculptures, art, and so many mementos of love and support started showing up on campus from people across the country and from people around the world. The most memorable messages came from the elementary schools and other universities. I had never seen or felt that kind of community and love before.

**Today we are all Hokies.**

*Cartoon by Ben Lansing*

We were in a strange haze. We felt love pouring in, but there were a lot of people still hurting and not knowing what to do. Some of the architecture students got together to tie orange and maroon ribbons around the Drillfield trees, but that didn't seem like enough. One musically talented student at some point wrote a very powerful song that captured how so many were feeling during that time, the main line in the song was *"Where do we go from here?"*

There were also artists that came to campus to perform to help us lift our spirits and move forward. Perhaps the best-known artists to perform were Dave Matthews Band, John Mayer, Phil Vassar, and Nas. On September 6th, 2007, they joined together for "A Concert For Virginia Tech" at Lane Stadium. They all waived their fees for the event. The concert was free to students, faculty, and staff.

It is difficult for me to describe how important art and music was in the wake of the Virginia Tech tragedy. Nikki Giovanni's poetic speech, the countless creative expressions of love that filled the Drillfield and the student center, and the Dave Matthews Band concert were sustenance for us. Art and music pulled us out of survival mode and back to learning and thriving mode. The excerpt below from Ethan Hawke's 2020 TED Talk resonates with me and articulates the importance of art in difficult times.

*"Most people don't spend a lot of time thinking about poetry. Right? They have a life to live, and they're not really that concerned with Allen Ginsberg's poems or anybody's poems, until their father dies, they go to a funeral, you lose a child, somebody breaks your heart, they don't love you anymore, and all of a sudden, you're desperate for making sense out of this life, and, "Has anybody ever felt this bad before? How did they come out of this cloud?" Or the inverse -- something great. You meet somebody and your heart explodes. You love them so much, you can't even see straight. You know, you're dizzy. "Did anybody feel like*

*this before? What is happening to me?" And that's when art's not a luxury, it's actually sustenance. We need it. …*

*And I believe that we are here on this star in space to try to help one another. Right? And first we have to survive, and then we have to thrive. And to thrive, to express ourselves, alright, well, here's the rub: we have to know ourselves. What do you love? And if you get close to what you love, who you are is revealed to you, and it expands."*

*- Ethan Hawke, June 2020 TED Talk*

Another grand gesture of kindness came from the New York Yankees who donated $1 million to the Hokie Spirit Memorial Fund and announced they would travel to Blacksburg for an exhibition game. This was a big deal in our small college town. I grew up rooting for the Seattle Mariners, and so Alex Rodriguez was one of my favorite players. Rodriguez was quoted the day of the exhibition game saying, *"There are certain things that happen that are so devastating that time stops. For me, this is one of them. This is probably the proudest day I've ever worn a Yankee uniform."*

There was a day a couple weeks after the massacre that my roommate and I again jumped into the same old black Jeep Cherokee to go play softball with our beloved intramural team. We were fairly certain that the remainder of the intramural season would be cancelled, but decided to practice anyway. "Gotta get ready for playoffs." That practice was the first time I had seen all the guys since the 16th. I've played a lot of sports, on a lot of teams, and had a lot of practices. I think that was the most important practice I ever went to, and not because we needed to prepare for a game or playoffs. There were no more games that season. There were no playoffs. That practice was the current short-term answer to the question – *"Where do we go from here?"* We all needed something normal and fun to do together.

# Chapter 3

## WHEN THERE IS NO PREVENTION MECHANISM
### May 4, 2007

*"We found a way to reason together. We found a way to
have common ground. We had true, honest, open dialogue.
And we agreed to disagree on some issues."*

*- Mayor Bob Dixson of Greensburg, Kansas speaking at TEDxHerndon
2016*

---

What would you do if your home was completely destroyed overnight? I don't mean what would you do the next day. I mean what would you do in the medium and long term? Would you move somewhere new and start a new life? Would you rebuild your home exactly as it was? Or maybe would you stay and build back better?

On May 4th, 2007 at 9:54 p.m., an EF5 tornado over 1.5 miles wide with winds over 200 miles per hour hit Greensburg, Kansas. The small rural town with a population of about 1,300 was leveled. The tornado took 12 lives and destroyed 95% of the town, including homes, businesses, and government buildings. The sirens went off 20 minutes before the tornado hit, but there was no mechanism to prevent the disaster from happening. Put yourself in the shoes of the residents of Greensburg: What do you do when your plans and your way of life and everything you know is destroyed overnight? What do you do as an individual, as a business, as a government, or as a community?

I grew up in the suburbs of Washington, D.C. in Northern Virginia, which is about as insulated from natural disasters as you can get on this planet. While Washington, D.C. will always be a target for terrorism, the Mid-Atlantic is subject to more mild extreme weather events and less frequently than most places in the United States. We've had a handful of EF1 tornadoes, tiny earthquakes, a number of tropical storms, and a couple manageable blizzards in my lifetime, but nothing as devastating as what Greensburg experienced. Northern Virginia has never seen an EF5 tornado. There are no seasonal city-destroying hurricanes, no major flood or drought risks, no consistently harsh winters, no wildfires, no landslides, no recurring earthquakes, and certainly no tsunamis.

I remember watching the 1996 movie *Twister* numerous times growing up. Helen Hunt and Bill Paxton play two storm chasers trying to deploy an experimental technology to understand tornadoes better. The film has undoubtedly inspired a generation of weather enthusiasts and scientists interested in advancing our understanding of storms. The film was certainly engaging as a kid, but perhaps it was because tornadoes were so foreign to me. The movie is generally classified as science fiction, but it is a depiction of reality for those that live in tornado alley in the United States. It just seemed unreal to kids like me that lived far from a region where tornadoes are a common occurrence.

The Mid-Atlantic United States is a relatively safe place when it comes to weather events. In fact, there have been zero Category 1 to 5 hurricanes that have made landfall in Virginia, Maryland, and Delaware over the last ~175 years. If you were to plot the landfall location of the last 175 years of hurricanes that have hit the Gulf Coast and East Coast of the United States, there would be a glaring gap in data points along the coast of Virginia, Maryland, and Delaware. This is because the coastline of North Carolina juts out into the Atlantic, which acts as a natural barrier for Virginia, Maryland, and Delaware since storms don't typically take hard left hand turns after passing North Carolina. By contrast, Kansas has had an average of 4.4 tornadoes for every 100 square miles since 1950, and an average of over 60 tornadoes per year since the 1990s. Every community, town, and city in Kansas has to worry about tornadoes.

Pause for a moment and think about all of the natural disaster risks that your community faces from year to year. In project management, risk registers are used to document and track all of the known risks associated with a particular effort. Communities can use risk registers to understand the many potential rainy days, their likelihood, and the probably impact of such events on quality of life.

Natural disasters are another example of how *geography is destiny* – how your zip code can determine various outcomes in life. What Greensburg, Kansas experienced in 2007 was the most concentrated community-wide natural disaster in the United States in my lifetime. The built environment of Greensburg was 95% destroyed. When I first heard this, I thought it was miraculous that so few people died.

In 1955, there was an EF5 tornado that completely destroyed Udall, Kansas, a town of about 500 people, killing 80 and injuring 250. Udall lost about 16% of its population (and also had about 50% injured), and Greensburg lost less than 1%. Any loss of life is tragic, but it is somewhat miraculous that a roughly equivalent tornado 52 years later, in the same area, resulted in significantly less lives lost.

What can we attribute this reduction in loss of life to? Better early warning systems? Better tornado shelters? More emergency preparedness drills and training? Luck? Both towns were completely destroyed, so the structural engineering of the built environment was likely not that much better 52 years later. Imagine a powerful EF5 tornado over 1.5 miles wide going through the place where you are sitting right now. How many people are within 1.5 miles of where you are sitting that would be able to find sufficient shelter within 20 minutes? In order to survive something like an EF5 tornado, you must at least know its coming. You must be able to get a text on your phone, a message on your television, or hear some sort of alarm go off in your neighborhood in order for you to know to seek adequate shelter.

Michael R. Smith, a researcher from Wichita, Kansas, actually looked at what changed from 1955 to 2007. The Udall tornado in 1955 occurred long before smart phones and modern early warning systems that exist today. In 1955, people were not constantly listening to the radio or watching television. As Smith remarks in his 2008 paper, it may have been the case that some of the victims in Udall watched the ten o'clock news 30 minutes before the tornado arrived, but television was not ubiquitous in 1955. So, most of the people of Udall likely had zero warning and very little time to get to shelter.

Fast forward to 2007, about an hour and 45 minutes before the EF5 tornado hit Greensburg, Kansas, the National Weather Service's Dodge City WSSR-88D radar and National Lightning Detection Network recorded cloud-to-ground lightning strikes and were able to measure the polarity of the lightning. About an hour and 15 minutes before the tornado struck Greensburg, storm spotters had begun reporting rotating wall clouds. According to Michael Smith's paper, *"The tornado warning for the City of Greensburg was issued at 9:19pm, more than 30 minutes before the tornado struck at 9:54pm. The tornado siren in Greensburg was activated at approximately 9:30pm. Normal practice for a tornado warning was to sound the siren once for five minutes then turn it off. Local emergency management, alarmed by the reports of damage in rural areas to the south, radar, and blow-by-blow reports from media allowed the siren to continue to sound until power was cut to the siren as the tornado arrived."*

Greensburg's story is an example of technological progress and our societal systems getting better. As Smith points out, if Greensburg had been subject to the same fatality rate as Udall (about 16.3%), 230 additional lives would've been lost. The combination of the federal government's weather service monitoring, on the ground communication from storm spotters in the area, and early warning systems in the town saved lives.

~1,500 exposed population in 2007 x 0.163 fatality rate in 1955 = 243 potential fatalities in Greensburg
Potential fatalities – actual fatalities = 230 saved lives

This estimation is calculated by simply multiplying the exposed population in the 2007 Greensburg event by the previous fatality rate from the 1955 Udall event, which results in a number that represents potential fatalities. To get the notional number of saved lives we can subtract the actual number of fatalities from the potential number of fatalities. The fatality rate was significantly less in Greensburg, but the loss of life is still tragic, and we should strive to achieve a zero percent fatality rate to continue to save lives in the future.

> ***Rainy Day Economics Design Prompt 4:*** *Design a tornado early warning system and shelter guidance that minimizes fatalities in a small town in Kansas. Identify the conditions and indicators necessary to minimize fatalities. Focus on the elderly and consider proximity and accessibility of the early warning system and tornado shelters.*

## *Emergency Medical Training, Books, and Triage*

In May 2007, the Greensburg tragedy was not on my radar. Before the massacre at Virginia Tech, I was thinking about how to go on more trips to the Gulf Coast to help with Hurricane Katrina recovery, and I think that mindset just got baked into my thinking on how I could be helpful in the world. I remember one of the volunteer teams we met on one of the trips to the Gulf Coast was a similar group of college students from Kansas State University in Manhattan, Kansas. Greensburg is only a few hours from Manhattan, Kansas compared to the over 15-hour drive from Manhattan, Kansas to the Gulf Coast. There are two questions that come to mind when thinking about the Kansas State team of volunteers. The first is how does the proximity to disasters impact the number of people that volunteer to help with the recovery? The second question is what is our country's capacity to handle multiple disaster recoveries simultaneously?

Over the course of the next couple years after the massacre (2007-2008), I meandered a little bit academically and in life. I didn't care as much about grades anymore, and I was more concerned with leading a meaningful life. I remember working for a bookstore called Bookholders in downtown Blacksburg. The business model was simple. They'd buy used books for significantly less than what they could sell them for the next semester. There were times when there was nothing going on in the store, and other times when many customers would arrive at the same time. When there weren't many customers coming in, I would walk through the thin, dimly lit aisles of bookshelves and read a few pages of something that looked interesting. I think there is something therapeutically distracting about books, and maybe also uniquely centering, focusing, and stimulating at times. When there were a lot of customers though, there was no time to read.

During a summer when many of my friends were doing corporate internships, I decided to take more classes at a community college. One class was a low-level comparative religion course that satisfied my last remaining general education requirement. The other course was a time-intensive Emergency Medical Technician training program that included a clinical rotation at hospitals and paramedic units in the region.

EMS 111 – Emergency Medical Technician – Basic
EMS 120 – Emergency Medical Technician – Basic Clinical
REL 232 – Religions of the World

The religion course didn't really resonate with me. Looking back, religion wasn't providing me with the substantive solution-oriented answers I wanted. The EMT training, however, was giving me a lot to think about related to humanity, spirituality, leading a meaningful life, and also interestingly giving me insight into some of our societal systems that we often take for granted.

During the EMT Clinical rotations, I remember thinking that being an EMT in many parts of the country must be simply caring for old people that fall down or drunk people that are throwing up. Being an EMT generally does not include responding to massacres, terrorist attacks, or natural disasters. It is just showing up when people are hurting. On the other hand, the EMT training did include a section on how to triage during a mass casualty event. I remember thinking that everyone should get basic triage training to know what to do in the case of a mass casualty event. Millions of people get CPR training, but that is because of the prevalence of the need to give CPR. At what point do we scale up basic triage training? What would be the threshold or point at which we experience so many mass casualty events so frequently that we need millions of people to know how to respond quickly and triage?

## Natural disasters, Black Swan events, and futurism

There are two reasons early warning systems exist for natural disasters. The first reason is that natural disasters, particularly tornadoes, are not preventable. In some cases, like flooding and wildfires, there is at least partial prevention possible and we can mitigate some of the impacts, but we currently can't stop hurricanes, tornadoes, tsunamis, and earthquakes from happening. The second reason early warning systems exist is that natural disasters are not Black Swan events.

What is a Black Swan event? This is referring to a theory developed by

Nassim Nicholas Taleb that described how we as a society think about and rationalize low probability, high impact events. The three characteristics of Black Swan events are 1) they are outliers that are outside the realm of normal expectations, 2) they have extreme impacts, and 3) we as humans describe the events after the fact as explainable and predictable. Taleb's book, *The Black Swan*, was published April 17, 2007 the day after the massacre at Virginia Tech (not sure why I find that interesting). The terrorist attack on September 11th may be considered to be a Black Swan event, but natural disasters, while they have extreme impacts, are not outliers. They are within the realm of normal expectations.

The notion of normal expectations is related to the idea of a societal risk register. As a society, we should develop a robust understanding of the risks we face, their likelihood, their potential impacts, and the costs of those impacts.

Simply understanding that most rainy days are not Black Swan events can help us think about the future and how we design the system of systems that make up our societal architecture. The related growing field of futurism, or future studies, provides a framework for thinking about rainy day economics and designing our societal architecture. Andy Hines and Peter Bishop wrote a book called *Thinking about the Future*, which explores futurism and strategic foresight. Hines and Bishop outline a number of strategies that are useful for rainy day economics, including:

- Knowing our biases
- Identifying wishful thinking as barriers to foresight
- Building teams with cognitive diversity
- Embracing complexity alongside linear thinking
- Understanding that different changes occur at different rates and have impact at different times

Futurist Jeremy Pesner also pointed out in his 2017 TEDxHerndon Talk that *"Unlike most of our jobs, which require technical, precise, and convergent thinking towards a specific solution, futurism requires creativity, interdisciplinarity, and divergent thinking to dream up different futures that could be."* He goes onto describe how scenario planning can be used to navigate different possibilities. There are four basic steps to scenario development that can be utilized in rainy day economics, as follows:

1. Identify driving forces
2. Identify critical uncertainties
3. Develop plausible scenarios
4. Discuss implications and paths

Scenario planning allows us to move beyond what we'd normally consider in preparing for and designing the future. In the case of the tornadoes in Kansas, we are trying to achieve an outcome where we minimize fatalities. We can apply futurism and scenario planning by starting with the outcome that we want and working backwards to create the necessary conditions and indicators in our societal architecture. We want zero fatalities, and we know tornadoes give people very little time to react, so what systems can we create to overcome the spontaneous nature of tornadoes?

## Federal Assistance and State Rainy Day Funds

Perhaps the most obvious critique of government in the wake of any tragedy will always be *the response time*. On September 11th, 2001, the official response time of the New York City Fire Department (FDNY) was 5 seconds. That is truly amazing and a testament to the people and the support system of New York City. However, that is a local government response in America's most densely populated city. Federal assistance for local and regional tragedies has often taken much longer than 5 seconds to be activated. The federal government clearly provides significant value to communities that are impacted by natural disasters, but there is definitely room for improvement when it comes to response time.

> ***Rainy Day Economics Design Prompt 5:*** *Design a method, policy, and/or system for the federal government to quickly deploy emergency resources to communities and regions impacted by natural disasters. Set a goal for ideal response time. Consider the most remote locations in the country.*

After Greensburg was hit by the EF5 tornado on the night of May 4th, 2007, it took over 24 hours to be declared a major disaster by President George W. Bush on May 6th, which is what triggered the deployment of federal government resources from various agencies including the Federal Emergency Management Agency (FEMA), the U.S. Small Business Administration (SBA) and the U.S. Environmental Protection Agency (EPA). Once federal resources started flowing, a lot more help started showing up in Greensburg.

The federal government invested more than $100 million for emergency response, temporary housing, assistance to individuals, families and businesses, and repairing or replacing tornado-damaged public infrastructure such as government buildings, schools, emergency services and a hospital. More than 7,600 volunteers registered via AmeriCorps to help clean up and rebuild Greensburg. About 75,000-80,000 truckloads of tornado-generated debris—totaling more than 800,000 cubic yards— were hauled from the town. If we divide $100 million in federal assistance by the population of about 1,300, we find that the federal government invested over $75,000 per citizen of Greensburg, Kansas.

I use the word *invested* intentionally, but at the same time I don't think it is the most accurate word to describe the money that we as a society allocate towards those impacted by rainy days. Something about the word investment implies the phrase "return on investment". The money we allocate to those impacted by rainy days isn't money we should expect to come back to us in significant ways, but we should recognize that if we don't allocate money for rainy days, then our society will slowly erode. In other words, the federal government should allocate money to Greensburg in the wake of a tornado because the federal government has a unique capability to do so, not because the federal government expects the federal tax receipts will be higher as a result of the allocation.

Imagine for a moment the federal government didn't invest $100 million in Greensburg after the tornado in 2007. Greensburg's operating budget is less than $5 million today. So, there was no way the town could've invested $100 million in a major response and recovery effort. What about the state government? Could the Kansas state government invest $100 million in a major response and recovery effort for Greensburg?

Every state government has a different approach to rainy day funds. Some rainy day funds are focused on natural disasters, but most rainy day funds are actually designed for more general budget stabilization of state finances particularly during economic downturns. The National Association of State Budget Officers (NASBO) does extensive research on state budget processes and publishes reports that compare the approaches of every state and territory.

There are wide-ranging differences in how states approach and utilize debt as well as how states optimize and maintain stabilization, disaster, and emergency funds. In NASBO's reports on state budget processes, there are a few tables that are particularly useful to a discussion about rainy day economics. If we look at the comparison of 2019 Unexpected, Natural, or Manmade Disaster Funds, we can see that Kansas had a relatively low balance of less than $1 million when compared to Colorado's $94.7 million. So, to answer the earlier question of whether or not the Kansas state government could've invested $100 million in a major response and recovery effort in Greensburg, I think the answer is likely no. It is conceivable that a state legislature could pass some sort of emergency bill to allocate funds in the wake of a disaster, but likely not very quickly.

For every type of rainy day, the federal government is best suited to provide targeted resources at scale. Every other type of organization is constrained by either a lack of resources or a lack of time. A corporation can't devote staff time for years after a natural disaster. A small town can't fund a complete rebuild of its infrastructure. Nonprofits can help, but they too must be funded somehow. Some state governments have the ability allocate sufficient resources for natural disaster response and recovery, but even in the best-case scenarios, there are budget and staffing limits to how much a state government can support before they need federal assistance.

## Rebuilding with Sustainability in Mind

Greensburg had a lot of decisions to make together related to rebuilding infrastructure, schools, and government buildings, revitalizing businesses, and creating spaces for creativity, joy, and community. One of the simplest things that FEMA did to help Greensburg recover was set up a big tent for the town to come and talk about what to do next. The town did everything under that big tent for a while. That's where they mourned together, but it is also where they did their planning, including their Long-term Recovery Plan and their Sustainable Master Plan. In a town of about 1,500, there were 300 to 400 people showing up twice a week to contribute to the planning effort. That is a high participation rate for a local government planning effort.

> *"We found a way to reason together. We found a way to have common ground. We had true, honest, open dialogue. And we agreed to disagree on some issues."*
>
> *- Mayor Bob Dixson of Greensburg, Kansas speaking at TEDxHerndon 2016*

People weren't just showing up to plan though. They were also showing up to be a part of their community. As a starting point, the town focused on what was unique about Greensburg. Greensburg is home to the largest hand-dug water well in the country and one of the largest in the world. But that's not the only thing Greensburg wanted to be known for. Mayor Bob Dixson described it as a discussion about values and character. What did the community care about? And what kind of community did they want to leave for their children? In his TEDxHerndon presentation years later, Mayor Dixson remarked *"Don't let realities of today cloud your vision of tomorrow."*

> *A Common Vision: A Sustainable Future*
> *The root of sustainability is based in common Kansas values. A Kansan thinks in terms of generations and harbors a sincere belief that decisions should build strong communities for our children. We still believe in the power of community, and in our rural areas neighbors still gather at the coffee shop to talk about the issues of the day. A Kansan's character is rooted in the agricultural industry prominent in the region. We understand the natural systems that power a sustainable economy and know what it means to live off, and with, the land.*
>
> *- Greensburg Sustainable Comprehensive Plan, May 2008*

The recovery of Greensburg was successful because the community was committed to rebuilding together and creating a town where the people could thrive. The rest of the country can learn a lot from Greensburg about community involvement and planning for long-term sustainability. The rural agricultural community embraced the U.S. Green Building Council's LEED certification program for all of their buildings. The Greensburg City Hall building used over 75,000 bricks reclaimed from the rubble of the town after the tornado. The first LEED Platinum building in the state of Kansas was the art center built after the tornado in Greensburg, another testament to the importance of the fifth pillar of Rainy Day Economics – the arts. The 5.4.7 Arts Center, whose name comes from the date of the tornado that devastated Greensburg on May 4, 2007, has been a catalyst for creativity, entrepreneurial thinking, and new beginnings in Greensburg. In the face of extreme hopelessness, Greensburg continues to be a shining example of resilience and sustainability.

# Chapter 4

## WHEN BRIDGES COLLAPSE
### August 1, 2007

*"The quality in our standard of living is in direct relation
to the well being of our physical life lines."*

*– Jesús de la Garza, TEDxHerndon, May 21, 2016*

---

In 2007, I was starting to become disillusioned with architecture as a profession. My 2nd year architecture studio had been the first opportunity to design buildings and think about potential real world applications of form and function, and how those buildings interacted with the places where they existed. Over the course of a couple years, I would see the disconnect between the practice of suburban architecture, where I was headed after graduating, and the more idealistic architecture that I was learning about in Virginia Tech's architecture program. After shadowing a couple Northern Virginia architects, it became apparent that my career would in all likelihood become designing slightly more livable cookie cutter apartment buildings or slightly more sustainable corporate office buildings.

Some of my peers in the architecture program have since proved me wrong by becoming leading designers at the most innovative architecture firms in the world. However, in 2007, I was still in an existential haze after the massacre, and there was starting to be signs of duress in the economy. Getting a meaningful job became more important than pursuing an architecture degree even after working so hard to get into Virginia Tech's prestigious program.

For the Fall semester of 2007, I decided not to take the six-credit architecture studio course, which inherently meant I would fall behind a year or ultimately transfer out of the architecture program. As a result, I was able to add more variety to my course schedule. In aggregate, these were the highest-level courses I had taken to date, which I knew would make for a challenging semester. The course lineup was as follows:

ARCH 4055 – Environmental Building Systems
ARCH 4076 – Building Structures
CEE 3014 – Construction Management
ECON 4014 – Environmental Economics
MGT 3304 – Management Theory and Leadership

This particular semester was where I began to consider a multitude of divergent paths instead of one singular path. I was suddenly on "the road less traveled by" instead of the clear and known path that led to becoming an architect. That poem "*The Road Not Taken*" by Robert Frost had a double meaning for me at that time. The first meaning was related to the paths we take in our careers and lives. The second meaning related more closely to the lives of the roads. Sometimes I wonder if the main character in that poem is not "*I*", but rather the "*two roads*". Or maybe the poem is entirely about the last two words – "*the difference*" – and the difference is referring to our impact on the paths we take rather than the impact that the paths we take have on us.

*The Road Not Taken by Robert Frost*

*Two roads diverged in a yellow wood,*
*And sorry I could not travel both*
*And be one traveler, long I stood*
*And looked down one as far as I could*
*To where it bent in the undergrowth;*

*Then took the other, as just as fair,*
*And having perhaps the better claim,*
*Because it was grassy and wanted wear;*
*Though as for that the passing there*
*Had worn them really about the same,*

*And both that morning equally lay*
*In leaves no step had trodden black.*
*Oh, I kept the first for another day!*
*Yet knowing how way leads on to way,*
*I doubted if I should ever come back.*

*I shall be telling this with a sigh*
*Somewhere ages and ages hence:*
*Two roads diverged in a wood, and I—*
*I took the one less traveled by,*
*And that has made all the difference.*

## *The Deterioration of America's Infrastructure*

On August 1ˢᵗ, 2007 at 6:05pm during rush hour, a bridge on Interstate 35 in Minneapolis, Minnesota experienced a catastrophic failure that resulted in 13 deaths and over 140 injured. The bridge had been in service for less than 40 years with about 140,000 vehicles crossing every day. In 1990, 2001, 2005, and 2006, the bridge had been reported as structurally deficient with a lack of redundancy in the main truss system and signs of cracking and fatigue. Those inspections, research, and reports came from the U.S. Department of Transportation, the University of Minnesota, and the Minnesota Department of Transportation. Everyone knew the bridge was deteriorating, as all infrastructure does, and Governor Tim Pawlenty stated after the collapse that the bridge was scheduled to be replaced in 2020. So, if everyone knew the bridge was structurally deficient, then why wasn't it scheduled to be replaced sooner? Most bridges are designed to have an 80-to-100-year life, so why didn't the I-35 bridge in Minneapolis last even half that time? There are five stages of the life of a bridge starting with the design and ending with the dismantlement.

Stages of Bridge's Life

- Design
- Construction
- In Use
- Maintenance
- Dismantlement

The five stages above provide a simple framework to analyze a bridge's life and also the lifecycle of other infrastructure assets like buildings, roads, transmission lines, and water pipes. This is not the same as an environmental life cycle analysis of a bridge, which can give us a better understanding of how to make bridges last longer without catastrophic failures and also how to build bridges more sustainably. These analyses look at all of the materials used, the chemistry of those materials, and where those materials go after the end of the bridge's life.

Phases of Environmental Life Cycle Analysis

- *Material Production* – including raw material acquisition, transportation to production site and construction site, and production of the construction materials.
- *Construction* – including the use of construction equipment, the construction processes, and the traffic congestion during the process of construction.
- *Use* – including maintenance and rehabilitation operations and daily traffic congestion.
- *Decommission* – including the demolition of the structure, transportation of materials and waste to a disposal site, and the associated traffic congestion.

There are various ways to approach an Environmental Life Cycle Analysis, but the process outlined above provides visibility that allows us to identify what causes bridges to fail before the end of their intended life. Retrospectively, we can ask questions to investigate why a bridge is being deemed structurally deficient with less than 25 years of use. Was the material sourced correctly? Was the concrete mixed correctly? Was preventative maintenance performed at the appropriate times? However, even if a bridge is designed, built, and maintained perfectly, it will still deteriorate to a point where it needs to be decommissioned and replaced.

At the time of the I-35 bridge collapse in Minneapolis in 2007, there were approximately 75,000 bridges in the United States that had been deemed structurally deficient. This represented over 10% of all bridges in the United States, which is a scary statistic. From 2007 to 2021, there was significant investment in the rehabilitation of infrastructure that included roads and bridges. This investment came in large part from the American Recovery and Reinvestment Act of 2009 signed into law by President

Barack Obama. In 2021, the American Society of Civil Engineers published their Infrastructure Report Card giving bridges a grade of C-minus overall. At the time of the report's publication, there were over 46,000 bridges known to be structurally deficient, which represented about 7.5% of all of the bridges in the country. That was a major improvement from 2007, but there was, and is, still a lot of work to be done.

Rainy Day Economics focuses on long-term sustainability, which allows us to understand society's portfolio of ever-deteriorating infrastructure assets. While the reduction in structurally deficient bridges from 2007 to 2021 was impressive, the number of bridges that were over 50 years old was an alarming 42% of all bridges in the United States. This is alarming for a few reasons. The first reason is that maintaining older bridges costs more than maintaining younger bridges. This means that states are being forced to increase their gas taxes to pay for infrastructure maintenance. In 2021, 37 states had increased or reformed their gas taxes since 2010, and the federal Highway Trust Fund, which has been a major source of funding for the nation's road and bridge projects, has been trending toward insolvency for over a decade. In my opinion, the Highway Trust Fund, along with other societal safety nets and endowments, should be under the purview of the Federal Reserve instead of being subject to the pendulum of politics in the United States.

All infrastructure deteriorates over time, and so as a society, we need to commit to being good stewards of the natural and built environment. During Andrew Yang's 2020 Presidential campaign, he advocated for the adoption of an American Scorecard. When I heard this, I immediately thought of the American Society of Civil Engineers (ASCE) Infrastructure Report Card as a reference point. The ASCE Infrastructure Report Card assigns a letter grade to each of the major types of infrastructure assets, including bridges, roads, power, and water infrastructure.

Andrew Yang was advocating for a scorecard that would measure a broad set of metrics that we could use as continuous indicators of the quality of life in America. Just like the ASCE Infrastructure Report Card gives us an idea of the state of our infrastructure in a given year, the American Scorecard would give us a snap shot of the quality of life in the United States from year to year. The American Scorecard represents the fundamentals of the third pillar of Rainy Day Economics – human-centered capitalism. *The central tenets of human-centered capitalism are:*

1. *Humans are more important than money*
2. *The unit of a Human-centered Capitalist economy is each person, not each dollar*
3. *Markets exist to serve our common goals and values*

The adoption of an American Scorecard, in my opinion, should include metrics on the state of infrastructure and the built environment in the United States, as well as the state of the natural environment. This would be a significant departure from using Gross Domestic Product (GDP) as a singular measure of economic growth, performance, and improvement. I'll talk more later about why GDP is a truly terrible measure to use to evaluate the performance of our economy. For now, just know that when the I-35 bridge collapsed, the GDP of the State of Minnesota was barely impacted (about 0.01%) while the quality of life for thousands of Minnesotans was significantly reduced for months, and that is in addition to the hundreds of lives impacted by death and injury on the day of the tragedy.

## *Response, Recovery, and Rebuilding*

The City of Minneapolis and the State of Minnesota responded quickly to the event and rescued over 90 people from the collapsed bridge in the span of just a couple hours. This included about 20 people rescued by the Minneapolis Fire Department from the Mississippi river by boat. There were 75 local, state, and federal agencies that supported the response. The

U.S. Army Corps of Engineers lowered the river level by two feet downriver at the Ford Dam to allow easier access to vehicles that were submerged under water. The U.S. Navy sent divers to recover bodies from vehicles that were under the bridge deck and other structural pieces.

The response to the bridge collapse was a massive effort focused on a single point in space and time. This is unlike responses to most natural disasters where search and rescue efforts are spread out over miles. The fact that there are thousands of bridges that have been deemed structurally deficient means that cities need to prepare for emergency responses to bridge collapses. As a society, we must be proficient at maintaining, rehabilitating, and replacing bridges and also be proficient at emergency preparedness for when bridges collapse. Every structurally deficient bridge should have an emergency response plan with associated preparedness drills designed by state and local first responders.

The fourth pillar of Rainy Day Economics – resilience – is all about how we respond and recover from disasters and tragedies. We strive to reduce probability of failure, consequences of failure, and time to restoration, and we assess resiliency using the 4Rs – robustness, redundancy, resourcefulness, and rapidity.

At a community or city level, recovering from the tragedy of a collapsed bridge is in many ways one of the most straightforward among all of the rainy day events that could impact a city. After the initial response, a city can simply divert traffic and begin the process of designing and building a new bridge. Communities can feel the impact of diverting traffic in two different ways, 1) the benefits of traffic and 2) the hindrances of traffic. The I-35 bridge in Minneapolis supported over 140,000 vehicle crossings every day at the time of its collapse.

This means there will be disruptions to businesses and communities during the transition period while the new bridge is built. And it is not so simple as saying what one business loses, another gains. The impacts of any shock to an economy at any scale are rarely as simple as one party gains and another loses. And, because it is a short-term diversion of traffic, the loss or gain to businesses will be temporary and thus only serve to create a shock to the local system and uncertainty for those businesses. Will the businesses that gain traffic add employees and then have to let them go later? Will businesses that lose traffic need to let employees go and then hire them back later? Will the businesses that lose traffic survive the transition period? Will the businesses that gain traffic be able to sustain some growth momentum after the traffic goes back to normal? These are all questions that make the future less certain for local communities and their businesses.

Small businesses near the I-35 bridge collapse lost between 25% and 50% of their income. And, the cost to commuters was estimated to be in the neighborhood of $400,000 per day for gas for the extra miles driven. These are not trivial numbers. Bridges connect places efficiently and thus when they are out of commission, things become inefficient. The U.S. Small Business Administration offers low-interest loans to those that are impacted by disasters, but it is still difficult to sustain operations when traffic is diverted away from what might've been a once thriving small business.

How long does it take to design and build a bridge? In the case of the I-35 bridge in Minneapolis, everything was fast tracked, because the bridge was deemed to be of vital importance to the city. When the I-35 bridge was first built it took from 1964 to 1967 just for construction, but after it collapsed in 2007, it took only a year after the announcement of who would be the contractors responsible for the construction. Less than 14 months from the collapse on August 1st, 2007, the I-35 bridge replacement project was complete and commuters and truck freight were back to normal. As part of the design requirements for the new bridge, all of the new bridge's superstructures, joints and bearings were made accessible for long-term inspection and maintenance.

*One bridge versus many bridges and temporary regulatory relief*

Rebuilding one bridge is easy, right? But what if a region finds itself in a situation where hundreds of vital infrastructure assets are damaged or destroyed? This obviously happened in the cases of Hurricane Katrina and the Greensburg tornado. It can also happen as a result of major flood events. The state of Vermont has faced this challenge in recent years experiencing major flood events in 2023 and 2024 that overwhelmed roads, bridges, wastewater treatment plants, and buildings. For a small state like Vermont, a major flooding event could create system-wide disruptions to the economy, and the response to such events can be slow due to capacity constraints.

In the case of the Minneapolis I-35 bridge, there were 75 local, state, and federal agencies that responded to the incident. This was possible, because it was one incident in one location. What if it were three interstate bridges in the Minneapolis region that collapsed on the same day? Would it have been 25 agencies responding to each bridge? That's simply 75 agencies divided by three bridges. That's likely not how it would've played out, but you can start to see where a state or region would run into capacity constraints quickly depending on the scale of the disaster or the number of locations represented in a given disaster.

When we think about who is responsible for rebuilding infrastructure, it is important to note that it is not always the state and federal government. For example, there are countless roads and bridges around your home that are funded, built, and maintained by your local government. There are also roads and bridges on personal properties, particularly in rural areas, that are funded, built, and maintained by those property owners. I have a friend that lives in a rural part of Vermont that experienced the recent floods in 2023 and 2024. His house was unharmed by the floods, but there was a bridge wiped out at the entrance to his property. The bridge went over a stream at the entrance to his and a neighbor's properties, and it was outside the scope of responsibility of the local, state, and federal government. So, he and his neighbor were responsible for funding and building a new bridge. They could of course decide not to rebuild the bridge, but then they would be trapped on their property or prevented from getting back on the property depending on which side of the stream they were on after the flood.

We often take for granted all the infrastructure that supports our daily lives. Likewise, we view the maintenance and rebuilding of infrastructure as someone else's responsibility. We don't often think about how much effort it takes to maintain our roads, bridges, water pipes, storm water management systems, power lines, and wastewater treatment plants. And when infrastructure systems fail, there is an often-unrealistic expectation that those systems are operational immediately after major rainy day events.

In the case of the 2024 flooding in Vermont, Governor Phil Scott authorized temporary regulatory relief to expedite emergency response and infrastructure rebuild. This is an executive action that a lot of citizens will support in the aftermath of natural disasters, because people want to get back to normal fast. However, this is a slippery slope, pun intended. It is conceivable that deregulation enthusiasts will use temporary regulatory relief during natural disasters to advance their political agenda after the recovery from those natural disasters. In the context of infrastructure, regulations exist to ensure worker safety, public health, environmental quality, and structural integrity.

As a society, we can be better about planning for worst-case scenarios. If we were to focus on long-term emergency preparedness, the need for temporary regulatory relief during natural disasters would decline. This would mean that the regulations that ensure worker safety, public health, environmental quality, and structural integrity would not be a hindrance to getting infrastructure systems operational quickly. The fact that temporary regulatory relief is being used to expedite emergency response and infrastructure rebuilds is not a justification for less regulation. Rather temporary regulatory relief being used to expedite emergency response and infrastructure rebuilds post-disaster is an indicator of a lack of emergency preparedness for large-scale events.

## Failure, performance, teaching, and learning

A significant aspect of all of the pillars of Rainy Day Economics is understanding the scale of human needs and also the capacity of a place's workforce to prepare and/or respond to rainy days. While I was at Virginia Tech's architecture school, I met a lot of future industrial designers. Industrial designers are those that design products, devices, objects, and services. Everything from phones and furniture to cars and shoes falls under the domain of industrial designers.

One of the industrial design students I met had started as a civil engineering student like me and had worked for a bridge engineering firm during a summer internship. He told me a story of when he was tasked with designing what he called "a pile of rocks". The pile of rocks he designed was apparently not up to the standards of his boss, and so this young intern got yelled at and embarrassed in front of the rest of the team. After the internship, he swiftly began the transition to becoming an industrial designer and eventually became a sailboat designer instead of a civil engineer. Now, the only piles of rocks he needs to worry about are the ones along the shorelines when he is out sailing.

In civil engineering, a "pile of rocks" is rarely an inconsequential part of an overall design. If a "pile of rocks" is being designed by a civil engineering team, then that pile of rocks is probably more important than a layperson would think. A pile of rocks can often be used as part of a structural support or a barrier to protect against erosion from water or wind. In the cases of bridges, everything that is being designed relates to the structural integrity of the bridge. And the structural integrity of a bridge is what keeps it from collapsing and causing a tragedy like the I-35 bridge collapse in Minneapolis. But, we also have a major shortage of civil engineers in the United States, and shaming young interns isn't going to help solve the workforce gap. So there is an inherent tension between creating learning moments for young engineers and designing infrastructure assets to not fail in the long term. We want young engineers to have the ability to fail and learn, but we don't want our bridges to fail.

Civil engineers play a vital role in maintaining a high quality of life for everyone in our society, in the good times and the bad. Discussing the workforce gap in the civil engineering profession is as important as discussing the workforce gap in medical professions. If we don't have sufficient numbers of people to design, build, operate, maintain, and rehabilitate our infrastructure systems, then our quality of life will slowly decline, and we will experience a growing number of catastrophic failures as well as a more insidious impact on our politics by way of increasingly tense budget and debt conversations.

We need more young people to want to become civil engineers. Increasing the salaries of civil engineers and the scholarships available to civil engineering students will help attract more young people to the profession. It would also be useful to increase the number of pathways to civil engineering. The road to becoming a Professional Engineer is rigorous and time-intensive, similar to the rigor and intensity of becoming a doctor. However, the undergraduate educational pathways to becoming a doctor are much more diverse than the pathways to becoming a Professional Engineer.

In medical school, there is a significant amount of real world training where future doctors are interacting with patients and practicing medicine with real patients under the supervision of experienced doctors. By contrast, the graduate education of civil engineers is mostly spent in a classroom. There of course needs to be significant classroom time for any profession to understand concepts and go deep on certain content, but the most engaging learning activities are often those outside the classroom. The American Society of Civil Engineers (ASCE) and the National Governors Association (NGA) identified the following five long-term strategies to grow the number of engineers and infrastructure workers in the United States. These strategies are particularly relevant to Rainy Day Economics as they focus on designing a workforce for a purpose-driven, resilient economy:

1. Increase the affordability of engineering education
2. Create multiple entry points to the engineering and infrastructure professions
3. Develop college programming for engineering student retention and support
4. Encourage high school students to enter infrastructure professions
5. Develop and support STEM curriculum in K-12 education

Before the I-35 bridge collapse in Minneapolis, there were other engineering failures that were and still are used in engineering classrooms to teach students how important their work is and how to engineer safe and high performing infrastructure. I remember in multiple engineering courses being shown the Hyatt Regency walkway collapse from 1981 in Kansas City that resulted in 114 deaths. This case demonstrated how non-deliberate structural failures can have devastating consequences, and it served as an example for young engineering students to remember when considering the impact of their work.

There is also a notable difference between how engineering educators and design educators talk about failing and performance. Design educators are generally more nuanced with discussions about failure, iteration, and performance. While engineering educators are direct and somewhat absolute with how they talk about failure, iteration, and performance. This makes sense. Consider the consequence of designing a structurally deficient chair. Perhaps a heavier person will sit in the chair, and it will break and the person will fall from a short height to the ground. Likewise, if a person buys poorly designed shoes, they may be more likely to roll their ankle while running. In most cases, the stakes are much higher in civil engineering than in industrial design. Generally, a structurally deficient building or bridge intended for use by hundreds or thousands of people at a single moment in time is more dangerous than a structurally deficient product intended for use by one or two people at a time.

> ***Rainy Day Economics Design Prompt 6:*** *Develop a new interdisciplinary program and curriculum to engage more high school students in the fields of design, engineering, economics, and sustainability. How might we build a purpose-driven workforce of the future?*

I think engineering educators and design educators can learn a lot from each other. Engineering educators can benefit from learning and teaching rapid prototyping, more iterative processes and methods, and divergent thinking. And design educators can benefit from learning and teaching deeper calculus-based optimization and more rigorous physics and material science. There are also ways in which the professions can drive a conversation about how to teach people to be high performers when lives are on the line, but also be at peace with and grow from failures, even when those failures cost lives. Civil engineering and industrial design are also both at the nexus of discussions related to improving quality of life in the long term. The cross fertilization of the educational pathways of civil engineers and industrial designers will lead to a more robust and prepared workforce, higher performing, more sustainable and resilient infrastructure, and better products in our society and by extension a better quality of life.

For the Rainy Day Economics framework to be effective, we need to build bridges across disciplines to develop a purpose-driven workforce focused on design, sustainability, and resilience.

# Part 2:
# The Complexity of
# Rainy Day Economics

# Chapter 5

## JOE THE PLUMBER AND THE GREAT RECESSION
### October 12, 2008

*"Money is not the only answer, but it makes a difference."*

*- President Barack Obama*

---

At the beginning of 2008, I was 20 years old. The year began with an unusually cold night in Miami, Florida at the 74th Orange Bowl, a close game between Kansas University and Virginia Tech. We lost 24 to 21. By the beginning of the Spring semester, I had officially decided to shift away from pursuing an architecture degree to pursue a degree in economics. The classes I took in 2008 were relevant to the national conversation at the time. My Spring semester in 2008 included courses that fundamentally shaped how I think about cost estimating and economics at the individual and firm level. Perhaps more importantly, the courses I took shaped my perspective on the Great Recession. Spring semester 2008 was as follows:

CEE 4014 – Estimating, Production, and Cost Engineering

CEE 4994 – Undergraduate Research

ECON 3104 – Microeconomic Theory

ECON 3214 – Money and Banking

MATH 1114 – Elementary Linear Algebra

STAT 3005 – Statistical Methods

I also started working as a research assistant in January 2008 within the civil engineering department. I was the sole economics major working in a research center with mostly graduate civil engineering students. The work was focused on Virginia's first performance-based road maintenance contracts. Most states at the time used means-based road maintenance contracts, and the research we were doing was trying to see if performance-based contracts would lead to better outcomes in the context of road maintenance.

In the "means-based" road maintenance approach, a contractor is paid based on the methods and materials used to complete a repair, like the number of potholes filled or tons of asphalt laid. In the "performance-based" road maintenance approach, a contractor is paid based on the achieved outcome or quality of the road after maintenance, incentivizing them to deliver better results rather than just completing tasks, and also encouraging innovation. My Fall semester in 2008 reinforced a lot of what I was learning at the research center. Fall semester 2008 was as follows:

CEE 4024 – Construction Control Techniques
CEE 4994 – Undergraduate Research
ECON 3254 – Analysis of Economic Data
ECON 4044 – Public Economics
ECON 4424 – Theory of Games and Economic Behavior

During the 2008 Presidential election cycle, the economy was center stage. Numerous large banks had engaged in unethical and irresponsible mortgage lending practices, which had brought their businesses to the brink of collapse. And, because those large banks were so integrated into the entire American economy, we were at risk of a system-wide failure, which could've led to a second Great Depression. In September of 2008, while the Presidential campaigns were in full swing, Congress was forced to take action and provided relief to the large banks to avoid nation-wide devastation. The two leading Presidential candidates, Senator Barack

Obama and Senator John McCain, released a joint statement saying, *"The effort to protect the American economy must not fail."*

It was a different time when there was still some level of respect between the two leading Presidential candidates. Looking back, the composure of Senator Obama and Senator McCain seems even more impressive today. In the last eight weeks of the 2008 Presidential election, Senator Obama was publicly being called a terrorist by the far right, and Senator McCain defended his political opponent in a Town Hall. The two candidates were tasked by fate with collaborating on high stakes legislation while competing against each other in a heated Presidential election. And somehow they figured out how to do it.

As if the financial crisis wasn't complicated enough, tax policy was also emphasized in the national conversation that year. This made sense as there were many Americans experiencing economic hardships. On October 12th, 2008, just days before the final Presidential debate, President Obama engaged in a conversation with a man in Toledo, Ohio who introduced himself as Joe Wurzelbacher and indicated that he was getting ready to buy a company that made $250,000 to $280,000 per year in revenue. The conversation started with a question about how Senator Obama's tax plan would impact Joe. Senator Obama responded directly with specifics.

*Senator Obama: "Well, here's what's going to happen. If you're a small business, which you would qualify, first of all you'd get a 15% tax credit. So, you'd get a cut on taxes for your healthcare costs. So you would actually get a tax cut on that front. If your revenue is above 250, then from 250 down your taxes are going to stay the same. It is true that for say 250 up, from 250 to 300 or so, for that additional amount you go from 36 to 39 percent, which is what it was under Bill Clinton. The reason we're doing that is because 95% of small businesses make less than 250. So what I want to do is give them a tax cut. I want to give all these folks who are bus drivers, teachers, autoworkers who make less, I want to give them a tax cut. And so what we're doing is we are saying that the folks who make more than 250 that the marginal amount above 250 they're going to be taxed at a 39 instead of a 36 percent rate."*

That is a pretty detailed response for a simple question on the campaign trail, and in a typical town hall event with a moderator, that might've been the end of that particular conversation. But this wasn't a town hall event. This was a random campaign stop in Toledo, Ohio standing outside in the middle of a crowd of people. The question was straightforward, and could've been asked in any election cycle in good times or bad. Joe Wurzelbacher's follow up question allowed the conversation to go to a deeper philosophical level, and also allowed Senator Obama to highlight his focus on the long-term sustainability of our economy.

*Joe Wurzelbacher: "Well the reason why I ask you about the American Dream, I mean, I work hard. I'm a plumber. You know I work 10 to 12 hours a day. And I'm buying this company, and I'm going to continue to work that way. Now, if I buy another truck and add something else to it and you know build the company you know I'm getting taxed more and more for fulfilling the American Dream."*

*Senator Obama: "Here is a way of thinking about it. How long you been a plumber? How long you been working?"*

*Joe Wurzelbacher: "15 years."*

*Senator Obama: "Ok, so over the last 15 years, when you weren't making 250, you would've been getting a tax cut from me. So, you would actually have more money, which means you would've saved more, which means you would've gotten to the point where you could build your small business quicker than under the current tax code. So, there are two ways of looking at it. I mean one way of looking at it is, now that you've become more successful through hard work, you don't want to be taxed as much, which I understand. But another way of looking at it is, 95% of folks who are making less than 250, they may be working hard too. But they're being taxed at a higher rate than they would be under mine.*

*So, what I'm doing is, put yourself back 10 years ago when you were only making 60 or 70. Under my tax plan, you would be keeping more of your paycheck and you'd be having lower taxes, which means that you would've saved and gotten to the point where you are faster.*

*Now look, nobody likes high taxes. Of course not. But what's happened is we've cut taxes a lot for folks like me who make a lot more than 250. We haven't given a break to folks who make less. And as a consequence the average wage and income for just ordinary folks, the vast majority of Americans, has actually gone down over the last 8 years. So all I want to do is, I've got a net tax cut. The only thing that changes is I'm going to cut taxes a little bit more for the folks who are most in need, and for the 5% of folks who are doing very well, even though they've been working hard and I understand that, and I appreciate that. I just want to make sure that they are paying a little bit more in order to pay for those other tax cuts.*

*Now, I respect the disagreement, but I just want you to be clear, its not that I want to punish your success. I just want to make sure that everybody who is behind you that they've got a chance at success too."*

This is the type of conversation and the level of detail that should happen every election cycle. The Presidential candidates should be able to engage with a random citizen in a crowd in any state in the country. It was a respectful interaction, and the candidate unpacked a policy position in detail and discussed the philosophy behind that policy position. Following that interaction between Senator Obama and Joe Wurzelbacher, the media machine started to focus on "Joe the plumber" as some sort of archetype of the average American small business owner. That week, "Joe the plumber" became the focus of national conversations and was a focal point in the last Presidential debate. Given my name, a number of my friends and family made sure to ping me with commentary. So, naturally, I started to be a little more intentional about how I developed and communicated my opinion.

When I was asked by friends and family in mid-October 2008 about what I, Joe Plummer, thought about the "Joe the plumber" tax policy debate, I had a foundational and growing body of knowledge to participate in meaningful conversations. I was lucky to have had recent and relevant classes and work experience so that I could attempt to navigate policy conversations a little. There were plenty of people in 2008 that compared Joe Wurzelbacher to Bud Johnson, Kevin Costner's character in the movie *Swing Vote*, which had been released earlier that year. I think it was really just the situation that reminded people of the movie.

In the movie, Bud Johnson somehow becomes the singular focus of a Presidential election in America, and the candidates from both major parties work to garner favor with Bud attempting to secure his vote. The candidates abandon some of their values and make outlandish promises to Bud in the hopes that the end justifies the means. Bud Johnson of course enjoys the attention he gets from the two powerful Presidential candidates. The movie culminates with a final Presidential debate where Bud Johnson is the sole moderator. After some soul searching, Bud decides to take his role seriously. Kevin Costner delivers a speech that I think candidates and voters can be inspired by in every election cycle.

*"We need someone who's bigger than their speeches. The kind of*

*President we learned about in school. America needs a big thinker. You know, like a giant, really. Someone who has the good sense to get in front of our problems. Somebody who has the wisdom to lead us to a place where we're at peace with ourselves and the world."*

That scene really resonated with me in a serious way after what was mostly a comical movie. I think it is easy to sit in the comfort of a single-family home in a middle class neighborhood and complain about how the federal government isn't writing and implementing policies that will make you better off. What is more difficult is understanding that there are a lot of people in this country that are suffering, and need the help of the federal government. Rainy days disproportionately impact the poor in negative ways, and it is the responsibility of the federal government to look at the whole system of systems on those rainy days and figure out who needs help the most. In the Rainy Day Economics framework, the third pillar – human-centered capitalism – must be part of every policy debate.

## Limits and Abundance

The Spring semester of 2009 was my last semester as an undergraduate. Despite the state of the economy, I was feeling good about where I was. I had a job working for a research center in a place with a low cost of living. I was about to graduate with honors and a degree in economics. My last semester included a light course load and allowed me some time to reflect on what the near future might look like. The courses that semester were as follows:

CEE 4994 – Undergraduate Research

ECON 3204 – Macroeconomic Theory

ECON 4074 – Labor Economics

PHYS 2206 – General Physics II

PHYS 2216 – General Physics II Lab

Those last two undergraduate economics courses – macroeconomic theory and labor economics – were well timed with the Great Recession of 2008. The courses from the previous year included microeconomics, money and banking, and public economics, which explained to some extent what caused the Great Recession. The big banks had taken on excessive risks and exploited low-income homebuyers, and that combined with the lack of regulation and oversight led to a system-wide failure. Unemployment reached 10% in October 2009. The immediate question was how to get millions of people back to work, and bail out the banks that were deemed too big to fail. But the longer-term question was more complex. How do we prepare for system-wide failures so that Great Recessions never happen again? The first two pillars of Rainy Day Economics – design and sustainability – are core to answering this question.

> ***Rainy Day Economics Design Prompt 7:*** *Architect a societal system that maximizes homeownership, minimizes risk of mortgage defaults, and doesn't allow low-income homebuyers to be exploited by banks. How might we design our economy such that more people are able to buy homes without substantially increasing the risk of defaulting on mortgages?*

We can of course add regulation and oversight to make sure big banks don't exploit low-income homebuyers again. We can maintain state and national rainy days funds so that a major economic slowdown in the housing market doesn't impact other areas of the economy. We can do a better job teaching financial literacy so that homebuyers are less likely to be exploited by banks. There are a lot of obvious "low-hanging fruit" ideas that we can implement to help avoid or mitigate rainy days similar to the 2008 housing crisis and recession. There are also less obvious ideas that leverage seemingly unrelated disciplines that could be helpful as we navigate increasingly complex economic downturns.

As I was taking the labor economics and macroeconomic theory courses, I was also taking a physics course, which had some curious parallels. In physics, all energy is accounted for and we know how to control energy flows through different kinds of systems. In the economy, we understand some of the basics of how money flows, but often times the government and the general public will turn a blind eye to money accumulating in the hands of a few people and corporations. This is problematic when there are millions of people that adopt a scarcity mindset while a powerful few are able to operate with a mindset of abundance. Our societal systems stop working when money doesn't flow to every part of the system. When people don't have money, when our institutions aren't properly funded, when nonprofits are starved, our society is made worse off.

And when we bail out the rich and powerful, but not the people, the institutions, and civil society, we invite entropy, chaos, and deterioration into our societal architecture. Economists can learn a lot from physics and ecological systems. I've noticed in a lot of the economics courses I've taken that instructors will intentionally remove some of the humanity from the equation. Humans are irrational, which makes traditional economic models difficult to apply unless there are assumptions made, and so traditional economic models will treat humans like robots with easy to understand preferences. This is not the kind of economics that I am advocating for.

The Rainy Day Economics framework embraces complexity, and then focuses on humanity. Traditional economics, particularly market-worshipping traditional economics, has become obsolete mostly because the real world is infinitely more complex than the oversimplified assumption-rich equilibrium models that traditional economists are clinging to. Traditional economists also will often ignore limits, which is problematic when considering the constraints associated with people, places, and the planet.

When designing societal architecture, there are obvious limits. Sometimes the laws of the natural world impose those limits. For example, resources, gravity, and time are all limits imposed by the natural world. There are also limits imposed by humans and human behavior. For example, property arrangements, contracts, willingness to pay, willingness to work, and willingness to produce are limits imposed by humans. There are also elements of the natural world and our humanity that seem limitless. For example, light from the sun and the moon's orbit both seem to be reliably limitless many years into the future. Likewise, human ingenuity seems boundless.

The basis of good science, good engineering, good architecture, and good economics is the ability to understand limits and to be able to measure and observe. If we can't measure and observe something, then we can't understand it and likewise we can't explain it. And if we can't understand something, then we can't understand how something impacts our quality of life. Likewise, if we can't understand and measure a limit, then we won't be able to figure out how to push the limit or maneuver around a constraint.

Pretend for a moment that we've found a way to inhabit Mars. Scientists, engineers, and architects have figured out how to sustain life on Mars. They know all of the tools, materials, food, water, and people they need to make life on Mars possible forever. Given all of that information, *how much money should exist on Mars?*

You may be thinking that Martians won't need money at first, because everyone will just do everything required of them, and there will be a plan to share resources and food in a structured and planned way. What happens when the population grows to the point where there are multiple cities on Mars? What happens when trade and industry develop? What happens when there is conflict on Mars? What happens when the government on

Mars wants to enact changes and incentivize or tax the citizens? How much Martian money will be required?

This thought exercise is useful to us, because it creates a framework for thinking about monetary theory on any planet at any stage of development, including Earth. Updating our societal thinking related to monetary theory and economics could lead to the greatest sustained improvement to quality of life on Earth ever.

Limits and constraints can also be observed and navigated on a micro-scale at the level of products.

Consider this book. This book may or may not be a tree, but probably is. When books are published in our society, they are usually printed on paper. Paper today is generally produced through an energy- and chemically-intensive process where thin sheets are manufactured using pulp derived from wood. However, in 2002, architect William McDonough and chemist Michael Braungart published a book called "*Cradle to Cradle: Remaking the Way We Make Things*", and it was not printed on paper that was derived from wood. McDonough and Braungart found a way to publish their book on infinitely recyclable paper that isn't made of trees. This is a true testament to human ingenuity and intention.

As McDonough pointed out in his TED Talk, trees make oxygen, sequester carbon, fix nitrogen, distill water, accrue solar energy as fuel, make complex sugars and food, create microclimates, change colors with the seasons and self-replicate. Can you imagine attempting to design and build a machine that does everything that a tree does naturally? Why would we cut down trees to write on them? Pause for a moment and think about that. Let me try to reframe the question a few times. Why are trees not sacred to us? How valuable are trees to us before they are cut down? How has our view of the value of living trees changed over time? Ah ha! Let's go deeper on this question.

When did we find out that trees make oxygen and sequester carbon?

It was the 1770s when Jan Ingenhousz discovered photosynthesis, the process by which plants absorb carbon dioxide and release oxygen. Also in the 1770s, Joseph Priestley discovered that humans need oxygen to live. And, in that same decade, America declared its independence and Adam Smith published "*The Wealth of Nations*", which would later earn him the title of "Father of Economics". So, imagine for a moment you are living during that era. You are probably not immersed in everything that is going on in the global scientific community. The world was at war, America was in its infancy, and there were major new scientific discoveries that weren't immediately understood by the general public. And even if you are exposed to any of the work of Jan Ingenhousz, Joseph Priestley, or Adam Smith, it is probably going to take you some time to fully grasp the work of each of those individually, and then potentially weave them together and then apply them to your values, your work, and your everyday life.

Likewise, governments of the time were busy dealing with social revolutions and international conflicts. Imagine being told at a convening of national leaders that scientists just discovered that trees produce oxygen and that humans need oxygen to breath. There is no action item after that announcement. Paper at that moment in time wasn't being made from trees. As a society, we didn't start printing on paper made from trees until the mid-1800s after the advent of sulfite processing. Before that, paper was made from cotton and linen rags, and only important documents used parchment made from animal skin. And trees were everywhere in abundance. The discovery that trees make what humans need to breath would never have been on any meeting agenda of the time, and there would have never been a reason to include any language in America's founding documents related to the value of the natural environment.

The use of paper today would seem almost archaic if it weren't so ubiquitous. What if the long-term realization of Adam Smith's early thoughts on labor specialization made it so that the only way a book today could be printed and not be a tree is if an architect and a chemist teamed up on a book about sustainable design? In other words, as labor has become so specialized, so too has production resulting in more difficult changes to the status quo. This is one of the reasons we should morph the economics profession from one that only analyzes and predicts to one that creates, optimizes, builds, and writes what our societal architecture looks like.

Traditional economists will often articulate market equilibrium as synonymous with the current status quo. They'll say the corporations and the wealthy have accumulated wealth by way of providing products and services that people value, and so the current state of society makes sense. Except it doesn't make sense when those corporations put profit ahead of people, places, and the planet. The Rainy Day Economics framework helps us strive to design a societal system that works for all people, places, and the planet.

# Chapter 6

## PEOPLE, PLACE, AND PLANET
### April 20, 2010

*"Spirit of place! It is for this we travel, to surprise its subtle-
ty; and where it is a strong and dominant angel, that place,
seen once, abides entire in the memory with all its own
accidents, its habits, its breath, its name."*

*- Alice Meynell*

---

In June 2010, I journeyed to New Orleans for a wedding. This was my first real opportunity to experience the city of New Orleans. I spent a lot of time that week absorbing the spirit of the place that is New Orleans. On one of the nights preceding the wedding, a group of friends and family went down to the French Quarter and walked around to different places listening to music. It was a beautiful night. I don't think I had ever been to a place that was so itself. I had been to cities and towns along the East Coast and in the Midwest, but New Orleans was unique because it didn't feel like it was drawing on any references from any other place in the United States. The architecture, the food, the music, the people – they were New Orleans, and only New Orleans, especially in the French Quarter.

At some point in the night, some of us arrived at a place on Frenchmen Street called The Spotted Cat. We had just listened to a brass band playing outside, and meandered into The Spotted Cat at the suggestion of someone in the group. We found some open space and continued conversations. Not long after we arrived, an attractive woman was looking at me and making her way through the crowd as if she knew me. Then, at the last second, I realized she was looking at someone behind me. "Story of my life," I thought to myself. And then I overheard her asking for a picture with someone. I turned around and saw Anderson Cooper casually talking with some of his friends. I didn't try to introduce myself. Nor did I say anything to anyone in our group. I had never met anyone remotely famous (except maybe ice hockey players), and I was content knowing that we were both sharing approximately the same experience of a night out with friends and family in the heart of New Orleans.

The night continued naturally, and eventually I decided to head back with some friends and family to where a group of us were staying. When we arrived back, my Great Aunt and Great Uncle were on the balcony next to mine in rocking chairs. They had just arrived back from Preservation Hall in the French Quarter. Preservation Hall is a well-known jazz venue that was a rare space in the South where racially integrated bands and audiences shared music together during the Jim Crow era. My Great Uncle Art brought national public radio (NPR) to Indianapolis in 1971, and he was a lifelong jazz musician that had played with a diverse jazz group in Indianapolis for decades. Preservation Hall had been a bucket list destination of his for a long time. I sat in the rocking chair on my balcony and talked to my Great Aunt and Great Uncle as a cool gentle breeze quietly danced the night to a peaceful end.

Thinking about that week reminds me of how much I love New Orleans, and how strong the spirit of place is there. It is also a place where the pillars of the Rainy Day Economics framework are at times on vibrant display. The intentional design of the city, the culture of sustainability, the thriving entrepreneurial ecosystem, the resilient people, and the abundance of art – all weave together in a city that is no stranger to disasters and tragedies. No stranger to rainy days.

*The class that came after Katrina*

A couple weeks before the wedding, Anderson Cooper was at Tulane University in New Orleans giving the commencement speech. In his deeply moving address to Tulane's Class of 2010, he acknowledged those young people that showed up and served and became part of the story of New Orleans – the vibrant, resilient, and joyful place that we all love. Consider their decisions for a moment. Pretend you are deciding on where to go to college or where to move to start your career. You are 18 to 23 years old, and you can live, study, and work wherever you want. Where do you go? These people moved to a place that had been devastated by a hurricane, a place that was still recovering, a place that had plenty of faults. They moved to New Orleans, because New Orleans has a spirit of place that they fell in love with, and they brought with them an entrepreneurial service mindset, which helped New Orleans grow out of disaster.

> *"You are the class that came after Katrina, and I'm sure you've heard this often, but that doesn't make it any less true. You saw this city on its knees in those weeks and months after the storm, and yet you still applied to Tulane. You could have gone elsewhere. A lot of folks probably said you were nuts to commit to New Orleans - some of your parents probably said the same thing.*

> *But you came anyway. You took a chance. You made a tough choice, but look at you now, look at what you've accomplished, not just for yourselves, but for New Orleans. Your choice helped this city rebuild, renew, restart.*

> *...*

> *In your time at Tulane in addition to studying, and working, and (all the other things you've done that I don't need to mention in front of your parents), you've also built homes, you've worked in schools, manned*

*clinics, volunteered with church groups and charities. You've reached out to strangers, and you've helped change people's lives.*

*Nearly five years after Katrina and New Orleans is back…yes, there is still much work to be done, wrongs to right, families that need healing, neighborhoods that need revival, but this city has risen, and its done so because you, and many others like you, did not give up. Local, state, federal governments, politicians, often failed in the wake of Katrina, but you and the people of this city did not.*"

*- Anderson Cooper, Tulane University 2010*
*Commencement Speech*

The commencement speech at Tulane wasn't the only reason Anderson Cooper was in New Orleans in May 2010. He was also interviewing survivors of the Deepwater Horizon explosion. Anderson Cooper had developed a reputation for on-the-ground reporting in New Orleans during the days and weeks following Hurricane Katrina. In his interview with some of the Deepwater Horizon survivors, one of the men remarked about the explosion, *"It looked like you was looking at the face of death. I mean you could hear it, see it, smell it."* It was a visceral personal account of the beginning of the worst environmental disaster in our country's history.

## An explosion off the coast of Louisiana

After graduating from Virginia Tech on time with a bachelor's degree in economics, I decided to continue working for the research center while taking some graduate level engineering classes. The Town of Blacksburg was a fun place to be. The cost of living was low. And, I was considering pursuing a graduate engineering degree, since the work I was doing was at the intersection of economics and engineering. From Fall 2009 to Fall

2010, I took the following courses while continuing to do research on performance-based road maintenance contracts:

ENGR 5104 – Applied Systems Engineering

ISE 5174 – Engineering Program and Project Management

ISE 5434 – Project Evaluation

CEE 5080 – Infrastructure Asset Management

CEE 5684 – Rehabilitation of Transportation Structures

CEE 4804 – Professional and Legal Issues in Civil Engineering

These courses were particularly relevant to the research I was doing, and they allowed me to dive deeper into the dynamics of maintaining infrastructure and our quality of life in the United States. The complexity of my research increased as I layered on different aspects of maintaining our societal systems. In addition to considering if the roads were being maintained at a sufficient level, I was also considering things like cost of maintenance, likelihood of innovation, labor required to maintain high levels of service, and the impact of natural deterioration cycles and unforeseen shocks to the system. It was a lot to analyze, and I was only skimming the surface of the multitude of potential research paths.

While I was asking the economics questions, other graduate students in the research center were diving deep on data collection technology. They were asking questions about how to efficiently and safely collect the data necessary to determine the condition of an infrastructure asset. I supported a couple of studies at Virginia Tech's smart road facility, which is a 2.2-mile long controlled-access test track section of road built to Federal Highway Administration standards. The studies looked at things like radio frequency identification (RFID) tags and readers attached to highway assets and multi-view cameras mounted on data collection vehicles. The goal was to find ways for the condition of the infrastructure assets to be determined accurately, quickly, and closer to real time. The civil engineering research at Virginia Tech has time and again proved to be relevant to environmental and public health disasters over the past 25 years.

On April 20th, 2010, the Deepwater Horizon oil rig exploded off the coast of Louisiana. The platform was being used to extract oil from a well about three miles under the surface of the water. There were 11 crew members killed and 94 that were rescued by the U.S. Coast Guard. On the morning of April 22nd, 2010 (Earth Day), the Deepwater Horizon drilling rig sank, and then later that day a massive oil leak was discovered. The drilling rig was owned by BP (British Petroleum), a multinational oil and gas company that has continued to have record setting profits in the 15 years since the oil spill in 2010.

According to BP, the oil leak was flowing at a modest 1,000 to 5,000 barrels per day, but an unbiased third party estimated the initial flow rate to be closer to 62,000 barrels per day. Over the next 87 days, approximately 4.9 million barrels of oil were spilled into the Gulf of Mexico. The result was catastrophic and despite extensive clean up efforts, there was still oil washing up on shore for years after the oil spill. There were devastating impacts to the wildlife in the region, including to some endangered species. The people that worked on the cleanup efforts were exposed to toxic carcinogens that caused health impacts for months and years after the disaster. The event also cost the Gulf Coast economy an estimated $22.7 billion just through 2013.

To put into perspective the scale of our society's oil addiction, the United States uses about 20 million barrels of oil every day. There are multiple ways to look at the scale of the event. One could frame the estimated 4.9 million barrels that spilled into the Gulf of Mexico as a tiny percentage of all of the oil that was later burned and spewed into the environment through normal economic activity. In my opinion, it is more useful to think about it in the opposite way. Every day, the United States uses four times as much oil as was spilt into the Gulf of Mexico in the largest environmental disaster in history. How can we expect the environment to support life on Earth, when we are so recklessly emitting greenhouse gases and toxic chemicals into our atmosphere and oceans?

I know I'm not going to convince the majority of Americans to significantly reduce their fossil fuel consumption overnight, so perhaps it makes more sense to focus on preventing catastrophic drilling rig explosions and oil spills. At the time of Deepwater Horizon explosion, the U.S. Department of Interior's Minerals Management Service (MMS) was responsible for regulating the oil and gas resources on the outer continental shelf (OCS). Unfortunately, the Minerals Management Service provided poor regulatory oversight due to a number of reasons including being understaffed, a culture of unethical behavior, and a revolving door with the oil industry that made it difficult for the agency to be effective at regulating.

As you can imagine, poor regulation has caused more ripple effects than just the Deepwater Horizon disaster. The National Oceanic and Atmospheric Administration's (NOAA) Office of Response and Restoration responds to over 150 oil and chemical spills annually that occur as a result of equipment breaking down, people making mistakes, and natural disasters. Even in the years following the BP oil spill, NOAA has had to respond to numerous smaller oil and chemical spills. Deepwater Horizon garnered the country's attention in 2010, but only because of the scale of the event.

My economics journey started at George Mason University, home of the Mercatus Center. Mercatus means market, and George Mason University's Economics Department is well funded by numerous wealthy Libertarian donors, such as Charles Koch, that believe regulation is bad and the market is infallible. In a recent presentation open to the public, one tenured economics professor at George Mason University remarked that the famous Dr. Seuss story of *The Lorax* would never be a reality, because as the trees became more and more scarce, the market would value them more and more until the trees would be so valuable that they wouldn't be chopped down, because no individual or firm would be willing to pay the obscenely high price to purchase the tree or its inherent resources.

This argument is of course deeply flawed, and I think the tenured professor knows it, but his students might not yet. One of the first concepts every economics student learns is the *"Tragedy of the Commons"*. This concept describes situations where a shared resource is depleted by individuals acting in their own self-interest until the resource is overused or completely exhausted, thus making everyone worse off. Adam Smith, considered by many to be the father of economics, also identified the "Diamond-Water Paradox", which acknowledged that there are some things that the market values highly that are *not* essential to life like diamonds, and there are things that the market doesn't value highly that *are* essential to life like water.

The purpose of regulation is to protect society from individuals and firms acting in their own self-interest. The Deepwater Horizon explosion and the months long oil spill that followed could have been prevented by adequate regulation. The three corporations involved, BP, Transocean, and Halliburton, were of course held responsible for the explosion and the oil spill, and they paid billions of dollars in cleanup expenses and lawsuit fines. But at this moment in time, about 15 years after the Deepwater Horizon explosion, it seems like a large portion of America has bought into the idea that we as a society are overregulated.

I think advocates for deregulation will argue that unfortunate tragedies will happen from time to time, but corporations will learn from their mistakes and avoid risks, because they want to make a profit. BP can't keep making a profit if their drilling rigs keep blowing up. That's true, but BP can also make a profit while taking on risks that probably make a lot of coastal communities uncomfortable. Keep in mind that the corporate executives at BP don't lose homes and livelihood when oil spills happen.

They take on none of the risk that their corporation does, and the risk that the corporation takes on is measured in dollars not lives. Corporations care about dollars, and society cares about a lot more than money.

> ***Rainy Day Economics Design Prompt 8:*** *Identify a technology for monitoring critical infrastructure assets so that catastrophic failures are prevented. How might we use technology to achieve high levels of safety during construction and operation of infrastructure assets?*

The corporations involved in the Deepwater Horizon event didn't even have an immediate solution for capping the well that was spilling into the Gulf of Mexico. They were drilling three miles underwater, and they didn't have the technology to fix the most predictable emergency, at least not in a timely manner. It is tough for me to believe that BP, Transocean, and Halliburton have society's best interest in mind when their infrastructure asset maintenance was so far behind the research I was seeing done in Virginia Tech's civil engineering department. A state university with a tiny fraction of the budget and staff of those massive corporations had a far better understanding of infrastructure asset maintenance and the necessary data collection technology.

The second and third pillars of Rainy Day Economics – sustainability and human-centered capitalism – address the need for robust infrastructure asset monitoring and effective safety measures in society, but there is still a question of who is responsible and willing to pay for robust infrastructure asset monitoring and effective safety measures in society. Corporations have time and again proved to be unwilling or unable to put people, places, and the planet ahead of corporate profit.

## *Is government an instrument of good?*

I've been cynical about the news media at many points in my life, but there have also been many inspiring moments where journalists have shown up in the wake of disasters and helped people and communities tell stories that would otherwise never have been heard by the rest of the country. Some of the rainy days in this book could have easily been ignored were it not for the journalists telling the stories of those survivors and communities.

In June 2012, Aaron Sorkin's television series "The Newsroom" was released. The premise of the show followed a fictional cable news network team as they tried to report the news with integrity amidst conflict with the network's corporate and political interests. In the first season, each episode was based on a recent major news event in the real world. On the surface, the first episode was about Deepwater Horizon and the BP oil spill. However, at a deeper level, the purpose of the first episode was to lay the groundwork for the entire show and engage the viewer in a vital real world conversation. MacKenzie McHale, played by Emily Mortimer, was the heroic executive producer that asserted in the first episode, *"There is nothing that is more important in a democracy than a well-informed electorate."*

As information about Deepwater Horizon slowly trickled in, MacKenzie McHale is arguing with Will McAvoy, a moderate Republican news anchor and the main character of the show. In the process of trying to convince Will McAvoy to buy into her quixotic vision, MacKenzie McHale is also activating the minds of the viewers.

> *"America is the only country on the planet, that since its birth has said over and over and over that we can do better. It's part of our DNA. People will want the news if you give it to them with integrity. Not everybody, not even a lot of people, 5%. And 5% more of anything is what makes the difference in this country. So we can do better!"*

Will McAvoy is not convinced early on in the show, at least that's what he says. He argues that the country is too polarized to have any meaningful conversations at a high level. He then asks a question that, in my opinion, led to Emily Mortimer delivering the most important speech in the show. *"What does winning look like to you?"*

> *"Reclaiming the fourth estate. Reclaiming journalism as an honorable profession. A nightly newscast that informs a debate worthy of a great nation. Civility, respect, and a return to what's important. The death of bitchiness, the death of gossip and voyeurism. Speaking truth to stupid. No demographic sweet spot. A place where we all come together.*
>
> *We're coming to a tipping point. I know you know that. There's going to be a huge conversation. **Is government an instrument of good or is it every man for himself? Is there something bigger we want to reach for or is self-interest our basic resting pulse? You and I have a chance to be among the few people who can frame that debate."***

I believe we've arrived at the point in our history where our society in America is actively deciding if government is an instrument of good or if it is every person for themselves. I want to believe that there are some things that are bigger than ourselves that we want to reach for together. Maybe self-interest is our basic resting pulse, but it is from there that we invite adrenaline into our lives to pursue exciting endeavors that benefit our communities and humanity. I believe America is in the process of understanding how we as a society can do better together. Hopefully, Rainy Day Economics can serve that conversation.

# Chapter 7

## THE COST OF PREPARING FOR THE WORST
### March 11, 2011

*"Even if you encounter opposition, have conviction and finish what you start. In the end, people will understand."*

*- Kotaku Wamura, Mayor of Fudai, Japan*

---

From first grade through high school, I was a part of a Japanese immersion program. In elementary school, I was taught math, science, and health in Japanese by a Japanese teacher. In middle and high school, the Japanese class became solely about the language, but for the six years of elementary school, me and about 25 other kids spent half of each day immersed in Japan's language and culture. The Japanese Immersion program was only available in two elementary schools in western Fairfax County, and there were no other language immersion programs in those two schools.

Why did we have a Japanese immersion program? I really don't know, but I think there could have been a number of good reasons. There were numerous Japanese companies emerging in the United States during the 1990s when I was in elementary school, and I was growing up in the suburbs of Washington, D.C. I could see how the local elected leaders of Fairfax County may have seen an opportunity to develop a subset of students into uniquely capable global citizens as the ecosystem of technology companies grew worldwide, but especially in Japan. The Fairfax County School Board of the 1990s probably expected the Floris

Elementary School Class of 1999 to go on to negotiate trade deals with Japan, but none of us ended up using our Japanese education in our careers, at least not directly.

Does that mean the investment in the Japanese immersion program was a waste? That depends on your view of the value of teaching global perspectives. I started writing this chapter on January 20th, 2025, the day we honored Dr. Martin Luther King, Jr. Once a year, we remember the civil rights leader and reflect on his words more intently. Dr. Martin Luther King, Jr.'s words have stood the test of time over and over again, and they continue to provide society with wisdom and guidance.

*"It really boils down to this: that all life is interrelated. We are all caught in an inescapable network of mutuality, tied into a single garment of destiny. Whatever affects one directly, affects all indirectly."*

*- Dr. Martin Luther King, Jr.*

Those words are particularly relevant today in early 2025 as nationalism and self-interest have spread quickly and globally, like a terrible wildfire burning through a societal garment that took decades to weave. It has become difficult to articulate a collective vision that an overwhelming majority of citizens can rally behind. The question we have arrived at is *— how do we relate to a global community of nations?* This is an important question in the context of Rainy Day Economics as it implies the scope and scale of our work.

Americans can learn a lot from Japanese culture. Minimalism, cleanliness, respect for the environment, and efficiency are elementary foundations in Japanese society. When you visit Japan, the streets are clean, the infrastructure is well maintained, and the systems are efficient. When you come home to America after visiting Japan, you realize how dirty, disorganized, and inefficient our societal systems are here in the United States.

American society is driven by consumerism and profiteering with the singular aim of increasing Gross Domestic Product (GDP). Some might argue that American society is driven by freedom, but I think at this moment in time it is difficult for Americans to break free from the influence that corporations have over their lives. From the food we eat to the products and services we use to the information we receive, corporations have far more control and influence than any fundamental cultural principles, government and academic institutions, or even community- and faith-based organizations.

There are three concepts from Japanese culture that I think are particularly relevant to Rainy Day Economics. These are concepts that will help us reframe our minds and develop more creative approaches to designing societal systems enabling us to navigate an uncertain future. The first concept is *wabi-sabi*, which refers to an awareness and appreciation of the transient nature of earthly things and an understanding and acceptance that plans go awry. This is an important mindset, because as we are designing societal systems, there will always be imperfections, and the responses to disasters will rarely go precisely according to plan. In the context of recovery, beautiful unplanned moments can occur often, and appreciating those moments can help communities find peace and joy as they rebuild.

The second concept that is useful for reframing our thinking for Rainy Day Economics is *kaizen*, which is a Japanese business philosophy signifying continuous improvement or change for the better. This concept might seem too general, but it is really referring to incremental change. It isn't suggesting we continuously start from scratch with our societal designs, rather kaizen is about iteration and rapidly addressing issues while they are small. The political pendulum has been swinging more drastically over the past few election cycles, which is creating more uncertainty in our societal systems. A more logical approach to changing our societal systems for the better is *kaizen* or continuous incremental improvements.

The third concept from Japanese culture that I think is perhaps most relevant to Rainy Day Economics is *ikigai*, which refers to that which gives us as individuals a sense of purpose in life. There will always be rainy days, and it is conceivable that the scale and frequency of rainy days will grow over time. If we as individuals know that rainy days are going to happen, then we should also be intentional about how we want to live our lives in relation to those rainy days. How do we as individuals navigate rainy days when they happen? How do we serve our communities when rainy days happen? How do we relate to the world when rainy days happen far away from us? These are all questions that require deep personal reflection, but they are also questions that could lead individuals to and through a deeply meaningful life.

## To strive together

There is a conversation going on right now in 2025 about tariffs. Tariffs are taxes on goods and services imported from other countries. The argument for tariffs is that they can be good for raising revenue, making America more competitive, and incentivizing companies to produce goods and services in America as opposed to in other countries. However, each of those arguments for tariffs has a counter argument that basically proves that tariffs are ineffective, inflationary, and inflammatory.

Let's start with what makes tariffs ineffective. The goal of some tariffs is to encourage more American manufacturing, but the manufacturing in other countries is often significantly cheaper and, in some cases, better quality. Taxing imports doesn't suddenly reduce the cost of American manufacturing. Nor do tariffs automatically increase the quality of American manufacturing. The way you reduce the costs associated with American manufacturing and increase the quality of American manufacturing is by investing in American manufacturing, as well as, research and development. Manufacturers abroad have at times made significant advances through state sponsored efforts similar to how America invested significantly in manufacturing capabilities around the time of World War II.

Tariffs are also inflationary and inflammatory. When America adds tariffs to goods and services, those costs are passed on to the consumer or end user. What makes tariffs inflammatory is when other countries decide to respond or retaliate by creating tariffs of their own, and then it becomes more costly for American manufacturers to sell to other countries. A tariff war can also create more tensions between countries outside the context of just commerce. We shouldn't be testing the limits of goodwill in a time when so many countries are dealing with their own internal constraints and pressures that are likely far more intense than those in the United States, a country with more purchasing power and more access to natural resources than most smaller nations.

Tariffs are just poorly thought out attempts at feeding a nationalist agenda. I believe we need to evolve beyond nationalism as a global society. John Nash, the mathematician that pioneered game theory, gave us the start of a roadmap for success in his dissertation in 1950 where he described how to navigate non-cooperative games. Non-cooperative games model a competitive environment, which is useful to us in our global economy. One of his many useful discoveries was depicted in the movie *A Beautiful Mind.*

A beautiful blonde woman walks into the bar with a group of her friends. John Nash's colleagues start to strategize how they will compete for the attention of the beautiful blonde woman. They all remember and recite Adam Smith's words *"individual ambition serves the common good."* And then John Nash, played by Russell Crowe, eloquently refutes their affirmation with his own.

*"Adam Smith said, 'the best result comes from everyone in the group doing what's best for himself.' Incomplete. Incomplete. Because the best result will come from everyone in the group doing what's best for himself and the group."*

*- John Nash's character in A Beautiful Mind*

This was John Nash's thinking in the 1950s. Game theory has evolved for decades since that early work. So, what do we as a society have to show for it? It might be the case that some high level policy makers and elected officials have adopted some form of advanced game theory, but as a society, it seems like we are going backwards. Game theory, particularly when making use of Nash's work, is all about making other people's decisions irrelevant to our own. In other words, it is about making it so that no matter what someone else does, you have a plan that leads to an optimal outcome for you and them.

At a societal level, we need to navigate away from conflict and towards better outcomes for America and the rest of the world. In his 2005 TED Talk, Architect William McDonough articulated a vision for how competition can be used in a cooperative way to help our global society get fit together.

*"Now if we look at the word 'competition', I'm sure most of you've used it. You know, most people don't realize it comes from the Latin 'competere', which means 'strive together'. It means the way Olympic athletes train with each other. They get fit together, and then they compete. The Williams sisters compete -- one wins Wimbledon. So we've been looking at the idea of competition as a way of cooperating in order to get fit together."*

*- William McDonough, 2005 TED Talk*

The challenge for elected leaders is to navigate global cooperative and non-cooperative games simultaneously competing and collaborating with many nations as they do the same; all while constituents are critiquing the work and sometimes voting people out of office. If America's overarching societal goal is simply to compete with other countries, then even if we win, we will lose. On the other hand, if America's overarching societal goals are more purpose-driven, then meaningful success is possible. I believe that if America wants to lead a global community of nations, then it has to be willing to care for and invest in that global community of nations.

## *The courage of one's convictions*

Kotaku Wamura was the mayor of the small coastal village of Fudai, Japan for four decades from 1947 to 1987. During his tenure as mayor, he convinced the village council to fund the construction of a floodgate and seawall to protect the village from any potential tsunami. Kotaku Wamura had lived through an earlier tsunami in 1933, and so it was important to him that he protect his community from the devastation that he had seen. During his tenure as mayor and for years after, the investments in the floodgate and seawall were considered to be a colossal waste of money. The structures were built from 1972 to 1984 for the equivalent of about $30 million, which was a significant amount of money for a small village during a time when the global economy was not doing well. Kotaku Wamuro was at times ridiculed for wasteful government spending.

It wasn't until over 25 years later that the investment paid off. On March 11, 2011, a powerful earthquake in the Pacific Ocean caused a tsunami with waves said to start at over 100 feet high traveling at over 400 miles per hour and continuing inland at heights up to 20 feet. The waves traveled up to 6 miles inland and flooded and destroyed everything in their path. Almost 20,000 people were killed and hundreds of thousands of people had their homes damaged or completely destroyed. However, the small coastal village of Fudai was virtually untouched, and it was because of the infrastructure that the government had invested in to keep the people of the village safe in the face of the worst disaster conceivable.

This is the type of long-term thinking that the second pillar of Rainy Day Economics – sustainability – seeks to inspire. What can we learn from this story? The obvious lessons learned relate to how we think about conceivable large-scale natural disasters in the long-term, and how those potential events in the distant future shape our decisions in the short-term. There is some infrastructure that we build to get thousands or millions of people from point A to point B, but there is also infrastructure that we as a society must build in order for thousands or millions of us to get from time A to time B. That is what sustainability is all about. Scientists know that the worst natural disasters won't be the ones that originate on Earth. NASA keeps an inventory of asteroids, comets, and meteors that could hit Earth and cause catastrophic events. But there aren't many local, state, and national governments or elected leaders that take large scale natural disasters seriously. Kotaku Wamuro was an exception.

In order to navigate an uncertain future, global leaders need to develop a societal risk register and find ways to allocate resources to effectively prepare for disasters that could occur on massive scales. It is conceivable that the habitability of the planet could change in the coming decades, and this presents a global challenge, not just to fix the associated problems, but also how to fund the efforts. A societal risk register would allow us to think long term and get ahead of future large scale rainy days.

Tsunamis and earthquakes are common enough in certain parts of the world that it makes complete sense for governments at various levels to fund major infrastructure projects to protect citizens from the terrible impacts. Before the tsunami in Japan in 2011, there was an earthquake in Haiti that killed somewhere between 100,000 and 160,000 people. And, before that there was an earthquake and tsunami in the Indian Ocean that killed over 225,000 people. This book that you are reading right now started with the September 11th terrorist attacks that killed about 3,000 people. And some might argue that we spent trillions of dollars after those attacks trying to prevent similar attacks from happening again. In that regard, Kotaku Wamuro's courage seems completely reasonable when you consider that he saved about 3,000 people in his village at a cost of about $30 million, far less than the trillions America spent reacting to September 11th. Sometimes being an elected leader is about the courage of one's convictions, but I think more often it is about articulating costs, benefits, risks, probabilities, impacts, scenarios, alternatives, timelines, and the value of human lives. So often elected leaders fall into the trap of only thinking about the budget of today rather than thinking about the people of the future.

## Humanitarian Aid

In the aftermath of the tsunami that hit Japan on March 11th, 2011, over 340,000 people were displaced and the country faced shortages of food, water, medicine, and fuel. The United States and many other countries sent search and rescue teams to help with the response. Fairfax County's world-renowned search and rescue team was deployed as they often are to natural disasters. The Japan Times reported a year later that over 900,000 people had assisted with recovery efforts. The Japanese Red Cross also reported receiving over $1 billion in donations from all over the world. The massive scale of the response and recovery efforts was truly remarkable. However, the long-term cost of rebuilding was considerably larger, estimated to be over $120 billion.

> ***Rainy Day Economics Design Prompt 9:*** *Brainstorm what an international rainy day fund might look like and how it would be created and managed. How might we prepare as a global community of nations for massive natural disasters that overwhelm the response and recovery capacity of individual countries?*

The majority of Americans seem generally supportive of humanitarian aid particularly in the early days after a major disaster. However, as the conversation shifts to how much we invest in helping other countries build or rebuild their economies, Americans become a little more hesitant to support investments abroad. This is also similar to how many Americans think about international trade. I think for towns in the Heartland of America there is a sentiment that before money flows to other countries, it should first be invested in communities in America that have been impacted by technological progress and the outsourcing of jobs.

How do you convince a person in middle America that globalization and international trade are good for society when that person just lost their manufacturing job because of either automation or globalization and international trade? The famous conservative economist Milton Friedman once said, *"Most economic fallacies derive from the tendency to assume that there is a fixed pie, that one party can gain only at the expense of another."* For those that aren't familiar with Milton Friedman, he was President Ronald Reagan's go to economist and influenced a lot of conservative thinking starting in the 1980s.

This is a curious statement from the conservative economist. But, it actually seems like something advocates for Modern Monetary Theory (MMT) might assert today in the context of the creation and flow of money, particularly in relation to a global community of nations. Advocates for MMT have argued that we can print money to spend on societal problem sets, particularly complex problem sets that are not easily solvable at the local or regional level. Michael Metcalfe, the Head of Macro Strategy at State Street Global Markets, has advocated for an approach to international aid that I think Milton Friedman would support. In Michael Metcalfe's TED Talk in 2013, he unpacks an idea that is actionable and deserves at least some low-risk experimentation on a global scale. His idea is simple – *What if we print money for foreign aid?*

At first glance, people may have a predictable knee jerk reaction and argue that this would inherently cause inflation or the devaluation of currency. But Michael Metcalfe, a globally respected expert in macroeconomics and financial markets, doesn't see it that way. When looking at the quantitative easing that was executed during the 2008 financial crisis, there was no inflationary impact in the years that followed. Likewise, the dollar got stronger in the decade that followed the 2008 financial crisis.

Milton Friedman was also the economist that championed the *quantity theory of money*, which said that increasing the money supply would cause a proportional increase in prices. In other words, he suggested that if we increase the money supply by 10%, then prices across the entire economy would also go up 10%. It is important to note that prices rarely go up uniformly across the entire economy. But, for a moment, let's pretend that the quantity theory of money is correct. What would've happened if the United States printed $120 billion to help Japan rebuild after the 2011 tsunami? The United States money supply was approximately $10 trillion at the time of the tsunami, so adding $120 billion would've been an increase of about 1.2%. So, if Milton Friedman was right, then prices in the United States would've increased by 1.2%, which I personally would've been proud to endure knowing that our aid was helping Japan rebuild. I believe Milton Friedman's quantity theory of money is wrong though, and MMT may be the key to deploying Rainy Day Economics on a global scale, particularly for planetary problem sets.

# Chapter 8

## LIVE TO LEARN AND LEARN TO LIVE
### October 29, 2012 - April 15, 2013

*"Tragedy is a tool for the living to gain wisdom, not a guide
by which to live."*

*- Senator Robert F. Kennedy, March 18, 1968 at Kansas State University*

---

The middle school I attended growing up was named after Rachel Carson, the famous conservationist credited with starting the movement that led to the creation of the Environmental Protection Agency (EPA). Our mascot at Rachel Carson Middle School was a black panther, and our rival middle school, particularly for track and field, was Langston Hughes Middle School. I have a feeling that some of my interests in writing, social activism, and environmentalism were seeded during those formative years in middle school.

From 2009 to 2010, I volunteered to help my alma mater middle school pursue a solar installation that would serve a few different functions. The solar installation was the idea of an environmental club at the school that was led by a legendary environmental educator named Mr. Treakle. When I was a student at Rachel Carson Middle School from 1999 to 2001, Mr. Treakle had offered to shave his head if our school won a recycling competition, and as a result many more students participated in the recycling competition. Then, almost ten years later, when students in the environmental club said they wanted to get solar panels installed on the school's roof, Mr. Treakle took the idea seriously and supported their endeavor.

It was a small group of 10 to 15 students that took responsibility for making the project happen. They called the initiative the "Future Renewable Energy Effort" or FREE, referring of course to the free electricity that the school would receive if the project was a success. They made a video, a brochure, a website and a model. They presented their project at the school's Showcase Night. They also presented at the school's Parent Teacher Association (PTA), and then the PTA decided to give them some money to actually make the project happen. I worked with Mr. Treakle and the students to find more money for the project. Most notably, Dominion, Lowe's, the Earth Day Network, and my mom's small business supported the project through grants and donations. After months of effort, the student-led project had raised about $40,000.

In November 2010, a 2.6-kilowatt solar array was installed on the roof of Rachel Carson Middle School. This included 11 solar panels, the associated mounting system, all of the electrical work, and a connected data monitoring system in one of the science classrooms. On December 27th, 2010, the panels started contributing clean power to the school, and they have been doing so ever since. The students hosted a "Flip the Switch" event and celebrated the completed project.

At the time of writing this book, that little 2.6-kilowatt solar array had produced about 47 Megawatt-hours of electricity over about 14 years. That's the equivalent of about 560 trees being planted or about 33 tons of carbon dioxide emissions avoided. But I am more curious about how many students have since had lessons in their science classes at Rachel Carson Middle School where the solar array and data monitoring system were part of the learning moments. The school graduates about 700 students every year, so perhaps a conservative estimate would be 500 students multiplied by 14 years, which is 7,000 students that have since had learning moments about renewable energy from that little demonstration project.

I was in the Boy Scouts growing up, and my Eagle service project was planting two trees, building a few wood benches, and a pedestal for art in my high school's courtyard. The benches and pedestal from that Eagle service project have probably since deteriorated, and the two trees likely struggled to get enough annual sunlight given their location in a courtyard where they were often in the shade depending on the time of year. The courtyard was also not utilized a lot by teachers and students. So, when comparing my Eagle service project in high school to the Rachel Carson Middle School solar project, it was clear that the solar project was going to be far more impactful for far longer. After the solar project went live at the end of 2010, the question in my mind quickly became *"how can I replicate this project?"*

## Three Birds

About six weeks into 2011, my big sister dragged me to what I thought was going to be a boring teaching conference. The event was the Teach For America 20th Anniversary Summit, and it was definitely not a boring teaching conference. There were numerous inspiring speeches, conversations, and performances, including a memorable performance by John Legend. But what I remember most from the whole event was the moment one of my questions was answered. I was sitting in the middle of a large room listening to a panel of powerful people speak about the future of education, and then they opened up the conversation to questions from the crowd.

They asked those interested in asking questions to write the questions down and hand the questions to runners who then took the questions up to the moderator. To my surprise, the moderator asked my question, which was something like *"what is the role of creativity?"* Looking back, I could've been more specific, but in any case, one of the panelists responded, and that panelist was Donald Graham, the CEO of The Washington Post. In his response to my question, Donald Graham asserted that Teach For America was the most creative nonprofit organization ever. That was the moment when I decided to start a nonprofit organization. I think it was a little bit a challenge in my mind, but more so after experiencing the Teach For America 20th Anniversary Summit, it was the culmination of a day that whispered, *"look what one nonprofit organization can do"*.

Within a couple weeks of the Teach For America 20th Anniversary Summit, I had prepared all of the paperwork to set up a nonprofit organization. As it turns out, you can actually complete most of the paperwork to create a nonprofit organization and apply for 501(c)(3) status without talking to a single person. However, before you are granted nonprofit status, your organization must have a board of directors. This begins the expansion of an individual's vision to other accepting hearts and minds. At first, I just called up friends and family and told them about what I was doing, and then I began talking to schools, nonprofit leaders, elected officials, corporate representatives and university professors with the hope of spreading my vision: *solar panels and a classroom data monitoring system at every school in America.*

The name of my beloved nonprofit was poorly thought out. I wanted to speak to the effectiveness and multi-faceted impact of having solar demonstration projects at every school in America. I thought of the old saying - *"hitting two birds with one stone"*. My nonprofit was going to have a massive positive environmental, educational, and economic impact, and so I decided to name the organization *"Three Birds"* alluding to the effectiveness of addressing three societal problem sets with one organization. On my initial website, I explained what that meant, but eventually I stopped explaining the name of the organization. The time it took to explain what the name of the organization meant was valuable time that I could've been getting deeper into the elevator pitch. Also, using a metaphor about killing birds was a bad start to a conversation about an environmental nonprofit organization. Some people just thought I was referring to the Bob Marley song.

During the summer in 2011, as I was setting up my nonprofit organization, I became concerned that I wasn't doing everything I needed to be doing, particularly related to the governance of the organization. So, I signed up for two graduate-level night classes at Virginia Tech that allowed me to get a deeper understanding of the nonprofit sector and nonprofit governance.

UAP 5364 – Non-governmental Organizations in Development
UAP 5454 – Nonprofit Organizations and Management

By the fall of 2011, I received the coveted Determination Letter from the IRS granting my organization 501(c)(3) nonprofit status. I had built an initial website, formed a Board of Directors for governance, as well as a Board of Advisors for more guidance, and I had connected with five local low-income schools to pilot programs in the upcoming school year. I spent the 2011 to 2012 school year going into classrooms and after school clubs with renewable energy demonstrations, things like a set of small solar panels connected to a water pump or a KidWind wind turbine or a bike connected to a light bulb. These educational demonstrations were the hook to get students engaged. While I was doing that, I was also talking to teachers and administrators about pursuing grants that would allow the schools to get real solar installations on site with data monitoring systems in the classroom the way Rachel Carson Middle School did.

That first year, I realized that Rachel Carson Middle School had a lot of things going for it that the low-income schools didn't have. For starters, Rachel Carson Middle School had an identity associated with environmentalism. There were pictures of Rachel Carson, the famous environmentalist in the building and students knew who she was and what she was about. Rachel Carson Middle School also had years of momentum when they started their solar project. They had done about 8 to 10 years of other smaller projects like recycling challenges, tree plantings, energy audits, and the like. But perhaps the biggest difference between Rachel Carson Middle School and the low-income schools was that Rachel Carson Middle School had an active and relatively wealthy PTA (Parent Teacher Association) that could invest seed money in a renewable energy project and connect the school to other sponsors. The low-income schools had PTAs, but many of the parents were working two jobs, and the schools had other priorities that they wanted to focus on with the PTA. Solar panels were considered by some to be a luxury investment for schools with more resources.

These low-income schools were all less than ten miles from Rachel Carson Middle School, and they were all part of the Fairfax County Public School system. Fairfax County has been one of the wealthiest counties in the country for decades, but there is still poverty in Fairfax County. I think there is a sentiment in America that the Washington, D.C. metropolitan area is somehow insulated from economic hardships, but I can tell you that there are communities in Northern Virginia where parents still struggle to get by and provide for their kids. The Washington, D.C. metropolitan region is not recession proof, and certainly not when the current Administration is intent on tearing down the federal government and making deep cuts to the federal government's workforce. As I'm writing this chapter, it is only a week into the new Administration, and there is already a wide spread palpable fear of at least regional economic collapse in the Washington, D.C. area, and maybe even a nationwide Great Depression.

## *Entrepreneurship Immersion*

At the beginning of 2012, I had completed a number of teaching experiments with the five pilot schools and connected with dozens of others that were interested in our programs. We had also connected with quite a few other nonprofits, universities, potential sponsors, and local elected leaders. But I still didn't feel like I knew what I was doing or how to scale the work I was doing. As I got more and more connected to nonprofits and universities, I became aware of a number of programs that helped young social entrepreneurs learn and grow. Babson College's Lewis Institute for Social Innovation and a changemaker community called StartingBloc both captured my attention around the same time in early 2012. I decided to apply to both programs at the same time – the Babson College one-year Masters in Business Administration (MBA) program and the StartingBloc Fellowship.

Babson College was (and still is) considered to be the best university in the country to learn entrepreneurship. And the StartingBloc Fellowship was hosting one of its 5-day institutes at Babson the week before the start of the one-year MBA. I received notification that I was admitted to both programs around the same time in late March or early April of 2012, and promptly put in my two weeks notice and then moved up to the Babson campus, which is about 30 minutes outside of Boston.

In my first week on the Babson campus, I was immediately immersed in a culture of entrepreneurship. I had my MBA orientation followed by a five-day StartingBloc Institute, which was unreal. In one week, I met about 100 people that were committed to building new organizations or new initiatives within existing organizations. I was inundated with knowledge, resources, connections, and leads, which would make scaling my nonprofit organization's work possible.

The summer of 2012 was coursework overload, since I had opted to pursue the one-year MBA instead of the two-year program, because I wanted to keep my nonprofit's momentum. I continued to connect with interested K-12 schools in Northern Virginia and Washington, D.C. as I immersed myself in Babson's core classes over the summer. The summer course load included the following:

ACC 7200 – Financial Reporting

ACC 7201 – Measuring and Managing Strategic Performance

ECN 7200 – Managerial Economics

ECN 7201 – Business, Government, and International Economics

EPS 7200 – Entrepreneurship and Opportunity

FIN 7200 – Introduction to Financial Management

LAW 7200 – Business Law

MBA 7150 – Simulation Experience

MIS 7200 – Global Technology

MKT 7200 – Marketing

MOB 7200 – Creating and Leading Organizations

MOB 7201 – Managing Talent

MOB 7202 – Strategy

OPS 7200 – Technology and Operations Management

QTM 7200 – Data, Models, and Decision Making

Needless to say, the summer was academically intense, but I was still able to go to a couple Boston Red Sox games during what was Fenway Park's 100th Anniversary year. It was important for me to do the summer intensive deep dive to understand how to build and grow an organization, but I also noticed that the core curriculum didn't include much if any discussion about sustainability. That has since changed at Babson, as the program now includes sustainability as part of the core curriculum, but many other MBA programs still lag behind and don't teach sustainability in their core curricula. This is a problem.

Consider that the MBA is the most common graduate degree in the United States. According to the National Center for Education Statistics, there were over 200,000 MBA degrees conferred in the 2021-2022 academic year, which represented 23% of all masters degrees conferred. Furthermore, the purpose of the MBA is to develop current and future leaders and decision makers in businesses of all shapes, sizes, and sectors. There is no other graduate degree that has as much influence and decision making authority over our future economy's carbon footprint. One of my Babson classmates articulated perfectly why this is important.

> *"MBA grads hold the levers of capital and policy in nearly every sector. So if they're not being taught to think in systems, to consider ecological limits, or to question infinite-growth assumptions, we're going to keep repeating the same destructive cycles, just dressed up in ESG buzzwords as it often happens. In a world where wealth and influence are increasingly concentrated in private hands, future leaders must be equipped to understand the long arc of consequences. Beyond climate, it's about justice, about power, and about designing economies that don't cannibalize the future."*
>
> *- C.J. Acosta*

Integrating sustainability into the core curricula of MBA programs could create unprecedented and enduring positive changes in the way businesses operate and interact with the environment, which could enable long-term resilience of a human-centered global economy. Integrating sustainability into the core curricula of the most common masters degree in the United States is essential to advancing Rainy Day Economics.

> ***Rainy Day Economics Design Prompt 10:*** *Imagine you are in charge of deciding what courses future business leaders and policy makers will be required to take. Develop a core curriculum that integrates the five pillars of Rainy Day Economics – design, sustainability, human-centered capitalism, resilience, and the arts.*

Going into the 2012 to 2013 academic year, I had grown the number of schools my nonprofit organization was working with in the DC area. I had done quite a bit of planning to make it so that I could drive down to the DC area from Boston consistently to keep the momentum that my organization had gained in the first year of programming. I had also continued to meet with the Board of Directors, Board of Advisors, and team of volunteers on a regular basis. The courses that year were perfect for where I was at in the growth of my organization.

Fall 2012 courses

EPS 7500 – Entrepreneurship
MBA 7515 – Enterprise 2.0
MBA 9506 – Corporate Social Responsibility
MOB 7548 – Social Value Creation
MOB 7559 – Global Strategic Management

Spring 2013 courses

EPS 7510 – Entrepreneurial Finance
EPS 7520 – Managing a Growing Business
EPS 7574 – Marketing for Entrepreneurship
EPS 8573 – Entrepreneurship Intensity Track
FIN 7517 – Financing and Valuing Sustainability

The fall season also included a few opportunities to go into downtown Boston to attend sustainability and startup events. Boston is a thriving entrepreneurial hub, and it is also a city that is ahead of the curve when it comes to sustainability. The Boston metropolitan area also has more universities than any other city that I know of, so there were countless opportunities to attend educational and entrepreneurial events. And it has always been relatively easy to hop on a train in Boston and go to New York City for a weekend. When it comes to Rainy Day Economics, the Northeastern region of the United States has both unique capabilities and vulnerabilities due to the density of population and infrastructure.

## The Tragic Trifecta

There was a six-month stretch from late-October 2012 to mid-April 2013 in the Northeastern United States that just sucked. It was like one punch to the gut after another. To kick-off the six months of gut punches, there was a large tropical storm that formed in the Caribbean on October 22nd and began making its way up the East Coast of the United States. On October 28, 2012, President Barack Obama signed emergency declarations in advance of Hurricane Sandy making landfall so that states could start to request federal aid before the storm's impact. This simple action shortened response and recovery times, and probably also saved lives.

My college roommate was living in New York City when Hurricane Sandy happened. He had an apartment near the Myrtle-Willoughby subway station about a block away from the Marcy projects, which is a low-income community in Brooklyn. I had visited him there before. When I came to visit, it was relatively easy to get from Penn Station to his apartment thanks to the G train, which was one of the oldest subway lines. The G train connects Queens and Brooklyn on a North-South route. The

G train wasn't in the best condition in 2012, but my friend was always able to use it on his daily commute into Manhattan.

On October 29th, Hurricane Sandy collided with one of the most densely populated regions on the planet. It wasn't the strongest storm our country had ever seen, but as a society, we had more people and infrastructure in harms way than for any previous storm. Over 2.5 million people in the Northeastern United States lost power. There were billions of gallons of raw or partially treated sewage that got released into the waters in and around New Jersey and New York. There were numerous subway stations and tunnels that were flooded. And, as with any storm, there were downed trees and debris everywhere.

My friend recalled that after the storm there was a two- to three-day stand still where no one really knew what was going on. The neighborhood luckily had power, but the G train was out of service, and the roads were filled with tree limbs and debris. And the sentiment in the neighborhood was that the government wasn't going to help the Marcy projects first. Rather, the government was most likely going to help the more historically affluent neighborhoods on the Upper East Side in Manhattan first. After the first few days, my friend's employer started to communicate an expectation that everyone return to the office for work. This was nearly impossible for the first two weeks following the storms as the bus routes were overwhelmed with lines of people at every stop constantly.

My friend's job was a corporate job in Manhattan that could easily be done from his apartment, but many of his neighbors were not working corporate jobs where they could just call into meetings and do work from their apartments on their computers. A lot of the people in his neighborhood worked at restaurants, grocery stores, retail shops, and the like where being on location was necessary in order to do the work. Those workers were impacted even more for at least the first two weeks after the storm while the mass transit systems recovered. For many people that included losing income, because they couldn't get to work where they were paid by the hour.

My friend's neighborhood was also not exactly a hot spot for grocery stores and restaurants. At that time, the neighborhood had a bodega on the corner, a pizza spot about a block away, and maybe two or three other places within reasonable walking distance for the hundreds or perhaps thousands of nearby residents to get food. The neighborhood may have been classified as a food desert, but even if it wasn't, there was still about two weeks of food scarcity there following the storm.

A few weeks after the storm, my college roommate and his girlfriend made their way up to Boston. We went to see our beloved Virginia Tech football team play Boston College. It was another moment in time where doing something normal, like watching a football game, felt like what was needed for my friend to find calm after the chaos. Later in the year, there was a Concert for Sandy Relief held in Madison Square Garden. The line up included numerous famous musicians, and the event was streamed across multiple platforms to an audience of millions. Music was again part of the healing process for a region devastated by a rainy day.

A few years after Hurricane Sandy, New Jersey Governor Chris Christie was asked about the collaboration with President Barack Obama in the wake of the disaster. People had given Governor Christie a hard time for being friendly with President Obama during the response to Hurricane Sandy, because it was so close to the 2012 Presidential election, but Governor Christie has time and again expressed that our country is more important than party politics. In the interview on MSNBC, he recalled the positive collaboration with President Obama.

*"He made the instruction to his cabinet members in front of me. He said, 'If the Governor or any of his people call, it is unacceptable for that call not to be returned within 30 minutes.'"*

*- New Jersey Governor Chris Christie*

Country above politics. Governor Christie and President Obama understood this. Now, in 2025, it seems like our country is suffering from the relentless disease of politics. I wonder if our country would be less polarized if more of our elected officials acted as if they were leading on a rainy day and collaborated with their political opponents as if their constituents' livelihoods depended on it.

Two days after the Sandy Relief Concert at Madison Square Garden, the next gut punch arrived. On December 14th, 2012, another school massacre occurred in Newtown, Connecticut, which is on the route between Brooklyn and Boston. This time the massacre was at an elementary school, and 20 young children and 6 staff members were killed. The reports said that police arrived less than 4 minutes after the shooting started, and that the shooting lasted about five minutes in total. Five minutes, 20 children, six staff members. I wonder sometimes if we as a society could evolve to the point where guns just didn't exist, not because of any policy or law, but because every member of society using their own hearts and minds decided that they didn't want guns in their homes and communities. In my humble and certainly biased opinion, "bears, bad people, and big government" are all weak arguments for guns in a modern society. We need to evolve. What if we designed our societal systems to minimize death and maximize life? This is a fundamental question in Rainy Day Economics, and it is essentially a complex optimization problem.

In the days following the massacre, President Obama went and spoke to every child's family. I can't imagine the amount of pain and sorrow those families were feeling, but I bet it meant a lot to them to have the President of the United States take the time to listen to them and to honor their children. There are a number of stories like that about President Obama, where he would take the time to honor people. I remember a similar story of him saluting fallen soldiers as they were unloaded in flag-draped caskets from C-17 planes. One of the simplest and most important responsibilities of our elected leaders is just to be present when tragedies happen and to honor people.

When the Sandy Hook Elementary massacre happened, I was living on the Babson College campus in a community with mostly international students. My classmates talked openly about America's unique gun culture. There were a number of people in my cohort from India, which is a densely populated country that allows people to own certain types of guns (revolvers, rifles, and shotguns) after the age of 21 and after a robust licensing process that includes a background check. India only has five civilian firearms per 100 people. By contrast, the United States has over 120 firearms per 100 people, and that number has grown on average about 1% a year for the past 30 years.

I wonder what would happen if the highly influential National Rifle Association and the highly addictive Call of Duty video games and the highly entertaining Hollywood action movies all ceased to exist for one year. I bet we'd still have 120.5 firearms per 100 people, but maybe we would have successfully avoided growing that number by another one percent to 121.7 firearms per 100 people. The percentage of household gun ownership in America has actually gone down significantly over time, which is good, but it also means the households that do own guns are more heavily armed. According to the Violence Policy Center, the percentage of American households that reported having any guns in the home dropped by 28 percent from 1973 to 2021. Household gun ownership peaked in 1980 at 53.7%, and reached a multi-decade low between 2012 and 2016 at around one third of all households owning guns. In 2016, the trend reversed and household gun ownership started to go up again. We can and should design societal systems to stop bad things from happening.

The third gut punch in the 2012 to 2013 academic year was April 15, 2013 – the Boston Marathon bombing. The Babson campus is about a 30-minute drive from downtown Boston where the Boston Marathon finish line was. The Boston Marathon is the world's oldest annual marathon race, and it is held on the third Monday of April every year, which is Patriots' Day, the day that commemorates the inaugural battles of the American Revolutionary War. On the afternoon of April 15th, two homemade bombs went off on Boylston Street near the finish line of the Boston Marathon. The explosions killed three people and injured hundreds.

Pause for a second and digest this moment. There are hundreds of people injured around the finish line of the course, and hundreds of runners still running their race towards the finish line. There are thousands of people now running away. Law enforcement doesn't know if there are more bombs, and they don't know who is responsible for the first two explosions. First responders and emergency managers are tasked with making sure the scene is safe and getting the injured to area hospitals. Law enforcement now has to gather as much intelligence as possible, and while they do want all the innocent people to get to safety, they don't want the bombers to escape to potentially do additional harm.

People come from all over the world to run or even just attend the Boston Marathon. There were thousands of people at the event. How do you keep bad people from escaping while encouraging innocent people to get to safety? As with all rainy days in this book, hundreds of people were activated to respond to the bombing, and hundreds more were activated to search for the bombers. Local, state, and federal agencies once again had to collaborate quickly. I remember that Facebook had a new "marked safe" feature that was particularly useful that day. During the massacre at Virginia Tech in 2007, it was difficult to get word out to family and friends that we were safe until hours later. The cell towers were overwhelmed, and smart phones weren't mainstream. But during the Boston bombing, people were able to mark themselves safe on their Facebook account using their smart phones. So, if your friends and family knew you were running in or attending the Boston Marathon, and they were on Facebook, then it was possible for them to be made aware that you were ok.

The manhunt for the bombers took a few days, but luckily they were stopped before they proceeded to their next target, which was Times Square in New York City. The FBI concluded that the bombers weren't connected to known terrorist groups, but were influenced by Al Qaeda and stated that the attack was retribution for U.S. military action in Afghanistan and Iraq. It was over ten years after the September 11th terrorist attack, and there were still ripple effects and individuals being radicalized. How do we obstruct the ripple effects of terrorist attacks? How do we stop individuals from being radicalized?

When Robert F. Kennedy was running for President in 1968, he made a campaign stop in my father's hometown in Indiana. Hundreds of people attended Kennedy's speech in the small downtown including my father. One of the most important issues Robert F. Kennedy spoke about on the campaign trail was the Vietnam War, but he also engaged on a deeper philosophical level about tragedies. Below is an excerpt from a speech Kennedy made during that campaign.

> *"Let me begin this discussion with a note both personal and public. I was involved in many of the early decisions on Vietnam, decisions that helped set us on our present path. It may be that the effort was doomed from the start; that it was never really possible to bring all the people of South Vietnam under the rule of the successive governments we supported – governments, one after another, riddled with corruption, inefficiency, and greed; governments which did not and could not*

*successfully capture and energize the national feeling of their people. If that is the case, as it well may be, then I am willing to bear my share of the responsibility, before history and before my fellow citizens. But past error is no excuse for its own perpetuation. **Tragedy is a tool for the living to gain wisdom, not a guide by which to live.** Now as ever, we do ourselves best justice when we measure ourselves against ancient tests, as in the Antigone of Sophocles: "All men make mistakes, but a good man yields when he knows his course is wrong, and repairs the evil. The only sin is pride."*

*- Senator Robert F. Kennedy speech at Kansas State University, March 18, 1968*

I think Robert Kennedy's main point was that we aren't meant to live in fear of tragedy, but we as a society are meant to learn from tragedies and minimize their future impact. We shouldn't live in fear of natural disasters. Our kids shouldn't fear going to school. We shouldn't be afraid to attend large events. But as a society, together we are responsible for designing a better system than the system designed by the previous generation. There are so many tragedies that repeat in different ways over and over again in our society. When something in life repeats enough times, we can start to see trends, outliers, and opportunities to improve the way we prevent or react to tragedies. We also benefit as time goes on from technological progress and more advanced understandings of science, engineering, and mathematics.

***Rainy Day Economics Design Prompt 11:** Take a moment to envision what the cities of the future will look like. Brainstorm what a thriving city looks like during normal times, and then develop a plan for helping a city or community recover and heal after a disaster or tragedy.*

The backdrop of the Boston Marathon bombing was one of the most entrepreneurial and scientifically literate places in the world. Boston has a deeply engrained entrepreneurial culture, thriving higher education communities, a long history of scientific exploration, and some of the best sports teams in the country. Boston was, is, and always will be a great American city. Boston Strong.

# Part 3:
# The Humanity of
# Rainy Day Economics

# Chapter 9

## WATER AND TIME
### April 25, 2014 - August 2024

*"Flint still doesn't have clean water."*

*- Michelle Wolf, 2018 White House Correspondents' Dinner*

---

On Christmas Eve 2015, I was sitting at a restaurant in Kigali, Rwanda with a family friend having a great conversation. She is someone I've known my whole life. We were trading travel stories and talking about old times. I had just summited Mt. Kilimanjaro days earlier, and I had cleaned myself up for our dinner that night. She was a USAID worker and had served in various countries in East Africa. We hadn't talked in years, because she was abroad so much.

That night, she was the most interesting person in the world. She had such good stories, and I just wanted to listen to her tell them all night. I also wanted her to think I was at least mildly interesting too. I tried to match her story for story, but her tales were just far more fascinating than mine would ever be. I was on a six-week global tour that started in Geneva then zigzagged through East Africa and ended in Cape Town. Those six weeks were my little attempt in my late 20s to pursue a life well lived. My friend had years of travel stories across dozens of countries, and I was just getting started.

She asked me what country was next on my itinerary, and I perhaps too casually informed her that I was heading to South Sudan the next day, Christmas Day 2015. She was deeply concerned. She knew things

I didn't about South Sudan. My reasoning for going to South Sudan seemed illogical to her. I wanted to talk to people at the embassy there about infrastructure and international development and what was next for the world's newest country. South Sudan had only recently gained its independence, and I wanted to be there to see it and experience it. She saw through me and diagnosed my trip as a self-serving exploration to prove to myself and others that I was living a remarkable life. She was probably right. I had no business going to South Sudan.

The Republic of South Sudan is a land-locked country in East Africa a little bit smaller than the size of Texas. The country has a population of about 11 million people. It shares borders with Uganda, Kenya, Ethiopia, the Central African Republic, the Democratic Republic of the Congo, and Sudan. South Sudan has been subject to intense internal conflict since Sudan gained its independence from Egypt in 1956.

The Fund for Peace had recently ranked South Sudan as the third most fragile state in their annual Fragile States Index. In other words, according to The Fund for Peace, South Sudan was more fragile than most of the countries we were hearing about in the news at the time including Iraq, Iran, Libya, Syria, Pakistan, Afghanistan, Israel, Saudi Arabia, India, China, and Russia. And, the others that were ranked highest by The Fund for Peace that were also not being talked about in the news are conveniently positioned near South Sudan, namely Central African Republic, Sudan, Democratic Republic of the Congo, and Chad.

There are a number of easily identifiable global implications of conflict in East Africa. Obviously, any time there is significant conflict in any country in East Africa, it is easy for those conflicts to spill over into other nearby countries. Perhaps the most obvious implication is mass migration. Conflict in South Sudan over the past few years had resulted in over a million refugees fleeing to neighboring countries. This contributed to the overall instability of the region. In addition to conflict-related migrations, reduction in regional economic activity and increased strains on infrastructure and resources are also global implications of conflicts in East Africa.

Maybe that isn't relevant to the average American. But consider this - two of the top ten coffee producing countries are in East Africa, namely Ethiopia and Uganda, which of course share borders with some of the most fragile countries in the world. So, it is conceivable that conflict in East Africa could have significant impacts on the global coffee market. Now do you care?

Let's pretend for a moment that we as a society have some intention of making the world a better place for everyone. Let's pretend for a moment that we want a sustainable future and that our vision includes stability and world peace. How can we make South Sudan, and East Africa as a whole, less fragile?

As a society, we have actually made significant progress in reducing the amount of extreme poverty globally. In 1990, 37% of the world's population lived in extreme poverty. In 2012, 12.7% of the world's population lived in extreme poverty. And, within the context of South Sudan, the U.S. Government had given over $1.8 billion in support over a few years after major conflict broke out in Juba, South Sudan in December 2013. This included support for shelters, economic recovery and market systems, protection, food security, logistics, and infrastructure.

The United States was not the only country to support peace and stability in South Sudan. Funding and support has also come from the European Union, United Kingdom, Canada, and Japan. Other countries see value in this as well. The global community has adopted a strategy of hope. We are collectively deciding that we care about South Sudan and the people of South Sudan. Whether it be for moral, economic, or political reasons, we as a society should be investing in the future of South Sudan.

We have provided vital support to South Sudan over the past decade.

But, we can't stop supporting South Sudan now. As we look forward, we should consider what else we can do to help South Sudan and other fragile countries grow. Let's not just react to conflict, but also prevent future conflict by helping South Sudan with things like access to water and sanitation, agriculture and food security, and education.

There is still a lot more work to do to create a stable South Sudan. Buey Ray Tut's model for international development, suggests that aid is only the first step of the process that leads to sustainability. It is interesting to note that of all of the USAID funding for South Sudan in 2015, 27% was for the support of initiatives that developed access to water. As policy makers consider what to do next in South Sudan, they need only remember one thing- ***without water, nothing can grow***.

When I arrived in Juba, South Sudan on Christmas Day 2015, I was excited to be there. The newest country in the world, and I had an opportunity to tell its story from the beginning. That enthusiasm quickly faded as I walked out of the small airport building into a parking lot where I was supposed to be picked up by someone from the Juba Bridge Hotel. My ride was late, and as I assessed my options, I quickly realized that if anything happened to me in Juba, I was done. I was an American traveling alone with only a few people expecting check-ins from me, and only a couple people knew where I was staying. This was a fool's errand.

Eventually my ride arrived, and we made our way to the Juba Bridge Hotel where I had booked a room. On the way there, I quietly observed the landscape and the people. There was no reliable infrastructure - no electrical grid, no paved interstate system, no elaborate water supply system. It may as well have been Mars.

The number of young men, and even boys, carrying guns out in public spaces was enough for me to regret my decision to come to South Sudan. Kids probably half my age carrying guns that I had only seen in video games. I feared for my life in a way I never had before.

Once I had checked into the hotel, I locked myself in the room, and nervously evaluated the situation. My friend had told me that this was essentially a warzone. USAID officials only traveled in armored vehicles and in groups. What was I doing there alone? What was I thinking? I closed my eyes and tried to sleep.

I woke up to a loud bang on the metal roof of the room I was in. It wasn't the sound of a gunshot, but it was loud. It happened again and again. Something was dropping onto the roof. I had no idea what time it was. I opened my laptop and began trying to use the internet. It was spotty, but I was able to get a couple communications out to friends and family to check-in. Another loud bang on the metal roof. It was late at night. I wasn't going to leave that room, and there was no sleeping that night.

The next morning I left my room for the first time since I had arrived for the complimentary breakfast at the hotel restaurant, which was called Da Vinci's. I was so hungry. The complimentary breakfast was chips mayai and a mango juice. Chips mayai is a simple East African dish that is basically just a French fry omelet. While I was eating, I found out what had been making the loud banging noises. It was monkeys dropping mangos from the trees above. I had developed a love for mango juice while in East Africa, so I understood the monkeys' late-night craving. I was glad to have solved the mystery, and it put me in a better mood to start the day.

The hotel driver took me to the embassy where I was scheduled to interview some of the staff there about international development and infrastructure. I was glad to be inside the walls of the embassy compound for a couple hours. The number of questions I had for the staff there had ballooned. I wanted to know everything. What were their stories? What was their strategy for helping South Sudan? What was life like for them? What was next for South Sudan? Every question led to ten more follow-up questions. They were confused by me at first. I think they also wanted to know what I was doing in South Sudan, and what I was going to do with the answers to these questions I was asking.

Walking out of the embassy, I felt like I had accomplished at least part of what I came there to do. And then I found myself waiting for the hotel driver again. This time felt a little bit better, because I was 20 feet from a door that would lead me back to protection from the United States government. I didn't mind waiting this time, until I saw in the distance a truck full of young men with guns. They watched me as I stood there waiting for my driver to arrive. After a little while, the car approached, and they drove past. Every one of the young men in that truck looked at me as they casually held their guns. Was it a game? Was it a threat? Was I a threat to them? My driver showed up and apologized for once again being late. I was ready to leave South Sudan.

I had planned to be there for a week, but any desire I had to explore and interview people had evaporated at the sight of young men with their fingers on the triggers of machine guns. Back at the hotel, I started looking into if I could leave the country earlier than planned. After another night of sporadic banging from the hotel monkeys seeking mangos, I woke up and went to the Da Vinci's restaurant for the complimentary breakfast, chips mayai and mango juice, again. The chips mayai was so bland, but the mango juice was divine and made my body feel less neglected.

I was already getting skinny from eating less and walking everywhere during my first few weeks of travels, and the trek to the top of Kilimanjaro only made me skinnier. I felt weak and tired. As I reluctantly ate the chips mayai, a group of uniformed men with guns sat down at the tables across from me. I was less nervous about them than the young kids with guns. I don't know why, but the uniforms set my mind at ease. They looked over at me a number of times, but I kept to myself, and eventually returned to my room to finalize the plans to leave.

My time in Juba seeing South Sudan early in its formation as a country got me thinking a lot about Rainy Day Economics. There is so much that goes into designing and building the infrastructure of society as we know it. This includes everything from the water infrastructure that we take for granted in the United States to the institutions that countries build to create societal support systems. South Sudan was in the early days of designing the country it wanted to be. Thinking back now to when I saw the young men in Juba carrying around machine guns in public, I imagine how difficult it will be to transform a region so accustomed to intense conflict into an intentionally designed, sustainable, human-centered economy that is a resilient, art-filled thriving hub of innovation. But, even though it seems incredibly difficult, I believe Rainy Day Economics could be a good starting point for that transformation. How do we go from kids carrying machine guns in public, to kids leading their communities on complex design, engineering and infrastructure projects?

> ***Rainy Day Economics Design Prompt 12:*** *Imagine you are a building a new country from scratch after a terrible war. Develop plans for infrastructure, education, social services, and a thriving ecosystem of entrepreneurs. Consider how your plans can help people heal from the trauma of the war.*

## *The end of Three Birds and a pivot to global sustainability*

Rewind to the beginning of the 2013 to 2014 school year. I had fully launched my nonprofit, piloted programs for two years, completed an MBA focused on entrepreneurship, and raised a little bit of money to support our efforts. Running the nonprofit was my full-time job, except I wasn't getting paid. The organization was still in its infancy, and I was applying to grants as much as I could, but there was no guarantee that I would get sufficiently funded to pay myself a salary, not to mention other employees. The challenge was to find a way to keep building the nonprofit full-time while not going completely broke.

I had already financed most of my private school MBA degree, and so I had a substantial amount of student debt, but the ability to make income-based payments allowed me proceed with the nonprofit. After all, I wasn't making any money, so the required monthly payment was zero dollars. I was, however, concerned that I might run into cash flow problems down the road if I wasn't able to raise enough money for the nonprofit to grow. I came up with a genius (or perhaps idiotic) plan to extend my financial runway while I grew the nonprofit organization. I applied to another master's degree program that was mostly taught online and at Virginia Tech's Northern Virginia Center at night, and then I applied for another student loan to finance not only the tuition, but my room and board as well. It put money in my pocket, so to speak, when I was operating on a shoestring budget.

This would be my second masters, and it was a degree in Integrative STEM Education. STEM stands for science, technology, engineering, and mathematics. The program was designed to help educators teach STEM better and in a way that integrated curricula across multiple subjects. The classes were relevant to the work I was doing during the day supporting teachers and schools in their STEM efforts and working towards getting more renewable energy education tools into classrooms. So, from the fall semester of 2013 to the spring semester of 2016, I took classes at night and online while trying to get the nonprofit to a point where it could support a full-time or even part-time paid staff. The STEM education classes over those few years were as follows:

EDCI 5804 – STEM Education Foundations
EDCT 5604 – Foundations of Career and Technical Education
EDIT 5564 – Topic Study in Information Technology

EDCI 5774 – Human Growth and Development

EDCI 5775 – Readings in Technology Education

EDCI 5824 – STEM Education Trends and Issues

EDCI 5834 – STEM Education Research

EDCI 5964 – Field Studies in Education

EDCI 5814 – STEM Education Pedagogy

I'm one of those people that believes well-funded and well-supported formal education is nearly a panacea, and I think STEM education, which includes Career and Technical Education (CTE), should be one piece of the education conversation where it is easy to build consensus and make significant investments. Even if you don't believe in the transformative power of education broadly, it is still easy to see the numerous individual, community, and societal benefits associated with STEM education and more specifically Career and Technical Education.

While I was trying to advance my vision of solar panels at every school in America, I experienced a welcome expansion of scope when we started working with the DC Public Schools system. My nonprofit organization was focused on renewable energy education at schools in low-income communities, and so my outreach quickly extended beyond the borders of Fairfax County in Northern Virginia. Unlike the Fairfax County Public Schools system at the time, the DC Public Schools system actually had significant support for solar schools efforts and more broadly green schools initiatives across the District. So much so that the school system had integrated sustainability into their Capital Improvement Program (CIP) by instituting policies that required new school buildings to be certified at high levels of the LEED rating system.

LEED stands for Leadership in Energy and Environmental Design. The rating system was designed by the U.S. Green Building Council to advance sustainability in the built environment. Even though the Fairfax

County Public School system was ranked consistently as one of the best and wealthiest school districts in the country, in 2014 it was still lagging behind many school district sustainability efforts. At that time, there were only two schools out of about 200 in Fairfax County that had solar panels on their roofs. One was Rachel Carson Middle School and the other was the county magnet school – Thomas Jefferson High School for Science and Technology. Meanwhile DC Public Schools was putting solar panels on numerous school buildings as they renovated them, and not just small demonstration projects, some helped offset significant percentages of school electricity bills.

As I connected with more and more schools in the District of Columbia, I also began working with DC Public Schools on their annual science fairs. There was an elementary and a secondary science fair every year where students could showcase their science and engineering projects. These science fairs were incredible events, and they also served to engage the community, local businesses, nonprofits, and universities by asking people and organizations to serve as event volunteers, judges, and exhibitors. Organizations also gave out special awards to students that were doing work related to that of the organizations. And, every year the DC STEM Fair would send a few students to the Intel International Science and Engineering Fair where they would connect with other students doing similar work and compete for higher level awards and scholarships.

Organizing the DC STEM Fair was a considerable undertaking, but the impact of the event was massive. There was the impact of the day of the event, which included hundreds of students presenting their science and engineering projects, and there was also all of the work leading up to the event where thousands of students would compete at their individual school science fairs to then go to the District-wide STEM fair. Organizing a District-wide STEM fair helped teachers and students develop an annual rhythm to researching and exploring science and engineering topics, and perhaps most importantly, it helped develop students' early identities as scientists and engineers.

This is the power of grassroots strategies working in concert with top-down strategies. Imagine for a moment the hundreds or thousands of school district-wide STEM fairs being held every year. The Intel Science and Engineering Fair creates a draw for District-wide STEM fairs all over the world to send their best students, and likewise, the District-wide STEM fairs create a draw for individual school science fairs to send their best student researchers. And the teachers in every science classroom are able to create the structures and schedules for students to develop their research projects in time for the district-wide fairs and then potentially the regional and international fairs. This is just one example of how we can supercharge STEM education every year in the United States, and excite students from the community level all the way up to the global level. You'd be surprised how advanced some of the science projects are at just the high school level. I dare you readers of this book to volunteer at a school or district-wide science fair this year.

Despite the success and excitement surrounding the DC STEM Fair, my nonprofit organization was still struggling to survive. After a few years of trying to get my nonprofit off the ground and to a point where it could support a full-time staff, I decided to shutdown the organization. I was spending too much time on unsuccessful fundraising, and I couldn't sustain a living on a non-existent salary any longer. I had connected with hundreds of people, raised a modest amount of money, and spread my vision a little bit further. I can honestly say that starting my nonprofit was the best decision of my life. However, there was always a lingering question in my mind since starting my organization. I once heard someone say that nonprofits should try to make themselves obsolete. So, the question that lingered was: "Does your organization *need* to exist?" When I asked myself this question in 2011, the answer was indisputably "yes". This answer is, of course, a combination of truth, ignorance, and youthful spirit. However, after four years, the question was more difficult to answer.

When I approached nonprofit leaders in 2011 and suggested new initiatives, I received at best responses like "that's an interesting idea, good luck." When I approached the same nonprofit leaders four years later, the best responses were more like "how can we help?" or "we're in." Likewise, in 2011 potential corporate sponsors would rarely return emails or calls. Four years later, most companies with respectable corporate social responsibility (CSR) departments would at least take meetings with me, though they were still slow to give financial support. This progress was great, but it didn't answer the question of whether or not my organization needed to exist.

In 2011, a significant number of our partner organizations were also recently founded. I had seen some great organizations fizzle, for lack of a better word, over those four years. I had also seen some wildcard organizations grow into thriving nonprofits. In my humble opinion, success in the nonprofit sector is a function of access to capital and luck more than anything else. Creativity, hard work, smart work and intentional networking are also significant factors. In any case, my organization had a torturously mediocre amount of success. The organization had received dozens of letters of support from local leaders, numerous small grants ranging from $500 to $15,000, and a couple of awards for innovative programs. However, this mild success also did not answer the question of whether or not the organization needed to exist.

In mid-2015, I answered the question. No, my organization didn't need to exist. I came to that realization with pain in my heart, with pride in what I was able to accomplish, and with a precise understanding of how to create greater impact. In short, after four years, my organization had not been able to breach $100,000 per year in revenue. And, for the type and size of my organization, the amount of time devoted to unsuccessful fundraising really did not make sense. Furthermore, the connections I had made allowed me to keep the momentum toward impact that my organization had created by diverting opportunities to other organizations that had the capacity to capitalize on them in ways that my organization could not.

My nonprofit had reached the end of its journey, because I believed more impact could be achieved through the consolidation of efforts. Over the next few months, I transferred the momentum that my organization had created to other partner organizations. While I was deciding to shutdown my organization and how to do it, I was also trying to figure out what I was going to do next.

I discovered yet another masters degree through Virginia Tech's Center for Leadership in Global Sustainability. The natural resources master's degree was set up for working professionals. So, I knew even if I took on a new job, I would still be able to finish the program. The degree was focused on global sustainability and leadership. For about 18 months, from 2015 to 2016 I was again in an immersion program of sorts. Every month was spent collaborating on written assignments and small group projects, and then there would be an in-person multi-day intensive where we'd do deep dives into various topics related to things like energy, water, transportation, waste, international development, agriculture, food, and policy. The courses over those 18 months were as follows:

> NR 5014 – Constructing Sustainability
>
> NR 5884 – Topic Study: Leadership for Sustainability
>
> NR 5884 – Topic Study: Sustainable Enterprise
>
> NR 5714 – Ecosystem Management
>
> NR 5964 – Field Study
>
> NR 5114 – Global Issues in Natural Resources
>
> NR 5864 – Sustainability Science
>
> NR 5884 – Topic Study: Professional Practice

NR 5954 – Study Abroad – International Residency

The international residency was a unique feature of the program. When my cohort started our first classes in 2015, we actually didn't know where the international residency was going to be. About halfway through the program, it was revealed that we were going to South Africa. Our capstone research projects were related to water resources, access, and infrastructure. My team's project was specifically focused on water access and infrastructure in Khayelitsha.

## Some Assembly Required

Less than a week after I left Juba, I arrived in Cape Town a couple days before most of my cohort, and met up with a couple of my classmates to go hike the trail to the top of Table Mountain. There were days while we were in Cape Town when the clouds would pour over Table Mountain like a nebulous, almost weightless cascade. When my classmates and I reached the top of Table Mountain, we walked around for a short while and took some pictures. Eventually, we turned around and started to head back to the trail that would take us down the mountain.

Before leaving the top of the mountain, we ran into a lone hiker that happened to be American, and we chatted with him for a minute. We told him we were graduate students at Virginia Tech, and he introduced himself as a writer or journalist, which made me curious. I asked if we could read his work anywhere. He said we could just search Jeffrey Gettleman and East Africa. My classmates and I joked on the way down the mountain that he was probably a Pulitzer Prize-winning journalist. Sure enough, he was and is. Jeffrey Gettleman has covered numerous conflicts and atrocities in East Africa. I was oblivious to his work until meeting him on Table Mountain. But ever since then, I find myself thinking from time to time about his purpose-driven writing and specifically some of the stories in his memoir – *Love, Africa*. For those that are pursuing purpose-driven careers, *Love, Africa* will teach you the hard truth that being effective takes more than heart, it takes good strategy.

My master's cohort met in a nice part of Cape Town for class meetings before venturing out to talk to government, nonprofit, and community leaders about Khayelitsha. The Group Areas Act enacted under South Africa's apartheid government was used in 1983 to forcibly displace black residents that were deemed to be 'legal' from their communities in Cape Town to a large site to the south-east, which was called Khayelitsha, meaning 'New Home'. The plan was to give each of the displaced black residents a plot of land with a tin hut, a bucket toilet, and 1 water tap per every 4 plots. The government's original plans were to also provide streetlights, refuse removal services, schools, clinics, post offices, public telephones, and bus services.

> *"Remember Dimbaza,*
> *Remember Botshabelo/Onverwacht,*
> *South End, East Bank,*
> *Sophiatown, Makuleke, Cato Manor.*
> *Remember District Six.*
> *Remember the racism*
> *Which took away our homes*
> *And our livelihood*
> *And which sought*
> *To steal away our humanity.*
> *Remember also our will to live,*
> *To hold fast to that*
> *Which marks us as human beings:*
> *Our generosity, our love of justice*
> *And our care for each other.*

*Remember Tramway Road,*
*Modderdam, Simonstown*

*In remembering we do not want*
*To recreate District Six*
*But to work with its memory:*
*Of hurts inflicted and received*
*Of loss, achievements and of shames.*
*We wish to remember*
*So that we can all,*
*Together and by ourselves,*
*Rebuild a city*
*Which belongs to all of us,*
*In which all of us can live,*
*Not as races but as people."*

*- Posted in the District Six Museum in Cape Town, South Africa*

From the time the black residents were forcibly displaced in the mid-1980s to 2016 when my team was doing our research, the government had failed to provide a lot of the promised infrastructure, and Khayelitsha had experienced massive population growth. By 2018, there were an estimated 500,000 people living in Khayelitsha in an area of about 15 square miles. To give you an idea of how densely packed that is, my suburban hometown of Herndon, Virginia has about 25,000 residents in just 4.2 square miles, which equates to about 6,000 residents per square mile. Khayelitsha's population density in 2018 was about 33,000 people per square mile. This is a population density greater than New York City's, which is around 29,000 people per square mile.

Like in South Sudan and in many places in Africa, Khayelitsha continues to face extreme challenges associated with access to water, sanitation infrastructure, and public health services. However, when I was there in 2016, there were signs of hope in the form of productive cross-sector collaboration on societal infrastructure projects to support the communities in Khayelitsha. Markets fail when they are unable to allocate resources efficiently and governments fail when they are unable to build infrastructure equitably. Correcting these failures is one of the central challenges of development, and it is why participatory development and cross-sector collaboration are essential. The premise underlying participatory development is the power of the group—the notion that individuals are far more effective when they work together toward a common objective than when they attempt to achieve the same objective on their own. By mobilizing citizens to work together for their collective well-being, participatory development has the potential to redress some failures of the markets and the state while improving the capacity of individuals to organize and work together.

My team also explored the use of social audits to build trust between communities and the government. A social audit is an accountability mechanism where citizens organize themselves to evaluate or audit government's performance and policy decisions. It rests on the premise that when government officials are watched and monitored, they feel greater pressure to respond to their constituents' demands and have fewer incentives to abuse their power. Democratically elected governments face critical challenges in adequately representing their constituencies and responding to their needs and demands. This results not only from a lack of institutional and technical capacity to resolve long neglected and increasingly complex social and economic problems, but also from a failure to adhere to basic democratic governing principles, including transparency and accountability. Citizens react by developing disappointment, cynicism and apathy towards the democratic process further removing them from participation.

Participatory development and social audits aren't new ideas to the nonprofit sector in the United States. However, they may be new ideas to many Americans that don't work in the nonprofit sector or in international development.

As I'm finishing the draft of this chapter, it is the night of February 3rd, 2025, and I've just read a prominent member of the current Administration remarking that, *"USAID is a criminal organization. Time for it to die."* The U.S. Agency for International Development (USAID) is not a criminal organization. USAID has provided billions of dollars worth of humanitarian assistance to countries all over the world for decades. USAID is an organization that needs to exist. When you live in extreme poverty, every day is a rainy day. Countries and communities can't think about preparing for rainy days when they don't currently have access to clean water. The United States can and should help countries develop sustainably to lift people out of poverty. Helping other countries by providing humanitarian assistance, water infrastructure, and economic development support leads to a more prosperous global community with more innovation, better global health, and a more vibrant economy.

## The Flint water crisis

Before April 2014, the City of Flint had sourced its water from Lake Huron and the Detroit Water and Sewerage Department. On April 25, 2014, the City of Flint completed the switch to source its water from the Flint River. Within months, an outbreak of Legionnaire's disease began and continued for over a year. In 2015, a manager at the U.S. Environmental Protection Agency (EPA) detected high levels of lead in the home of a Flint resident. The level of lead was seven times that of EPA's acceptable limit. Then a few months later, a team of Virginia Tech scientists led by water expert Marc Edwards, found extremely high levels of lead in four homes in Flint. As all of this was happening, local and state-level public officials were telling everyone that everything was fine. Then in September 2015, the Virginia Tech water study team reported that 40% of the homes in Flint, Michigan had unsafe levels of lead, and the team recommended that the State of Michigan declare that the water in Flint was unsafe for drinking and cooking.

And then three months go by before the Mayor of Flint declared a state of emergency. And then three weeks go by before the Governor of Michigan declared a state of emergency in Genesee County. And then a week goes by before the Michigan National Guard is deployed to distribute water in Flint. And then a couple days after that, on January 14, 2016, the Governor of Michigan finally asked President Barack Obama to declare a state of emergency in Flint. President Obama then declared a state of emergency and authorized $5 million dollars in aid. Then, in February, the House Committee on Oversight and Government Reform held multiple hearings in which the Governor of Michigan was asked to testify. Despite numerous invitations from the Congress and demands from the public, the Governor of Michigan didn't testify for another six weeks. In November of 2016, a federal judge ordered door-to-door delivery of bottled water to residents in Flint that didn't have filters. Multiple state workers and public officials were charged with felonies and investigations continued into 2017.

I've only described a small portion of the ridiculously long and drawn out response and recovery to the Flint water crisis that still continues in some ways today in 2025. In just the two paragraphs above, you can start to see how urgently we need a STEM-literate workforce, better water infrastructure monitoring systems, and public officials that understand how to ethically and efficiently address civil engineering problems that impact the quality of life in their communities. Understanding the workforce necessary to maintain quality of life is a vital part of Rainy Day Economics. A comprehensive understanding of workforce demands is inherent in the first three pillars of Rainy Day Economics – design, sustainability, and human-centered capitalism.

It is also frustrating to hear people connect the failures of local and state government to the party affiliation of elected leaders. The Flint water crisis happened on the watch of leaders that were affiliated with both of the major political parties in the United States. And I think it is unproductive to insert politics into a civil engineering problem. We are better than that, and anything that isn't related to science, technology, engineering, and math, should be left at the door when coming to the table to solve these types of problems. It is also bizarre to me that so many people in the United States are strong advocates against the federal government and agencies like the U.S. Environmental Protection Agency. It is disturbing to think about where the residents of Flint would be without the help of the federal government during this crisis. There will continue to be times when local and state governments are overwhelmed by the scale of a problem, and the capabilities of the federal government will more often than not be more advanced than the capabilities of local and state governments.

It is also important to remember that governments in the United States are by and for the people. This means that everyone has a role to play in noticing, reporting, and addressing societal problems. As individuals, I believe we should adopt the mentality of societal designers. Designers today are tasked with making everything better. This means noticing what is and isn't working and noticing what does and doesn't exist. For many projects, the prerequisite to developing novel solutions to problems is observation of existing users, products, and systems. It is the job of the designer to improve the things of life, and so it is also the job of the designer to notice opportunities for improvement.

Tony Fadell is the co-founder of Nest Labs, which was acquired by

Google in 2014. He was also an early designer of the iPod and later served as Senior Vice President of the iPod division at Apple. In 2015, he delivered a TED Talk that is still very relevant to design today. He discussed the importance of noticing and observing. He compared this action to the way comedians notice every day things and illuminate them for us.

> *"It's seeing the invisible problem, not just the obvious problem, that's important, not just for product design, but for everything we do. You see, there are invisible problems all around us, ones we can solve. But first we need to see them, to feel them."*
>
> — *Tony Fadell, 2015 TED Talk*

In his Talk, Tony Fadell also highlights how every day things and process become habit. Unless we are intentional as designers about how we move through our days and observe the world, we won't see the sometimes very useful frustrations of everyday life that we are uniquely empowered to improve. We sometimes talk about looking at something with "fresh eyes" or having a "child-like sense of wonder". These are useful frames of mind, but it is also important to develop community-level methods of noticing and observation. The same way scientists in research fields have their own methods and processes for conducting experiments, it also makes sense for societal designers to have tailored methods of experimentation, user research, and observation that illuminate opportunities for improvements in society. If we as societal designers develop our noticing skills, it is more likely that we will be able to continue to develop effective solutions and systems that improve everyday life in our communities.

# Chapter 10
## DIFFICULT CONVERSATIONS
### March 14, 2015

*"I've come to TED, because I believe that many of you understand that the moral arc of the universe is long, but it bends toward justice; that we cannot be full, evolved human beings until we care about human rights and basic dignity; that all of our survival is tied to the survival of everyone; that our visions of technology and design and entertainment and creativity have to be married with visions of humanity, compassion and justice. And more than anything, for those of you who share that, I've simply come to tell you to keep your eyes on the prize, hold on."*

*- Bryan Stevenson, 2012 TED Talk*

---

At first glance, you may look at the Rainy Day Economics framework and easily agree with the first four pillars – design, sustainability, human-centered capitalism, and resilience. And then you might wonder, do the arts really make sense as the fifth pillar? Why do we need the arts? Why are creativity, self-expression, and imagination important? Pause for a moment and develop your own opinion. Do these things matter to you? Do they matter to you less after a bad day? Would the arts matter more to you on the worst day of your life or in the wake of a tragedy in your community?

> ***Rainy Day Economics Design Prompt 13:*** *Brainstorm a community arts event that could be easily planned and executed in the wake of a disaster or tragedy. Consider how you might design your event to help your community find joy and hope during a challenging time.*

TED is a nonprofit organization whose mission is to *"Discover and spread ideas that spark conversation, deepen understanding, and drive meaningful change"*. The organization was started in 1984 with a one-off event that highlighted the convergence of three fields – Technology, Entertainment, and Design. TEDx allows people to bring the spirit of TED to their communities to uncover new ideas and spark conversations at the local level. They do this by allowing individuals to apply to host independently organized events with their permission after a rigorous vetting process. The TEDx program, in my opinion, has massively expanded our society's global capacity to tell stories and share ideas in a consistently compelling format.

In 2014, after an inspiring conversation with the mayor of my hometown, I decided to apply for a TEDx license to host a local independently organized TED event.

After going through the process to obtain the TEDx license, I began designing my local event. TED places some constraints on first-time organizers in large part to protect their brand, but also because it makes sense to start with a small event and then grow. The 100-attendee limit imposed by TED was actually a welcome constraint, and my town had the perfect venue for an event that size. The NextStop Theatre Company in Herndon has a black box theater facility with approximately 100 seats and all of the lighting and stage set up that we needed. I worked with the NextStop Theatre Company to identify a date that didn't conflict with one of their shows. The date we chose was Pi Day 2015 – March 14th, 2015.

As I am writing this chapter in February 2025, the NextStop Theatre Company is showing a play called "Native Gardens" by Karen Zacarías.

It is a story about new neighbors and clashing cultures. NextStop Theatre Company seems to always be putting on shows that have a timely message. When I started recruiting speakers in 2014, I was hoping that I could curate a lineup that spoke at least a little bit to issues of the day. I wanted the event to be relevant and inspiring, and so I started talking to people about the event and asking around searching for "*ideas worth spreading*".

It wasn't long before my search led me to a guy named Tattoo Tom Mitchell. Our first meeting was at a Whole Foods in Northern Virginia. As you might have assumed from his name, Tom had a lot of tattoos. He looked like the mean motorcyclists you see in the movies, but Tom wasn't mean at all. In fact, Tom was one of the kindest people I worked with while organizing the TEDx events. Tom had lost his daughter to cancer during the Great Recession, and then shortly after started a nonprofit organization called Stillbrave that helped families navigate the extreme challenges associated with childhood cancer. Tom was known for being a tireless advocate, activist, fundraiser, and friend of kids with cancer. In his 2015 TEDxHerndon Talk, Tom told his story and brought the crowd to tears, but he also managed to inspire people at the same time.

> *"I wondered why somebody didn't do something.*
> *Then I realized, I am somebody."*
>
> *- Tattoo Tom Mitchell, TEDxHerndon 2015*

Tom was one of 15 speakers and performers, and he somehow became the glue of that first event. He was one of the older speakers and had far more life experience than many, but he committed to the process of developing his Talk and in doing so led by example with humility and an admirable work ethic. He also talked to everyone and made everyone feel seen and heard. I ended up asking Tom to speak two more times in 2016 and 2017, partly because of how he showed up as a member of the community. He wasn't speaking to extract value from the TED platform. He was there to help kids with cancer and to be a part of the community. I interviewed Tom a few years later, and he spoke candidly about how he viewed life in America. If Tom was still with us today, I'd ask him to do his 4th TEDxHerndon Talk on how we can redefine what life in America is really about. Below is an excerpt from that interview.

*"What does it say about how we prioritize things? Or how is it that we can prioritize certain things and the fact that we're not prioritizing children and children's lives, what does that say about us?*

*Well let's be honest. You know it is very much a, particularly now, it's very much a 'me, me, me' country that we live in, largely. I mean that's just what we've been brought up on, most of us. You know most of us who are you know whatever 10 to 60 have been brought up with this 'more is better' you know 'buy, buy, buy, get, get, get, consume, consume, consume'. And that's what we've all been brought up with since TV has been invented, because we certainly have it thrown at us ad nauseam on a daily basis. And so we've kind of been again we've kind of been blinded to what's really important, you know to the real authentic level of what's important in life. And we see a lot of shiny things. And just like a crow loves to fly and gather shiny things, people can be easily subjected to that too. And when you're constantly inundated with shiny things and those things become a value when the Administration is leading you to believe that amassing the most amount of money that you can is somehow your success. That's somehow how you've won, when you've got children dying on a daily basis. See I don't think that's true. I think if I'm bringing these children up and I'm helping these children to have a future and have a life and to get an education and to feel loved and to be seen and to be heard, that's how you measure success.*

*But it's not, I don't think it's anybody's fault at this point because it's just what we've all been force-fed for so many years. I mean fortunately for me I stopped watching TV ten years ago. I haven't watched a lick of TV in ten years. So I'm not getting that constant inundation in my living room of 'buy this, it's shiny' and then my focus or my needle goes there. You know, I spend a lot of my time in the hospitals in the chemotherapy clinics and my focus goes there.*

*And so I think if we had, it's kind of like an 'out of sight out of mind' thing right? Like if you had more people, I always tell people 'why don't you come to the clinic with me one day?' You know what I'd love to take some of these politicians to the clinic with me for one day just to see what I see and to hear what I hear and to feel what I feel. And I wonder if their priorities would change just a little bit.*

*You know the amount of money that we spend on certain things that I mean, if we spend five billion dollars on a wall, right, what could that five billion dollars really be used for on a raw humanitarian level? Now I'm not arguing whether or not you need to build, that's not my place to argue that. I'm just saying is there not a better prioritization of that money right now than that? And I would gather and say – 'yes absolutely'. Yes, you know, because I hold the hands of kids when they die, you know, and it puts things, for me it puts things in perspective that prioritizes things for me in a very matter-of-fact way.*

*And if we had less of that inundation and less of that shiny thing, 'buy this, buy this', and more of the connections, you know, the real raw honest authentic connections, then I think we would be in a better position. It says a lot about our country and the world, particularly our country. I think we're at the head of that because America is big and everything's big and grand and great in America, but is that really what life's about? No."*

*- Tattoo Tom Mitchell, 2019 Interview*

There were a few Talks at that first TEDxHerndon event in 2015 that related to rainy days in direct and indirect ways. We had Talks about green schools, solar technology, bees, cyber security, and public health. But the Talk that I think related most directly to rainy day economics was by a woman that I met when I was a student at Rachel Carson Middle School about 15 years earlier. Stephanie Buxhoeveden was an ICU nurse and had been pursuing a career as a nurse anesthetist. One day, while she was in the operating room, she experienced a loss of vision and the feeling in her legs. She was diagnosed with multiple sclerosis (MS), and then, as she described in her Talk, she had a few choices.

*"Life is going to challenge you at some point. It's going to hand you something unfair. It's going to take something from you. And, it's going to interfere with your plans. When this happens, you have a few choices – deny, cope, or thrive."*

*- Stephanie Buxhoeveden, TEDxHerndon 2015*

In the face of rainy days, we as individuals, as communities, and as a society are given these same choices – *deny, cope, or thrive*. We can choose to deny that rainy days exist, and just let them happen to us. This would mean we don't prepare for them, and we likely react poorly to them. We can choose to cope with rainy days. This would mean we make some effort to deal with them as they come our way. Or, we can choose to thrive on rainy days. This would mean preparing for and responding to rainy days in ways that allow us to maintain a high quality of life as individuals, as communities, and as a society.

After being diagnosed with MS, Stephanie Buxhoeveden became a subject matter expert. She worked as a nurse practitioner and treated thousands of other people living with multiple sclerosis. She then went on to earn her PhD, and today drives cutting edge research as the Chief Scientific Officer of the Accelerated Cure Project for MS, and is a member of the Board of Trustees for the National MS Society. Given the choices deny, cope, or thrive, Stephanie chose to thrive.

## *TED Active, TED Talks Live, and TED Global*

The main TED conference is legendary, and at the time in 2015, the event was being held annually in Vancouver. TED had also added a number of other TED conferences to their annual calendar. All of the main TED events were costly to attend. As you can imagine, organizing high caliber and increasingly engaging conferences every year is quite an undertaking. However, as a TEDx organizer and a student, I was able to apply for scholarships to the main events. In 2015, I applied to attend three of the main TED events – *TED Active, TED Live, and TED Global.*

TED Active was a satellite event held in Whistler just north of Vancouver at the same time as the main TED event. I think the goal of TED Active was to expand the capacity and impact of the main TED event and to make it more accessible to a broader audience. I attended TED Active the week after I had just executed my first TEDxHerndon event. When I arrived at the venue in Whistler, I was in awe of the scale and creativity of the TED Active conference. I met many other TEDx organizers, and it seemed like every person I met was a creative tour de force in their communities. I felt like an imposter or maybe just an amateur idea-haver. It felt a little bit like the first days on campus at Babson College during the StartingBloc Institute and MBA orientation when I was constantly meeting people with creative minds at work.

On one of the nights during the conference, there was an event held for TEDx organizers. It was incredible to see how many people from all over the world were committed to the vision of *ideas worth spreading*. That night there was a special performance by Aloe Blacc, and I heard his famous song "I Need a Dollar", which resonated on multiple levels as I was in the process of making the decision to shutdown my nonprofit largely because of lack of consistent funding. The experience of TED Active was visceral. I was constantly seeing, hearing, and thinking about new ideas about the world, about my community, about my life, and about how I could make my TEDx event better in 2016.

There were dozens of inspiring Talks that week, but the Talk that has resonated with me the most over the past ten years was delivered by Anand Giridharadas. He told the story of a hate crime where an individual was assaulted at a Texas mini-mart ten days after the September 11th terrorist attacks. In the Talk, he describes a tension between two Americas and the need for agents of reconciliation. The story is particularly relevant today. I believe we need more of the agents of reconciliation that Anand Giridharadas described in his Talk.

> *"We, the greatest inventors in the world, can invent solutions to the problems of that America, not only our own. We, the writers and the journalists, can cover that America's stories, instead of shutting down bureaus in its midst. We can finance that America's ideas, instead of ideas from New York and San Francisco. We can put our stethoscopes to its backs, teach there, go to court there, make there, live there, pray there.*

> *This, I believe, is the calling of a generation. An America whose two halves learn again to stride, to plow, to forge, to dare together. A republic of chances, rewoven, renewed, begins with us."*

*- Anand Giridharadas, TED 2015*

The next opportunity I had to attend one of the main TED events was in early November 2015 in New York City. TED Live consisted of six nights of Talks at the Town Hall Theater. There were three themes that week – *The Education Revolution, War and Peace,* and *Science and Wonder.* As a TEDx organizer, I was able to get a ticket to two of the nights, one of which happened to be the night Adam Driver delivered his Talk about his life journey from becoming a Marine to becoming an actor. Both Adam Driver and my father are Marines from Indiana that have an appreciation for the arts. In his Talk, Driver described the work of his nonprofit, *Arts in the Armed Forces,* and it has since made me think about how there are so many individuals and communities experiencing hardship that could be helped using the arts as a catalyst to facilitate self-expression and community conversations.

> *"So we started this nonprofit called Arts in the Armed Forces, where we tried to do that, tried to join these two seemingly dissimilar communities. We pick a play or select monologues from contemporary American plays that are diverse in age and race like a military audience is, grab a group of incredible theater-trained actors, arm them with incredible material, keep production value as minimal as possible -- no sets, no costumes, no lights, just reading it -- to throw all the emphasis on the language and to show that theater can be created at any setting.*

> *It's a powerful thing, getting in a room with complete strangers and reminding ourselves of our humanity, and that self-expression is just as valuable a tool as a rifle on your shoulder. And for an organization like the military, that prides itself on having acronyms for acronyms, you can get lost in the sauce when it comes to explaining a collective*

*experience. And I can think of no better community to arm with a new means of self-expression than those protecting our country."*

*- Adam Driver, TED Talks Live, November 2015*

A few weeks after the TED Talks Live event in New York City, I was in Geneva, Switzerland to attend the TED Global conference. I had once again applied to attend as a TEDx organizer, which meant I was able to go without paying the high registration price. I was still a graduate student at the time at Virginia Tech's Center for Leadership in Global Sustainability. I had shutdown my nonprofit months earlier and was searching for what I would do in the next phase of life. The TED Global conference was the beginning of a six-week trip that would end in Cape Town, South Africa for the international residency component of my natural resources masters degree program.

In the few years leading up to 2015, there was a growing refugee crisis in the Middle East and Europe as people were forced out of their home countries by a number of conflicts, including major wars in Afghanistan and Syria. Neighboring countries in the Middle East were the first to receive refugees, but in 2015, over one million refugees and migrants crossed the Mediterranean Sea into Europe. This was a significant increase from the previous years, and many European Union governments reacted by closing their borders. To give you a sense of scale, the population of the European Union in 2015 was about 550 million, and so the influx of 1 million refugees represented a population increase of less than 0.2%. But Europeans were afraid of so many refugees moving into their countries so quickly, and there were deep concerns about security.

When I was in Geneva in December 2015, I visited the United Nations office there where numerous important global agencies are headquartered. One of the most notable speakers at the TED Global event was António Guterres, who at the time was the UN High Commissioner for Refugees.

He is now the Secretary General of the United Nations. In his interview with the TED Global host, Bruno Giussani, Commissioner António Guterres explained how he thought many Europeans were viewing the refugee crisis.

> *"I mean, what does a European see at home in a village where there are no migrants? What a European sees is, on television, every single day, a few months ago, opening the news every single day, a crowd coming, uncontrolled, moving from border to border, and the images on television were of hundreds or thousands of people moving. And the idea is that nobody is taking care of it -- this is happening without any kind of management. And so their idea was, "They are coming to my village." So there was this completely false idea that Europe was being invaded and our way of life is going to change, and everything will -- And the problem is that if this had been properly managed, if people had been properly received, welcomed, sheltered at point of entry, screened at point of entry, and then moved by plane to different European countries, this would not have scared people. But, unfortunately, we have a lot of people scared, just because Europe was not able to do the job properly."*

> *- António Guterres, UN High Commissioner for Refugees,*
> *TED Global, 2015*

Americans can learn a lot from the European Refugee Crisis. Perhaps the most fundamental concept Americans need to understand is what a refugee is. There are many people that are being characterized in the United States as illegal immigrants when in fact they are refugees. By definition, refugees have been forced to leave their country due to persecution, war, or violence. Commissioner António Guterres also described how refugee crises are triggered and exacerbated.

*"And then the trigger was when all of a sudden, international aid decreased. The World Food Programme was forced, for lack of resources, to cut by 30 percent food support to the Syrian refugees. They're not allowed to work, so they are totally dependent on international support, and they felt, "The world is abandoning us." And that, in my opinion, was the trigger. All of a sudden, there was a rush, and people started to move in large numbers and, to be absolutely honest, if I had been in the same situation and I would have been brave enough to do it, I think I would have done the same."*

*- António Guterres, UN High Commissioner for Refugees,*
*TED Global, 2015*

This page you are reading right now was written on February 4th, 2025 as the new Administration in the United States is dismantling the United States Agency for International Development (USAID), freezing foreign aid, pausing grant and loan programs to nonprofits in the United States, and threatening to fire hundreds of thousands of federal government workers. As all of this is happening, I'm thinking about all the individuals and communities in America that have been devastated by economic hardship over the past two decades. I wonder how many of those folks are blaming the international community, foreign policy, and globalization. I wonder if those people heard the TED Talks of Anand Giridharadas, Adam Driver, and António Guterres, if they might see things differently. I wonder how many Americans believe in the words of The New Colossus poem that is mounted at the base of the Statue of Liberty.

### *The New Colossus*

*Not like the brazen giant of Greek fame,*
*With conquering limbs astride from land to land;*
*Here at our sea-washed, sunset gates shall stand*
*A mighty woman with a torch, whose flame*
*Is the imprisoned lightning, and her name*
*Mother of Exiles. From her beacon-hand*
*Glows world-wide welcome; her mild eyes command*
*The air-bridged harbor that twin cities frame.*
*"Keep, ancient lands, your storied pomp!" cries she*
*With silent lips. "Give me your tired, your poor,*
*Your huddled masses yearning to breathe free,*
*The wretched refuse of your teeming shore.*
*Send these, the homeless, tempest-tost to me,*
*I lift my lamp beside the golden door!"*

*Emma Lazarus*
*November 2, 1883*

Why do we share ideas? Why do we tell stories? Why do we create? Why do we express ourselves? Maybe there is no good reason. Maybe it is for our own catharsis. Maybe it is just to help us understand our world better. Maybe it is because sometimes ideas, stories, creations, and expressions have a positive impact on our lives and the lives of others. I think ideas, stories, creativity, and art make the world a better place where we understand ourselves and each other better. The arts help us navigate rainy days together.

# Chapter 11

## A SOCIETY BY DESIGN
## May 2016 - May 2017

*"If design is shaping our culture and our world and has
been doing it for centuries, then why are we not inviting
designers to the table to address these social justice issues that
are embedded within our culture?"*

*- Antionette Carroll, TEDxHerndon 2017*

---

In 2016, I renewed my license to organize a TEDx event in my hometown. After attending multiple events organized by TED in 2015 and seeing the incredible scale and impact of those events, I decided to attempt to make our TEDxHerndon event as big as possible. We were constrained in two ways the second year. The event venue had to be in the Town of Herndon, and the event could be no longer than a single day. The middle school in town had the best set up for a larger event, so we decided to host a full day event there. The middle school theater could seat nearly 600 people, and I wanted to fill every one of those seats. I also had a backlog of potential speakers that either I had connected with or that had reached out to me.

The second year of TEDxHerndon was a mixed bag of successes and failures. It was a full-day event as planned, but I was trying to do too much in a single day. I invited over 30 people to speak or perform, and didn't prepare all of them sufficiently, so there were more than a few speakers that went over their allotted time. This pushed us off schedule early in the day, which made the lunch break chaotic, and the lunch was held on the other side of the building, in the school cafeteria, which proved to be a logistical tripping point. The theater also proved to be an increasingly warm space as the day went on, which made the attendee experience less comfortable over the course of the event. And, while I had more volunteers in 2016 than in 2015, I still needed a lot more. At the end of the day, we had gone 2 hours over the scheduled time, and we also went over budget for production and editing. Despite all of these logistical failures, there were a number of Talks that did well on the day of the event and online afterwards. TEDxHerndon in 2016 was a high impact event, but I knew I could organize and execute better in 2017.

In the first two events, I hadn't been intentional enough about how I recruited speakers and performers. It was essentially just casting a wide net and talking to people I already knew. The problem with that approach was that the resulting lineup ended up being predominantly able-bodied straight white men. I wasn't trying to make the lineup predominantly able-bodied straight white men, and we did have a number of women and people of color speak and perform in 2015 and 2016, but the demographics of the speaker lineup did not reflect the demographics of Herndon. At the time, about one third of the population of the Town of Herndon was white, and two thirds were people of color. And yet, in 2015 and 2016, the speakers and performers were about 75% white and 25% people of color. Because I wasn't intentional enough, the speaker and performer lineup for the TEDxHerndon event wasn't a representation of my community. Rather, it was a representation of what my network looked like.

In an attempt to be more intentional about developing the lineup for the 2017 event, I added a self-imposed constraint to how I was going to do speaker recruitment. I decided that for the 2017 event, 50% of the speakers and performers needed to be people of color and 50% of the speakers and performers needed to be women. In the context of race, this was still not quite representative of the population of Herndon, but I figured 50% was a good start. The logistics of this self-imposed constraint proved to add a level of complexity to the speaker recruitment process.

I knew that the event was better as a half-day event, and that speakers were going to be limited to 12-minute Talks. I approximated that there would be 16 speakers and performers, which meant eight of them had to be people of color and eight of them had to be women, according to my self-imposed constraint. When I started speaker recruitment, I essentially had a surplus of potential white male speakers and a lack of potential speakers that were people of color and/or women. I wanted this third year to be the best TEDxHerndon after I had fumbled the 2016 event. So, the speaker lineup had to be the best in the history of the event.

Pause for a moment and think about how you would approach the speaker recruitment for this event. As I started speaker recruitment, I was hesitant to confirm any white male speakers, and I was eager to find speakers that were women and/or people of color. The immediate result was that I rejected more speaker proposals from white men. That was unavoidable. There were only 16 speaking spots, and only up to eight speaking spots for white men, and I wasn't willing to give one of those eight speaking spots to a guy that was just another "motivational speaker". There was also an element of time at play. I couldn't just wait for women and people of color to discover the opportunity of speaking at TEDxHerndon. I had to go find great ideas and stories that were being told by women and people of color.

I was on the clock to find great ideas and stories worth spreading within just a few months, and so I asked for help. A couple months into the speaker recruitment process, a miracle happened. Two world-renowned writers said yes to speaking at TEDxHerndon – Nikki Giovanni and Kwame Alexander. Both Nikki and Kwame meant a lot to the Herndon community. Nikki was the person that lifted the spirits of the Virginia

Tech community in 2007 after the tragedy. Kwame Alexander was an inspiration to so many people in Herndon, having recently won the Newberry Medal for his book "The Crossover," which he had written in town a few years earlier.

Having confirmed Nikki Giovanni and Kwame Alexander, the speaker lineup quickly filled out and manifested as the best and most creative group of speakers and performers in TEDxHerndon's short 3-year history. And I knew it before the event happened. In 2015, we barely filled the 100-seat black box theater for the first TEDxHerndon. In 2017, we sold 550 tickets for the third TEDxHerndon. There was a buzz in town before the event. And after the event, we got a measurable confirmation when our post-event survey showed a significant increase in our Net Promoter Score, which meant a higher percentage of attendees liked the event than in the previous year.

At least in the context of my little TEDxHerndon event, embracing the principles of diversity, equity, and inclusion resulted in much better results across multiple metrics. There was more talk about the event before it happened. There were more tickets sold. And, the event was enjoyed more than in previous years. But to me, the success was that it became a real community event. It was no longer just a fun thing that I was doing with my friends and professional network. It was an event that served the community. It existed in a place and time and effectively shared ideas and stories worth spreading.

## A society that works for everyone

We currently face a confluence of complex problem sets. Society has a lot to think about including, but not limited to, an epidemic of national debts, environmental sustainability, the deterioration of infrastructure systems, public health risks, and major gaps in the workforce. As if all those things weren't enough to understand, we also need to understand how to allocate money efficiently to adequately address all of those issues. Furthermore, we need to be able to determine if we even have enough money to adequately address those issues.

> ***Rainy Day Economics Design Prompt 14:*** *Take a moment to conceptualize society and the economy. Grab a blank piece of paper and a pencil. Sit down at your desk. Now, draw the economy. Think about the economy that you belong to. Think about how you exist in the economy. Think about all of the different elements of an economy. Consider the people, the organizations, the money, the infrastructure, the resources, and all of the connections. This exercise should take more than a couple minutes. Once you have a drawing that you are satisfied with, put your pencil down. Stand up from your desk, and look down at the economy that you have drawn. Now add all of our societal problems.*

As we seek to answer the thousands upon thousands of questions that need to be answered, we also need to remember that we are trying to design a society that works for everyone, not just able-bodied straight white men. And the only way to do that is to commit to diversity, equity, and inclusion. The third pillar of the Rainy Day Economics framework – human-centered capitalism – inherently embraces diversity, equity, and inclusion in order to design societal systems that work for everyone.

> *"We spend a lot time designing the bridge, but not enough time thinking about the people who are crossing it."*
>
> — *Dr. Prabhjot Singh, Director of Systems Design at the Earth Institute*

Diversity, equity, and inclusion is not just about race. In a Talk at

TEDxMidAtlantic in 2016, Elise Roy delivered a message that is imperative for societal designers everywhere to understand. The message is simple — *when we design for the disabled, everyone benefits.* Elise Roy is a deaf human-centered designer, and she has become an outspoken advocate for the notion of designing for disability. She is on the frontlines of design suggesting that solutions developed by designing for the disabled will outperform solutions developed by designing for the norm. This is a powerful idea. In her Talk, Elise tells the story of her time in a design school woodshop.

> *"As you're working with a tool, right before it's about to kick back at you — which means the piece or the tool jumps back at you — it makes a sound. And I couldn't hear this sound. So I decided, why not try and solve it? My solution was a pair of safety glasses that were engineered to visually alert the user to pitch changes in the tool, before the human ear could pick it up. Why hadn't tool designers thought of this before?"*

Her story is very personal, but it resonates, because it illustrates her point perfectly. There are so many things that designers will not naturally design for if they are only designing for the norm. The glasses Elise engineered are of course useful to people that are not deaf too. And, there are thousands of products that could be designed better by thinking about disability. And, there are quite a few products that exist because people designed with disability in mind. Elise's website identifies a few, *'The typewriter, audio books, remote controls, OXO grips, and closed captioning were all created by designing for disability.'*

> *"Humans aren't as good as we should be in our capacity to empathize with feelings and thoughts of others, be they humans or other animals on Earth. So maybe part of our formal education should be training*

*in empathy. Imagine how different the world would be if, in fact, that were 'reading, writing, arithmetic, empathy.'"*

—*Neil deGrasse Tyson*

Perhaps we should start to teach designers to design with disability in mind. Educating future designers to design for disability would likely lead to better design with more functionality. And, ingraining the empathy necessary for this work into new designers will make them better humans in the process of educating them. Likewise, we should encourage more people with disabilities to be designers. Having this perspective at the table of the design industry will inherently add an important perspective to conversations about how we should design products and experiences.

*"Designing for a user problem that you don't deeply understand is really hard to do. You're much more likely to successfully design for a user problem that you deeply understand. It also makes you more creative and more innovative when you do this kind of counterfactual thinking. It has a neurological effect that stimulates creativity."*

—*Katy Mogal*

It is conceivable that if we as a society decide to design with disability in mind, then the quality of life for everyone will increase. Also, designers can enable people with the systems, products, and experiences they design. If we leverage a deeper understanding of the human experience of everyone, we will be able to create a world that is more inclusive and better designed for everyone, especially on rainy days. This is an opportunity for designers to have a massive positive impact on the future.

Empathic design thinking is also something we should look for in our future leaders. There is a scene from the popular television show *Game of*

*Thrones* where Tyrion Lannister, played by Peter Dinklage, articulates a vision for who could be the one to unite and lead.

> *"What unites people? Armies? Gold? Flags? …Stories. There's nothing in the world more powerful than a good story. Nothing can stop it. No enemy can defeat it. And who has a better story than Bran the broken? The boy who fell from a high tower and lived. He knew he'd never walk again, so he learned to fly. He crossed beyond the world a crippled boy and became the three-eyed Raven. He is our memory, the keeper of all our stories. The wars, weddings, births, massacres, famines. Our triumphs. Our defeats. Our past. Who better to lead us into the future?"*

In 1921, Franklin Roosevelt's career was nearly derailed by an illness that caused him to be paralyzed permanently from the waste down. He remained active in politics through the 1920s while also going through extensive therapy and rehabilitation efforts. Then in 1928, he ran for Governor of New York and won. In October 1929, the Wall Street Crash occurred and the Great Depression began. In 1932, Franklin D. Roosevelt ran for President and won. Under his leadership from 1933 to 1945, the United States navigated and survived both the Great Depression and World War II.

## Community design moments

When I was a kid at Rachel Carson Middle School (1999-2001) in the suburbs of Washington, D.C., we were taught about the history of the Civil Rights Movement and the legacy of slavery. We were shown the images and told the stories of Emmett Till, the Little Rock 9, the Montgomery bus boycotts, and the student sit-ins. I made a video for a class assignment that was really just a slideshow with a song added in the background to evoke emotion. The slideshow included a set of images from the Civil Rights Movement that I found online. The song I added to this slideshow was "Bitter" by Nine Days, which was a popular band when I was in middle school. The chorus of the song resonated with me, and I thought was relevant to the struggles of the Civil Rights Movement. The last line of the chorus was and is a frustrating sentiment though.

> *"If I could change anything*
> *Then I would wipe the years away*
> *If I could change anything*
> *Then I would brush the time away*
> *If I could change anything*
> *Then I would change everything*
> *These bitter days shall remain"*

To this day, I don't know what the majority of kids in the United States are taught related to the history of the Civil Rights Movement and the legacy of slavery. When you're a kid, you think that the life you and your friends are living is the norm. I definitely thought that, at least in middle school. I knew that maybe not every student was going to hear as much about Rachel Carson, the famous environmentalist that our middle school was named after, but it never crossed my mind, at least not in middle school, that students my age in different parts of the country wouldn't learn as much about the Civil Rights Movement or the legacy of slavery. A 2020 CBS article also pointed out *"while states set expectations for what students learn, experts say in the end, it is up to individual districts to decide what and how students are taught—and up to teachers to bring those lessons to life"*.

As I was trying to get my nonprofit off the ground from 2011 to 2015, there was a new iteration of the Civil Rights Movement growing in America, and it was called *Black Lives Matter*. This movement was somewhat relevant to the STEM education work I was doing at schools in low-income communities, because the movement had a lot to do with the signals that we send as a society to kids of color to let them know that they are important to us. When you walk into a high school in Washington, D.C., you must go through metal detectors in order to get into the building. This is an experience that kids in Northern Virginia don't have growing up. The reason there are metal detectors in high schools in D.C. is to prevent weapons from being brought into the buildings. The metal detectors are there to protect kids. That is the type of societal design moment that says, *"the kids that are learning in this building matter to society"*. Outside of schools though, there aren't many societal design moments that tell young kids of color that they are important.

When I think about design moments in society, I think about the built environment, our social support systems, and the products and capabilities that public servants are provided to serve the public. You can tell a lot about what a society values by looking at how governments spend their money. For many local governments in the United States, the largest piece of the budget pie is education. Public safety is usually the third largest portion of the budget behind health and human services. So, if that is where we stop our analysis, we'd come to the conclusion that society clearly values the lives of young people, so therefore no change in how we think is necessary. Except local government budget pie charts only tell us a tiny part of our collective story.

What if we were to do a side-by-side embodied-investment analysis of a fully equipped local police officer on duty and a 17-year old person of color? You can follow along with this thought exercise by drawing these two individuals on a piece of paper side-by-side. The fully equipped local police officer went to a public school, had access to social welfare programs and affordable housing initiatives, and enjoys all of the well-maintained roads and bridges in his community. The same is true of the 17-year old young person of color. So, is that it? Are we done with our analysis? No.

The fully equipped police officer is fully equipped. What does that mean? The average police officer is armed with multiple weapons, an advanced communications system, a database of information about individuals in the community, a uniquely capable vehicle, a badge, and a tool belt that helps them navigate various situations. I'm sure there are other products and systems that I didn't mention that police officers have available to them as well. Also, a police officer can use his or her communications system to call other police officers, and they will show up to help. The 17-year old young person of color maybe has a cell phone that he or she can use to call people that might show up to help if they are available.

So now you might be thinking, based on this side-by-side embodied-investment analysis, society cares a lot more about police officers than kids of color. And frankly, I think there are plenty of stories to reinforce that assertion. Also, given our country's relatively recent history, it makes sense to me that kids of color are fearful of police officers. There are people alive today whose parents or grandparents were beaten by police officers during the Civil Rights Movement in the 1960s. But I believe community policing is transforming the way everyone thinks about police officers.

> *"Community policing is, in essence, a collaboration between the police and the community that identifies and solves community problems. With the police no longer the sole guardians of law and order, all members of the community become active allies in the effort to enhance the safety and quality of neighborhoods."*
>
> *- United States Department of Justice*

The side-by-side embodied-investment analysis changes when kids of color view a police officer as a societal investment in their own individual wellbeing and the quality of life in their community. We'll know progress is being made when young kids of color don't instinctually put their hands up out of fear of police officers, and instead reach out to shake the hand of the police officer that they've known as a member of their community for years. In the wake of disasters and tragedies, kids of color should be able to trust that police officers and other public safety officials will be there to help them. There shouldn't be a layer of fear between kids of color and police officers on rainy days.

Crys Matthews was the closing performance at the 2017 TEDxHerndon event, and the last song she performed was an upbeat, uplifting counterweight to the heavy issues of the day. The main line of the song was – *"We are imagineers. The ones who still believe in magic. The ones who rise above our fears."* I believe we will always need more imagineers, but particularly on rainy days in our local communities. Designers, or imagineers, can help build a sense of community that allows people to recover faster in the aftermath of rainy days.

# Chapter 12

## ISLANDS OF INNOVATION
### September 20, 2017

*"Resilience is a complex relational process that emerges not from our independence from each other, but from our deep interdependence."*

*- Soraya Chemaly*

---

Imagine for a moment that you live on an island. The island has roads, schools, businesses and a beautiful landscape. On this island, the people have decided they never want to be taxed more than 20 dollars. This worked well until recently when the per capita cost to operate and maintain the island and all of the public infrastructure increased to some amount over $20 per year. It is now projected that the cost to operate and maintain the island and all of the public infrastructure will soon reach $40 per capita. The government is now looking to you for a solution. What would you do?

In an ideal scenario, we want to be able to maintain the current quality of life on the island. So, what are our options? We could increase taxes above the 20-dollar threshold and risk the possibility of people leaving the island. We could stop funding certain public infrastructure and programs, risking the possibility of a major reduction in quality of life. Or, we could increase the money supply to pay for public infrastructure. This is only possible if we are able to increase the money supply. And, if we utilize this approach, we must be mindful of inflation possibilities. If increasing the money supply isn't a possibility, then the government will likely resort to deficit spending.

This scenario might seem obscure and unrealistic, but this is similar to the situation Puerto Rico was experiencing in 2015. Puerto Rico's debt was then well above $70 billion. That is not an insignificant amount of debt, and the Governor of Puerto Rico at the time admitted publicly that the debt was not payable and that if the economy didn't grow, Puerto Rico would be in a death spiral. Put yourself in the shoes of the Puerto Rican government. How would you pay that off? Paying that amount of debt off in any reasonable amount of time inherently means considering a significant increase in taxes and/or a significant decrease in government-funded programs. Just imagine an annual budget of $10 billion. To pay off the $70 billion debt in less than 15 years, it would take at least half of the annual budget committed to debt payments … *for 15 years*. And that's assuming a 0% growth in the debt from year to year.

Puerto Rican lawmakers approved an increase in the sales tax from seven percent to 11.5 percent. At the same time, the governor of Puerto Rico proposed a budget that included a $200 million cut to education. This resulted in protests, which were not covered by any major U.S. press. This was just the tip of the iceberg when it came to the effects of the island's massive debt. The island's population dropped drastically from 4 million in 2009 to less than 3.6 million in 2014. This drop in population was at least in part due to the direct and indirect impacts of the island's massive debt.

So what? Who cares what's happening in Puerto Rico? Well … I do, and you should too. Puerto Rico is family. No matter your perspective on the structural connection between the United States and Puerto Rico, Puerto Ricans are part of the fabric of America. Moreover, Puerto Rico's problems are very similar to the problems the U.S. federal government is facing, namely the massive debt. As a country, we should pay attention to and learn from the Puerto Rican debt crisis, because the U.S. federal government needs to solve the massive debt riddle too. Make no mistake; debt makes it harder to thrive on rainy days. Whether you are an individual, a community, or a country, your debt makes it more difficult to prepare for rainy days, to maintain long-term plans, and to recover from rainy days.

How does a country get out of massive debt? The obvious answers are increase taxes, decrease spending and don't take on more debt. But there is a limit to how much we can increase taxes and decrease spending. What is the next set of answers to this riddle? The next set of answers might include investing in an ecosystem of entrepreneurs, intentional research and development efforts, more efficient infrastructure, and actively recruiting top-tier talent from overseas. In the case of the United States, increasing the money supply should also be considered.

There is a clear opportunity to collaborate with Puerto Rico to develop high-impact strategies that will guide us all out of debt. Puerto Rico could be an entrepreneurial incubator. And, it is in the best interest of the U.S. federal government to help solve the Puerto Rican debt crisis. Helping to solve the Puerto Rican debt crisis will inform and help develop a set of strategies to effectively address the U.S. debt crisis without increasing taxes and/or cutting valuable government programs. It was clear in 2015 that Puerto Rico was a canary in the coalmine. What was happening in Puerto Rico was prologue. What happens next is up to us.

Rainy Day Economics can help a society burdened by debt by designing a more sustainable and resilient system and focusing on creating innovative mechanisms that maintain and improve quality of life. Think back to the beginning of this book about how the September 11th terrorist attacks set us on a course for massive national debt. Society can design hundreds of permutations of rainy day funds that manifest in different ways and effectively keep us from going deeper into debt. For example, endowments can be viewed as a type of rainy day fund that is capable of maintaining and improving quality of life without adding to the national debt.

*The Endowment Economy*

Since its inception in 1997, the Bill and Melinda Gates Foundation has made grant payments totaling more than $77 billion. These grants have gone to things like polio eradication, the Malaria Vaccine Initiative and targeted education efforts in low-income communities. The Gates Foundation's endowment is currently around $75 billion. Harvard's endowment is of a similar magnitude: around $52 billion, compared to the average university endowment of about $350 million. Harvard has used its massive endowment to fund professorships, financial aid and research. These endowments seem to be positive forces for good. Furthermore, they seem to provide perpetual funding for their chosen causes. So, why don't we have more massive endowments?

> *"An endowment model, if structured with integrity and accountability, could create long-term, locally-controlled support for essential systems— education, sustainable farming, climate adaptation, health, food sovereignty."*

> *- C.J. Acosta*

Most endowments are the result of wealthy individuals setting aside money for a particular cause or set of causes. Or, in the case of universities, it is the result of an accumulation of donations and grants. So, it makes sense that we don't have thousands of massive endowments of magnitudes similar to that of Gates and Harvard. On the other hand, we have witnessed numerous injections of capital into the economy by the federal government in the form of stimulus packages and quantitative easing.

The American Recovery and Reinvestment Act of 2009, which was introduced to the House on Jan. 26, 2009, and signed into law by the President three weeks later, injected roughly $800 billion into the American economy over ten years. The legislation funded things like infrastructure, energy efficiency, education, healthcare and scientific research. The Federal Reserve has also been active in recent years. The third round of quantitative easing (QE3) in September 2012 started at a rate of $40 billion per month and peaked in 2014 at a rate of $85 billion per month. This money is injected into the economy when the Federal Reserve buys securities from banks thus giving banks more capital to lend. Quantitative easing and federal stimulus packages are shortsighted solutions to our economic problems. We need an effective long-term solution. We need more massive endowments.

Consider the money associated with the American Recovery and Reinvestment Act of 2009 -- $800 billion. That amount of money is the equivalent to about 11 Gates endowments or 15 Harvard endowments. Similarly, at the starting QE3 rate of $40 billion a month over two years, we could create 12 Gates endowments. At the QE3 rate of $85 billion a month over two years, we could create 39 Harvard endowments. That amount of money could create a $40 billion endowment for every state and territory in the Union. Again, endowments provide perpetual funding streams. These wouldn't simply fund a road maintenance project and create jobs for a year. Endowments are designed to give ongoing support.

Advocates for smaller government should like this idea. While this wouldn't necessarily shrink government, it would inherently shrink the market share of the government sector (perhaps a more accurate term for this would be 'sector share'). Therefore, if newly injected money were funneled to the nonprofit sector, then the nonprofit sector would grow while the government remained close to the same size. It is also reasonable to assume that as the nonprofit sector grows, the government sector would not only shrink in sector share, but also in actual size. A lot of the work done by government agencies can be, and sometimes is, done by the nonprofit sector (think: education, healthcare and other social services).

It is clear that our societal challenges aren't getting easier. Issues relating to food, energy, water, poverty, infrastructure, education and justice are becoming more and more complex. A more robust nonprofit sector is necessary to address these challenges. Increasing the size and number of philanthropic and university endowments can very effectively address the social and environmental challenges of today and tomorrow. As governments consider future rounds of economic stimulus and quantitative easing, they should consider the effectiveness and longevity of endowments. Endowments can effectively be utilized as rainy day funds. This would also help facilitate cross-sector collaboration between government, philanthropic foundations, the nonprofit sector, and corporations. Increasing the number of public endowments across the United States has the potential to effectively address all five pillars of Rainy Day Economics.

## *Replicating the Michigan Office of the Foundation Liaison*

In mid-2017, I stumbled across an interesting cross-sector collaboration model in Michigan that I thought could be applied in Virginia. The Michigan Governor's Office of the Foundation Liaison was established in 2003 and had since brokered over $150 million in philanthropic investments in the state of Michigan in collaboration with the Governor's office.

> *"The Foundation Liaison is a cabinet-level position and helps to identify and broker innovative funding partnerships and strategic collaborations between the executive branch of state government and foundations to encourage programs or policy reforms that would improve the lives of all Michigan children, families and residents."*

The idea I had was to simply replicate that office in Virginia, and since there was going to be a new Governor starting in January 2018, I figured it was a good time to shop the idea around. I called every community foundation in the state and pitched the idea. I also connected with a handful of other private family foundations. Most of the leaders of the community foundations were immediately onboard, as they had been longing for more opportunities to collaborate with the state government to create more impact in the communities they served.

As I was doing this initial outreach and shopping the idea around, I asked for feedback from some of my previous mentors at Babson College who were particularly attuned to cross-sector collaboration efforts across the country. Naturally they thought of someone that I should talk to immediately, a fellow Babson alum and also a fellow Virginian interested in philanthropy and cross-sector collaboration.

When I pitched my idea to him, he was instantly supportive. I also realized in those early conversations how little I knew about the world of philanthropy and impact investing. My fellow Babson alum had an impressive depth of knowledge about impact investing, social entrepreneurship, and philanthropy, and like most Babson alumni, he also had and has a bias for action. Within a few months, we had over 30 philanthropic leaders in Virginia signed on to a letter to the Governor-elect to create something similar to the Michigan Governor's Office of the Foundation Liaison.

I also worked with state legislators to attempt to create by legislation a zero-cost commission to more formally engage philanthropy and impact investing leaders. At first it seemed like we had bipartisan support for this effort. However, when it came time to vote, the legislation didn't pass. The votes cast were along party lines, and I think the argument against this zero-cost commission was that it would just create more government bureaucracy. In my opinion, the benefits of the state government collaborating more with philanthropic foundations far outweighed the tiny bit of new government bureaucracy. Luckily, the Governor was still interested in advancing collaboration with the Virginia philanthropy and impact investing community, or "the Virginia Impact Community" as we called the group of leaders that had signed on. In June 2018, we received a letter from the Governor's Chief of Staff identifying a point person in the Governor's Administration that would serve as a liaison to the Virginia Impact Community.

It was a months long effort that resulted in a little bit more collaboration between philanthropic foundations and the state government. We didn't succeed in forming a formal office or commission in precisely the way I had originally envisioned (the way that Michigan had), but there was clear progress. In addition, we laid the groundwork for more work and momentum in the Virginia philanthropic community. At that point in time, Virginia didn't have its own grantmakers association. The grantmakers in the northern part of the state were members of the Washington Regional Association of Grantmakers, and the grantmakers in the southern part of the state were members of the Southeastern Council on Foundations. Two years after our push for a Virginia Governor's Office of the Foundation (or the like), the Virginia Funders Network was created and now has over 130 member funders.

The federal government also has a number of teams that are tasked with working with philanthropic foundations to help society. The Council on Foundations has a Federal Liaisons program that brings together a mix of political appointees and career employees from Cabinet Departments and various independent agencies, such as the Department of Housing and Urban Development, Department of Veterans Affairs, Department of Education, Federal Emergency Management Agency, Environmental Protection Agency, State Department, and the Corporation for National and Community Service. These kinds of offices that are focused on cross-sector collaboration can be ideal incubators for Rainy Day Economics and advancing conversations related to improving quality of life. They can also be particularly helpful on rainy days to coordinate cross-sector response to disasters and tragedies.

## *Food, community, and the urgency of 'right now'*

The 2017 hurricane season in the Atlantic was extremely active, which is to say that there were a lot of storms that year. Hurricane Harvey made landfall in Texas in August, and tied Hurricane Katrina as the costliest hurricane in American history. And then Hurricane Irma swept through the Caribbean a few weeks later eventually making landfall in Florida as the first Category 4 hurricane to hit the state in over a decade. Hurricane Irma knocked out power for tens of thousands in Puerto Rico, and for many the power hadn't been restored as the next hurricane approached. Soon after Hurricane Irma, on September 20th, Hurricane Maria hit Puerto Rico as the most intense storm the island had faced since 1928. The island was devastated.

Millions were without power immediately following the storm, 95% of the island didn't have cell service, and less than half of the population had access to tap water. In the days that followed, the Federal Emergency Management Agency (FEMA), the U.S. Coast Guard, the Federal Aviation Administration (FAA), the U.S. Air Force, the U.S. Army Corps of Engineers, the U.S. Marine Corps, and the U.S. Navy were all activated to support the response and recovery in Puerto Rico.

Puerto Rico may look small on a map, but it was a large area to provide support to in the wake of Hurricane Maria. The devastation was spread across the entire island. As a point of comparison, the land area of New York City is about 300 square miles, and the land area of Puerto Rico is over 5,300 square miles. As another point of reference, Puerto Rico is larger than Rhode Island and Delaware, but smaller than Connecticut. But unlike Rhode Island, Delaware, and Connecticut, Puerto Rico didn't have the benefit of immediate support from surrounding states or the hundreds of access points for response and relief teams to bring aid. The airports were temporarily disabled, and the roads and bridges on the island were full of debris.

Pause for a moment and imagine you are living in Puerto Rico after the island has been devastated by Hurricane Maria. You have no power, little food and water, and no ability to communicate with people outside of those nearby in your community. What do you do?

José Andrés is the founder of World Central Kitchen, which is a nonprofit devoted to providing food to people in the wake of natural disasters. In his TEDxMidAtlantic Talk in 2018, he told the story of how the amazing people of Puerto Rico came together to feed the people of Puerto Rico. When you listen to José Andrés speak, you can tell he is action-oriented. The World Central Kitchen website quotes him saying, *"When you talk about food and water, people don't want a solution one week from now, one month from now. The solution has to be now."* In those first days after Hurricane Maria made landfall, the people of Puerto Rico didn't have time to wait for a top-down plan from the government, and so the people took action to take care of their communities.

In José Andrés's story, he talks about how they just started feeding people in Puerto Rico. There was no power, no cell service, limited access to clean water, but they were determined to just start feeding people. They didn't have time for the meetings with the government. He started by providing 1,000 meals, and within days his team was providing 25,000 meals. And then his operation grew to 50,000 meals and then 70,000 meals. Eventually, José Andrés had established 18 kitchens across the island and provided two million meals. He asserts in his TEDxMidAtlantic Talk *"We cannot be planning how to give aid a month from now. We have to be ready to start giving help the second after something happens."* I completely agree with this sentiment. When natural disasters happen, we should be able to act immediately to respond and recover. The planning should be done before the storm by all of us at every level – as individuals, as communities, as organizations, and as a country.

A friend of mine that was in Puerto Rico during that time also reminded me that *"While José Andrés was heroic, what truly kept people alive was the strength of Puerto Rican communities themselves—neighbors cooking together, co-ops clearing roads, churches organizing supply drops, farmers sharing what little they had. That kind of hyperlocal resilience is not just inspiring, it's instructive, and it's exactly what your audience of young readers can see themselves in."* My friend also told me about how Puerto Rico has become a hub for innovation and experimentation and a shining example of hope and resilience. This has included a growing entrepreneurial ecosystem, solar energy co-ops, and agroecology networks transforming how food is grown and shared.

> *"We're not just surviving—we're testing the future."*
>
> *- C.J. Acosta*

Puerto Rico's resilience is both inspiring and instructive. If we combine Puerto Rico's story with Michel Brunaeu's 4R Resilience Framework, then we can start to lay the ground work for community resilience globally. The "4R Resilience Framework" is a relevant model that can be applied to rainy day economics at the individual, community, organizational, and national level. Michel Bruneau is a civil engineering professor at the University at Buffalo, and his research focuses largely on earthquake engineering. Bruneau and his colleagues have advanced this framework and defined resilience according to three outcomes.

- Reduced probability of failure
- Reduced consequences of failure
- Reduced time to restoration

Defining these three outcomes allows us to measure our success when thinking about resilience. The "4R Resilience Framework" suggests that there are four main characteristics of resiliency – robustness, redundancy, resourcefulness, and rapidity. Robustness refers to capabilities that allow us to resist the impact of a rainy day event. Redundancy is all about developing substitutes, alternatives, and layers of system capabilities, so that a single point failure doesn't cause a system-wide failure. Resourcefulness refers both to our ability to adapt and also be creative when resources are constrained. Rapidity refers to the ability to restore operations and systems quickly after a rainy day event.

> ***Rainy Day Economics Design Prompt 15:*** *Develop a plan to feed your community in the immediate aftermath of a natural disaster. Consider how much food and water you will need and for how long. Also consider the cross-sector partnerships that you should develop now before the disaster to prepare.*

Puerto Rico in the aftermath of Hurricane Maria is a useful context to think about how we might make remote communities more immediately resilient. More specifically, thinking about how we might reduce the time to response and recovery in remote communities on an island can help us design better solutions for all rainy days.

# Part 4:
# The Politics of
# Rainy Day Economics

# Chapter 13

## HUMAN-CENTERED, CONSENSUS-DRIVEN
### November 6th, 2017

*"Oh get a job? Just get a job? Why don't I strap on my job helmet and squeeze down into a job cannon and fly off into job land where jobs grow on jobbies!"*

*– Charlie Day, It's Always Sunny in Philadelphia*

---

From late 2016 through most of 2017, I was working for an infrastructure "consulting" firm. I put consulting in quotes, because the firm was actually lobbying more than consulting. The company survived by taking money from companies that thought they were going to get access to the Administration. I had networked my way into this job. The son of a former U.S. Senator recommended I apply to a role that had an inflated Director title. The salary though was closer to that of entry-level positions in the area, but the company seemed interesting, there was a ping-pong table in the office, and I needed a job. And so shortly after the 2016 election, I started working there.

For months after I started, I thought I was contributing meaningful analysis related to large infrastructure projects, but eventually I realized I was just developing fodder for infrastructure project developers that were trying to cozy up to the Administration. My office was two blocks from the White House. There were quite a few days when my lunch break or commute would include walking past a protest in front of the White House. Meanwhile, my boss was trying to help infrastructure project developers accelerate their projects by getting the Administration to "cut the red tape". They were all described as "shovel ready" projects that were facing long permitting timelines. The projects were being held up for good reasons. Some projects would have massive negative environmental and public health impacts if completed without regard for the "red tape."

For most of my short tenure at that company, I was kept out of meetings with high level project developers, top tier management consulting firms, and of course the meetings with the Administration. My job was to analyze large infrastructure projects, and in doing so, the direction that this work was heading was illuminated to me. The primary motivation for these projects wasn't improving quality of life. The primary motivation for these projects was profit.

You can tell project developers don't care about quality of life by the way they talk about the environmental impact assessments and the public health impacts of their projects. My boss clearly didn't care to maintain any data on environmental and public health impacts of the projects he was advocating for. His focus was on who was developing the project and how much money he could make by promoting the project by charging the project developer for access to the Administration. There was however one dataset I was asked to maintain that seemed more altruistic than the others, and that was the number of jobs that would be created by each project. If you are looking at a national portfolio of hundreds of large infrastructure projects, the number of jobs that would be created by each project and where those jobs would be created is useful information.

The Great Recession, for example, had a massive impact on the construction industry. The number of construction jobs peaked in 2007 at around 7.7 million, and then due to the Great Recession, was reduced to about 5.4 million jobs by the end of 2010. If not for the American Recovery and Reinvestment Act of 2009, the construction industry may have continued to experience a steep decline. The main focus of that legislation was to save people's jobs and invest in modernizing America's infrastructure. Ever since that legislation was passed, the construction industry has experienced consistent job growth, and at the end of 2024, employment in the construction industry hit an all time high of 8.3 million in the United States.

Have you ever wondered why politicians talk so much about jobs during their campaigns? It is simple. When people are employed, they are able to maintain and improve quality of life for themselves and their families. When people are unemployed, their ability to maintain and improve quality of life for themselves and their families goes down, especially on rainy days. Increasing jobs represents an intrinsic improvement to the quality of life in America. When there is a high unemployment rate in communities across the country, more people suffer.

After about nine months at the infrastructure "consulting" firm, I got fed up with the types of projects my CEO was supporting. Perhaps the most frustrating project that they were advocating for was the Atlantic Coast Pipeline. This was a natural gas pipeline that was being planned to run from West Virginia through Virginia's state and national parks to North Carolina. I have never bought into the idea of natural gas as a "transition fuel," and I was having a hard time convincing people that an equivalent investment in solar farms and offshore wind would be better for Virginia and the surrounding region. I decided to put in my two weeks notice, even though I didn't have another job lined up. It had become obvious that I wasn't going to be able to convince my boss or his clients of any meaningful changes to how they were thinking.

## Deciding to run

So there I was in late 2017, unemployed again as the holidays approached. Earlier that year, I had been getting increasingly involved in my town's sustainability efforts, and it felt like I could have a much more immediate positive impact at the local level. That fall season in 2017, I had plenty of time on my hands. All I was doing was volunteering for a couple nonprofits and looking for my next job. As I had more and more conversations with people in my network trying to find a job or figure out what to do next, I started to think seriously about running for town council. I would still need to find a job, because town councilmembers only got paid a few thousand dollars a year at the time. But the more I thought about it, the more I thought it made sense for me to run.

At the time, I was active in my community, I had grown up there, I had some unique work experience, I had accumulated three masters' degrees in relevant disciplines, I was kind of a nice guy, I had helped out on a local campaign in 2016, and I was aware of most of the issues in town. There was just one complication. The campaign that I had helped out with in 2016 had resulted in the election of the current town council. In other words, all of the sitting councilmembers were friends, or at least friendly, and so I wasn't sure if it made sense for me to run "against" the incumbents that were so willing to collaborate with me.

At the local level, it is pretty easy to get a meeting with an elected official. And if you generally agree on things, it is relatively straightforward to advocate for and advance certain policies. All of the incumbents were 10-30 years older than me with tons of work and life experience. They were also deeply engaged in the community and obviously aware of all of the issues in town. So, what business did I have considering a run for town council?

There are two dangerous sentiments that I want to call out. The first is the notion that if you run for an elected office and someone else also runs for that same elected office, you are against each other. This thinking doesn't make sense, but especially not when you are running for one of six at-large seats on a council or board. This is thinking derived from our two legacy parties and their campaigns for national offices. The sentiment has encroached on local politics and is harmful to community conversations and relationships. On rainy days, local elected officials should be able to instantly collaborate for the good of the community. There has to be a base level of respect among town councilmembers, particularly in hard times. At least at the local level, we should be able to have civil debates about issues related to our communities without the vitriol. Often times, at the local level, disagreeing with someone could be as mild as saying, "I think I have an idea that could be slightly better." We should be able to critique ideas, designs, and policies without insulting people and yelling at them. You can be against an idea, design, or policy without being against the person advocating for it.

The second dangerous sentiment is the "get in line" assertion and mentality. This is apparent when looking at the dynamics of both legacy political parties in the United States. An elected official can hold a public office for decades simply by maintaining the notion that in order to run for public office, the seat must first be voluntarily vacated by the sitting elected official, and if you ignore this, then you are running "against" the incumbent and serving the interest of the other legacy political party. This "get in line" mentality can neutralize an entire generation of candidates and convince them to disengage. This is insidiously destructive at the local and state level where our society should be supporting and engaging more candidates in meaningful conversations about the direction of our communities.

In December 2017, I announced I was going to run for town council, because I knew I would be a better champion of sustainability than any of the current council members. And in January 2018, I began collecting petition signatures during a particularly cold winter. I think some of the signatures I received were out of pity. When I knocked doors in January, there were a few people that invited me in for a conversation, which was a nice break from the cold. By mid-March, I had collected more than the necessary number of signatures, and I was the first to submit my paperwork, which meant my name would appear first on the ballot. I continued collecting signatures for all of the other candidates in the race that I knew about. This seemed like a good idea at the time. I've noticed over and over again that my efforts to collaborate are often negated by the toxic competitiveness and duplicitous nature of others. In the end, I'd rather lose while trying to be genuinely positive and attempting to collaborate with people I disagree with than win by being duplicitous and tearing people down.

The remainder of the town council campaign in 2018 was not fun. I got an inside look at how the legacy political parties operate, and I did not like the view. There were so many lessons learned from that campaign, but I think the most important lesson for me was to focus on the things that I could control. Some of the things I could've controlled included waiting to run until I was employed, attempting to self-fund my campaign (in a small town campaign, a candidate can get by on just a couple thousand dollars), knocking on more doors, talking to more people, hosting more events, and staying away from legacy party meetings.

There were also a handful of little moments where I should've charted my own path. There is a scene in the movie "A Few Good Men," where Tom Cruise's character is interviewing a member of a Marine Corps platoon and asking him how he knows where the mess hall is if it isn't in his training manual. The Marine replies simply saying, *"I guess I just followed the crowd at chow time, sir."* There were moments in my town council campaign in 2018 where *"I just followed the crowd at chow time"*, and those are the moments I regret the most. Those are also the moments where I didn't display the type of leadership that I wanted to see.

Perhaps the most frustrating of those moments was my decision to use the same printer as the other candidates to print thousands of flyers and door hangers. I had identified a more sustainable solution, but ultimately went with the cheaper option, partly because I hadn't raised enough money to fund the more sustainable option. I think most of the people in town disliked the amount of paper they got from my campaign, especially since I was advocating for sustainability. It was a clear contradiction that thoughtful voters noticed.

Making people aware of your campaign is tough. I also put a ton of effort into making my campaign website as thorough, easy to use, and visually pleasing as possible. I added a plug-in to make it so that the website could be read in every language. And after a ton of effort and 10 months of campaigning, less than 500 people in a town of over 25,000 had visited the website. Had I committed more money to digital ads, I think I could've saved some trees while more effectively increasing awareness of my campaign. Live and learn. Needless to say, I was not elected. I was 22 votes shy of becoming a member of the Town Council, but who's counting? There were countless lessons from my first run for public office, but perhaps the most relevant to Rainy Day Economics was the value of community-centered, consensus-driven politics, as opposed to divisive partisanship, particularly at the local level.

## The Yang Gang and the Humanity First Campaign

On November 6th, 2017, Andrew Yang announced his campaign for President of the United States. I remember I didn't recognize his name, but I recognized his organization, *Venture For America*. The organization's mission was admirable - *"to create economic opportunity in American cities"*. They did this by training recent graduates to be startup leaders. I had become aware of Venture For America through my Babson College and StartingBloc networks over the span of a few years. Venture For America was on the radar of most entrepreneurial ecosystems throughout the country by the time Andrew Yang made his announcement at the end of 2017, particularly in the cities where the hundreds of Venture For America fellows had been placed to launch businesses.

Over the course of 2018 and 2019, I slowly learned more and more about Andrew Yang and his campaign. By the end of 2019, I was ready for Andrew Yang to be President. I remember in 2019 telling my mom, "Mama, I'm thinking about joining a gang." My mom has always been hard at hearing, and also would never believe me if I told her I joined a real gang. She looked confused and waited for me to either repeat myself or explain myself. I was talking about joining the "Yang Gang," which was the name for the people across the country that had bought into Andrew Yang's vision for America – *Humanity First*.

In a field of very well qualified Presidential candidates, Andrew Yang found a way to stand out among the crowd. He was not a Congressman, a Senator, a Governor, a Mayor, or a billionaire, and yet he was polling well, raising a substantial amount of money, and garnering a significant amount of media attention. And he was also influencing other Presidential candidates, then, now, and in the future(s). In a world where we have been discussing many of the same issues for decades, Andrew Yang was running a data-driven campaign laser-focused on the future(s). While many candidates, past and present, have delivered soaring speeches with platitudes about the future, Andrew Yang seemed to be the first Presidential candidate that spoke as though he was familiar with the field of future studies.

The biggest clue that Andrew Yang was and is familiar with future studies is his stated motivation for his signature policy proposal. Andrew Yang's Universal Basic Income proposal, which he called the "Freedom Dividend," would give every American adult $1,000 a month unconditionally forever, and the primary driver for him suggesting this is automation and artificial intelligence trends. Universal Basic Income (UBI) is a form of social security that ensures income inequality doesn't get out of control. Yang communicated superbly why he thinks we need to implement a Universal Basic Income.

The reason Andrew Yang cites for UBI is that we are experiencing the greatest technological shift in our history. He argued (or simply observed) that four million manufacturing workers had already lost their jobs in 2015 leading up to the 2016 election. On Andrew Yang's campaign website it said, *"The smartest people in the world now predict that a third of all working Americans will lose their job to automation in the next 12 years. Our current policies are not equipped to handle this crisis. Even our most forward-thinking politicians are unprepared."* His campaign highlighted the plight of so many working class Americans that were experiencing economic hardship. Something about his campaign reminded me of that famous song from the musical *Le Miserables*.

*Do you hear the people sing?*
*Singing a song of angry men?*
*It is the music of a people*
*Who will not be slaves again!*
*When the beating of your heart*
*Echoes the beating of the drums*
*There is a life about to start*
*When tomorrow comes!*

Some might argue that Andrew Yang was just forecasting technology trends, and that other candidates have done just as much forecasting on issues related to the environment, healthcare, and foreign policy. It may be true that other candidates have done some futurist exercises, but at the very least Andrew Yang identified a massive blind spot that no one saw, and he validated the economic hardship of millions of Americans at the same time. And, how did he do that? Was it luck that he just stumbled upon a massive problem and the associated solution that virtually no mainstream politicians were talking about? Maybe. Or, maybe Andrew Yang is a new brand of candidate that is familiar with the fields of future studies and strategic foresight.

Andrew Yang's candidacy also represented the beginning of a new wave of candidates that will have the ability to understand and articulate the complexity of our society in ways that previous candidates hadn't been able to. We obviously need less career politicians and more of something else. Maybe that something else includes scientists, entrepreneurs, architects, engineers, and artists that are proficient at brainstorming and building the improbable solutions we need. I believe we need more elected officials with "once-in-a-generation" minds that have the intellect and imagination to identify blind spots and build consensus to inspire and implement effective solutions.

Andrew Yang told his story of coming to the conclusion of UBI as a process of discovery, like the way a scientist might uncover a new element or like the way an entrepreneur might discover a market opportunity. Imagine if more candidates were as curious and methodical as scientists, architects, and engineers or as resourceful and as creative as entrepreneurs and artists. Imagine electing 535 designers, engineers, and architects to the United States Congress. The creative societal designs of such a Congress would be an unprecedented step forward.

Andrew Yang may have been the first modern futurist to run for President of the United States. This was and is a big deal. Imagine a government thinking on 100-year time scales or 1,000-year time scales, and driving consensus for long-term solutions. The Founders of our country were probably aspiring futurists in their time, but somewhere along the way, it seems like our elected officials jumped on the short-term thinking bandwagon. Andrew Yang's candidacy gave current and future Presidential candidates a renewed permission to more ambitiously communicate long-term thinking and societal complexity to the American public at higher levels. Andrew Yang hasn't shied away from complexity and nuance. In his campaign for President, he faced it head on. Presidential candidates need to be able to communicate complex problems to the American public. Our society is only going to get more complex. Imagine how much more complex our society will be in 1,000 years. We need more Presidential candidates that are willing to communicate complexity and data, and we need them to be able to build consensus around big ideas. We need more candidates that identify as futurists. Hopefully, Andrew Yang is just the first of many.

Wayne Gretzky, the greatest hockey player of all time, was famously taught to skate to where the puck is going, not where the puck was currently or had recently been. Perhaps the most important conversation during any Presidential election is about where the economy is going and how we can get ahead of any potential rainy days. I believe the most valuable superpower in a Presidential candidate is the ability to authentically validate current economic hardships while seeing and articulating the future(s).

## Human-centered Capitalism

As I'm writing this chapter, I'm looking out the second floor window of the Lake Anne Coffee House in Reston, Virginia. The Lake Anne village center wraps around a small reservoir where people paddle board and kayak in nice weather. Reston is a planned community that was first developed by Robert E. Simon (a clue to the name R.E.S.-town). There are no chain restaurants or national brands represented in this little village center, just small local spots where people can experience the spirit of place. Robert E. Simon's vision was to develop a community that prioritized quality of life and giving people places to live, work, and play that were within walking and biking distance. Community planning is perhaps the purest form of both human-centered capitalism and rainy day economics.

*The central tenets of Human-centered Capitalism are:*

1. *Humans are more important than money*
2. *The unit of Human-centered Capitalism is each person, not each dollar*
3. *Markets exist to serve our common goals and values*

Sometimes people conflate socialism with human-centered capitalism. This conflation can be detrimental to societal progress. To be clear, the opposite of human-centered capitalism is profit-centered capitalism. There is broad agreement in the United States that a capitalist operating system of some kind will always be part of our societal architecture. In my humble and accurate opinion, conversations about capitalism versus socialism are outdated and less important than conversations about human-centered capitalism versus profit-centered capitalism. If consensus is a necessary prerequisite to meaningful societal change, then the starting point must be broad agreement on the three tenets of Human-centered Capitalism.

In Andrew Yang's book - *The War on Normal People* – he describes how the market systematically undervalues many activities that are core to the human experience. Most of the activities conducted by the government and by the nonprofit sector are undervalued by the market. The market also undervalues the activities that people do at home. The market will never pay you to take care of family and friends. The market undervalues art and creativity. The market only serves the poor when it is profitable. The market undervalues the environment, infrastructure, and local communities. So, it makes sense to me that we shouldn't give the metaphorical keys of society to billionaires that don't value humans and communities.

There are of course reasons billionaires don't like humans and communities. We humans are needy. As Andrew Yang cites in his book, there are countless ways in which humans need more from billionaires than robots do. Here are a few quick examples of how humans create headaches for billionaires:

- Humans need rest and time with family and friends
- Humans want overtime pay
- Humans need healthcare and sometimes get sick
- Humans have bad days and get bored
- Humans need to work well with each other

Robots on the other hand don't make billionaires think as much. Billionaires and robots go together like peas and carrots. I'm sure billionaires and robots will be happy together in the long run, but for the rest of us, we need to achieve broad consensus on the simple and compelling tenets of Human-centered Capitalism. How can we possibly achieve broad consensus though, when the country is the most polarized it has ever been?

## The Forward Party and Ranked Choice Voting

Since as far back as 1900, the United States has never had more than two thirds of eligible voters cast their votes in a Presidential election. In other words, for every Presidential election in the past 125 years, one third of all voters sat out and didn't vote, every single Presidential election. Why is this? Why do so many people disengage from democracy in America? It is simple – the two legacy political parties. They are powerful with systems that are designed to keep them powerful. And, we've been conditioned to think there are only two sides to every issue. You are either pro-this or anti-that.

We as individuals supposedly exist on a linear political spectrum that has end points on the far left and the far right. Except this linear spectrum isn't an accurate depiction of the amorphous four-dimensional blob that is our aggregate political perspectives. The linear spectrum really doesn't capture the complexity of the political views or how humans exist and think and believe. In the minds of the two legacy parties, you are either with us or against us, with them or against them. And so we perceive our elections to be a pendulum swinging from one side to another. I think it is time to settle the pendulum and move the ball forward.

The concept of the linear political spectrum is of course problematic for those that believe in nuance, complexity, and that there are more than two dimensions in politics, humanity, and life. Imagine for a moment you are looking at an object and all you can see is a circle. So, you tell the world that you see a circle. Then someone else refutes your assertion, because all they can see is a square. You are both looking at the same object, so how could you possibly have such opposite understandings of the shape of the object? If it is just the two of you holding your ground and standing firm in your opinion, then it will be a stalemate over and over again until the end of time.

Now imagine that, instead of just two people with two opposing perspectives, there are three people with three unique perspectives. One person says it is a circle, one says it is a square, and the third says it is a cylinder. This conundrum isn't about compromising beliefs and values. Rather, it is about understanding problems. It is clear that having the third perspective makes building consensus much easier. How does that translate to our political system though?

Right now, we have a political system that is designed to snuff out independent third perspectives. There are thousands upon thousands of bi-partisan rules baked into every state legislature and the United States Congress that keep those legislative bodies bi-partisan instead of tri-partisan. And when members of those legislative bodies don't tow the party line, the party finds someone that will. The two legacy parties don't want to relinquish any power, because it means that any progress that they've made will be negated by the other side. Why would either of the legacy parties ever risk allowing a third party to gain power? After all, both of the legacy parties stand to gain all of the power if they play their cards right… right?

Wrong. The never-ending battle between the two legacy parties is resulting in the mutually assured destruction of the **United** States. We need a strong, independent, data-driven, consensus-minded, nuance-loving, complexity-understanding, kind-hearted, willing-to-mediate-and-negotiate third political party in the United States. We need it like a heart needs a beat.

You might be wondering "why can't the legacy parties just have more independent thinking, more data-driven discussions, be more driven by consensus, navigate nuance and complexity, and be willing to mediate and negotiate in a more kind-hearted manner?" The legacy parties can! No person or political party has a monopoly on genius, good methodology, kind-heartedness, or anything for that matter. Both legacy parties are capable of driving consensus. Both legacy parties are capable of doing good things. But as every middle child knows, there is a fundamentally different dynamic when there is an argument with three parties compared to when there is an argument with two parties.

An argument between two individuals or parties will be more likely to lead to entrenchment. But, an argument with three people or parties has many more possible outcomes. Entrenchment is still possible, but much less likely. Also, when you are in the minority of a three-person debate, your argument gets much better or it falls apart. As a society, everyone would get better at articulating arguments if we didn't reduce them to the oversimplified falsely two-sided arguments that the two legacy parties have articulated to us. We need to evolve past this, and embrace nuance and complexity, and the legacy parties can't do that while they are facing off against each other. The legacy parties need a "middle sibling" to help them keep the peace in the family and actually get things done consistently. Middle children are the best. We all agree on this fact. So why don't we as a society give the two legacy parties a "middle sibling" for the country's 250th birthday in 2026?

This is an important part of Rainy Day Economics, because without a strong third political party, our society is destined to be divided by the two party system, which will inherently obstruct all five pillars of Rainy Day Economics.

How might we convince the two legacy parties that it would be beneficial to them to support the creation of a strong third political party and also agree to design their legislative rules to accommodate the new political party? The legacy parties might be excited by the third party's unique ability to increase voter turnout, if that is something the legacy parties truly care about. At the beginning of the tri-party system, the legacy parties might be excited to collaborate more regularly in a bi-partisan way while still keeping distance from the other legacy party. In other words, legacy party politicians could tell their constituents how they collaborated with another party, while also maintaining clear distinctions regarding their values versus the values of the other legacy party. Also, during years when a particular legacy party is not in power, it would still have the ability to potentially move legislation forward instead of being stalled for two to eight years.

Perhaps the most valuable aspect of having a strong third party right now, in 2025, would be to reduce the chaos of the upheaval of policies every four years as the two legacy parties gain and then lose control of the Executive and Legislative Branches over and over again. We'd have fewer threats of government shutdowns. We'd achieve long periods of consensus, which would result in predictability for individuals, businesses, communities, states, and regions. It would allow our country to maintain peace and reduce social unrest. It would make Thanksgiving a less stressful holiday. Happiness in America would increase, and anger would decrease. There would be less road rage, lower blood pressures, less alcoholism, less depression, less anxiety. America would chill out and cooler heads would prevail day in and day out. Your community would be more of a community. Our national community would be less bifurcated. Cities and states wouldn't be defined by the political affiliation of their elected leaders. And, perhaps most importantly, rainy days would be less bad.

If you are even a little bit convinced that a strong third party needs to exist, then the next question is *"how do we make this happen?"* Luckily, the founders of the Forward Party exist. Former Governor of New Jersey Christine Whitman, Michael Willner, and Andrew Yang co-founded the Forward Party and have been building support across the country for a couple years now. The Forward Party is gaining significant momentum and facilitating the transition to a tri-party system. There are about 500,000 local elected offices in the United States and about 70% have historically been uncontested and non-competitive. So, the Forward Party is at the beginning of a movement that I think is going to save America from itself.

> ***Rainy Day Economics Design Prompt 16:*** *Design a new methodology for driving consensus in your community. Test your consensus-building strategies in a small focus group. How can we build consensus around sustainability and resilience at the local level?*

The Forward Party is also advocating for the implementation of Ranked Choice Voting among other process-driven policies that will help navigate to a consensus-driven society. Ranked Choice Voting allows voters to rank candidates in order of preference. You can rank as many or as few candidates as you like. All first-choice votes are counted. If nobody wins a majority, the candidate with the fewest first choice votes is eliminated. Second choice votes from voters whose preferred candidate was eliminated are transferred to those corresponding candidates. If there's still no candidate with enough votes to win, the process is repeated until there's a clear winner.

The outcome of Ranked Choice Voting is that the candidate that is chosen is the most likely to build consensus. We can imagine a day in the future where there are a few strong candidates for any given elected office, and so Ranked Choice Voting would encourage more candidates to go on listening tours and to build coalitions and to truly understand the needs of the many people and communities they represent. As of 2024, there are already 62 jurisdictions in 24 states that use Ranked Choice Voting. Here in Virginia, the County of Arlington and the City of Charlottesville have voted to adopt Ranked Choice Voting. Ranked Choice Voting is gaining momentum, and that is good for Rainy Day Economics, and it is also good for the ***United*** States.

# Chapter 14

## A GLOBAL HEALTH EMERGENCY
### March 11, 2020

*"Those who contemplate the beauty of the earth find reserves
of strength that will endure as long as life lasts. There is
something infinitely healing in the repeated refrains of
nature -- the assurance that dawn comes after night, and
spring after winter."*

*- Rachel Carson*

---

Are there more stars in the Universe or grains of sand on Earth? If you asked Carl Sagan, or any astronomer, they would tell you there are far more stars in the Universe than grains of sand on Earth's beaches. Have the astronomers also considered the sand in the deserts of Africa, though?

This is the type of question you ponder when you have an hour and a half commute into work everyday. That was me in February 2020 – half asleep on the Washington, D.C. metro train being slowly teleported into a windowless office where I would sit in front of a computer screen for eight hours a day reading about mundane and outdated government processes and policies.

Months earlier, in 2019, it was slightly better. I was a stereotypical traveling public sector management consultant. The company would fly me into a city early Monday morning and out on Thursday night. Those were also boring government clients, but at night I could explore a new city. Also, you can accumulate a lot of points with airlines and hotels doing this work. But when you are single in your 30s and traveling alone, it isn't as ideal as you might think, and it gets old quickly.

Right before the holidays in 2019, I was "rolled off contract," which is a polite way of saying I was let go. Being unemployed around the holidays has become a recurring theme in my life. The holidays can actually be ideal timing to be recently unemployed considering that family, friends, colleagues, and strangers are more likely to be in a benevolent mood. That was the case in December 2019 when I met with a friend from high school for a holiday coffee.

My friend had retired from the U.S. Coast Guard and was doing well in the world of federal government consulting. In a matter of weeks, my friend had facilitated interviews with his company and his client, and I had a job offer in hand going into 2020. Not only that, it was the highest salary I had ever been offered. My start date was set for the first week of February 2020.

The timing would prove to be lucky to say the least, as the World Health Organization would declare a global pandemic the next month in March 2020. Though in mid-February around Valentine's Day, I didn't feel lucky at all. I felt like I had sold out, thrown my passion for sustainability to the curb for a nice salary, and now I was spending at least three hours a day commuting to and from work.

Three hours a day for approximately 250 working days a year meant I was going to be spending 31.25 days a year in transit to and from work. 8.56% of my life. Sure, I could read, write, listen, and study during that time, and to some extent I would, but that was never going to be truly joyful time spent. The time in commute was time away from a life well lived, and no one could convince me otherwise.

Millions of people have done that calculation and wished they could eliminate time spent commuting to and from work. And in March 2020, those millions of wishes were granted, unfortunately due to a global pandemic. At first, we were told that we should work from home for the time being and only come into the office if necessary. That quickly changed to a stay-at-home mandate. And then as the weeks and months passed, the guidance shifted, and we were told that we could plan to work from home for the foreseeable future. How long was the foreseeable future? No one knew.

With so much free time on my hands, I decided to buy a nice acoustic guitar and began learning to play. That lasted a few weeks, and then I had an idea that would change my life forever. For years, I had envisioned adopting a dog from a shelter that would be some obscure mix of breeds. He would have a unique name, and he would already be fully-grown and potty-trained, and he would be super chill. What actually happened? A high energy, purebred border collie puppy named Buddy.

I got hooked on the idea of training my potential future dog to do hundreds of tricks. He had to be a border collie or an Australian shepherd. I called around to shelters in the region, and without fail they'd always tell me the dog I was asking about was good except around kids. The thought of my dog biting a kid was enough for me to look elsewhere. Eventually, I let go of my "adopt, don't shop" mentality. I found an Amish breeder in Pennsylvania, and made arrangements to pick up Buddy in June 2020. There is something about a rural, self-sufficient life that has always appealed to me. I was looking forward to visiting the Amish community and appreciated that Buddy was coming from a place that had its own character and charm.

When I arrived at the Amish farm in Lancaster, Pennsylvania where Buddy was born, the farmer, Abraham, greeted me warmly with a smile as if I was an old friend. Abraham's kids brought Buddy and Buddy's siblings out. Buddy's mom showed up momentarily after Abraham whistled for her. Abraham said she was out tending to the field. I loved the idea of a dog safely enjoying the farm while still being obedient enough to respond to a simple whistle. Buddy was not interested in playing with his siblings. He was interested in the Amish girls and their long dresses. Buddy has always been a people person. I sat on a small stone wall and talked to Abraham for a little while. He asked a lot of questions about the pandemic, but seemed unphased with any update I gave him.

When I called and motioned for Buddy, he was so excited to meet me. He ran along the level grass leading up to the edge of the stone wall where we were sitting. He slipped and fell off the stone wall, face-planting and then standing up immediately and shaking it off. He was clumsy then, and he is still clumsy now. I picked him up and kissed him. We couldn't stop smiling at each other.

The ride home was fine at first. I had created a cozy bed for Buddy with some old towels in a large plastic bin in the back seat. Buddy was content for a short while, and then started to whine. We stopped at a nearby soccer field and ran together for the first time. Eventually, we got back on the road, and Buddy negotiated his way to falling asleep on a towel on my lap as I drove us home.

My mind wandered back to the farm where Buddy was born. Buddy's mom was free to roam the fields and lived most of her life off leash. Buddy was heading to the suburbs of Washington, D.C. where he would need to stay on leash whenever outside unless in a fenced in area. As I felt Buddy breathing on me while he slept, I knew we couldn't stay in the high traffic suburbs of Washington, D.C. Buddy needed safe places to run, fields to roam, and mountains to climb. And I had 31.25 days a year that I was still figuring out what to do with. Suburbia wasn't where our wolf pack was meant to be.

By the end of the summer, Buddy and I had moved to Charlottesville, Virginia. Charlottesville is the heart of Virginia. Not because of its central location in the state, but because of the irrepressible spirit of love that radiates from the city. Three years before Buddy and I arrived in

Charlottesville, there had been a tragic, hate-filled, and violent riot that resulted in multiple innocent lives lost. Charlottesville had been healing since August 2017, and throughout the city we could see the messages of hope and resilience. Despite what happened in 2017, Charlottesville made it clear that the people still believed in the state's mantra that *Virginia is for lovers*.

From August to November 2020, Buddy and I settled into our new home, which was a nice apartment at the base of Carter Mountain. The apartment was an easy hike to Monticello where Thomas Jefferson had designed and redesigned and built and rebuilt his house and gardens over more than four decades. The apartment was also walking distance to a grocery store, a mom and pop restaurant, and a local veterinarian. It was the perfect setup for our wolf pack.

I had committed myself to not owning a car when I was in Northern Virginia, because I care about the environment, and I could walk to metro bus stops and the metro transit station, which was what I used for my commute to work. I didn't really need a car for that monotonous life in the suburbs. Things were different now though. Buddy and I loved hiking in Central Virginia in the fall weather, and there were a growing number of places that we wanted to explore, but we needed a car to get to those places. I began researching electric vehicles. Then, in November 2020, I bought my first new car. It was an electric vehicle – a blue 2020 Nissan LEAF. There was just one tiny hiccup. I didn't really research where or how I was going to charge.

Before you buy an electric vehicle (EV), you should know how and where you're going to charge it. It is important to know that you will be able to charge your EV from home, work, or at a public charging station out in the world. The first place I charged my new electric blue Nissan LEAF was in a parking garage next to Charlottesville's charming downtown mall. The charging station was a fast charger, and it was part of the EVgo charging network. EVgo names all of their chargers, and the name of my first charger was Abraham. Buddy watched as I fumbled through the process for the first time. Once the charging had started, we left the parking garage. I commented to Buddy that the charger's name was Abraham, and I could see him remembering his Amish roots.

Downtown Charlottesville was a perfect place during the pandemic to take Buddy for a walk and grab a meal outside at one of the local restaurants. We frequented a long-standing diner there called "The Nook" where we would sit in the middle of the historic downtown mall and watch the other people and dogs walking by while we waited for the car to charge. In 45 to 60 minutes, we could walk to The Nook, order, enjoy our meal, and walk back to find the car fully charged.

In December 2020, I was employed, working remotely, living in a nice apartment in the middle of Virginia's wine country, with an adorable young dog, and a brand new car. I was also more physically fit than I had been in a long time. I could tell a noticeable improvement to my quality of life since leaving Northern Virginia. I was thriving during a global pandemic. But the rest of the world wasn't doing so well. In fact, a lot of people were living lives that were much worse than they were before the pandemic. This contrast is important to digest to understand Rainy Day Economics.

## *Nursing and the K-shaped recovery*

At the start of the pandemic, in March 2020, student loan payments were paused to provide temporary relief to people across the country during the pandemic. During this pause, student loans would not accrue interest. Up until this point, I wasn't sure I would ever pay off the massive amount of student debt I had accumulated from 2012 to 2016. It was a sum of money that would make a medical student blush, and I didn't have the in demand doctor's skills or salary that came with a medical degree. But the student loan payment pause that started in 2020 gave me an opportunity to think about my future differently.

I surmised that if I took on a second job, I could pay off my student loan debt in less than 10 to 12 years and also miraculously buy a small home in the same time period if I took advantage of low-interest government-backed loans through either the U.S. Department of Agriculture (USDA) or the Federal Housing Administration (FHA). I had previously entertained the idea of becoming an Emergency Medical Technician (EMT) years earlier, and had met a number of other types of medical professionals over the years. I started to look into Certified Medical Assistant (CMA) and Certified Nurse Aide (CNA) programs, and began taking introductory classes online at night through Northern Virginia Community College, and then eventually Piedmont Virginia Community College once I had moved to Charlottesville. I completed Certified Nurse Aide training and the following courses in the first year of the pandemic:

> BIO 141 – Human Anatomy and Physiology I
> HLT 110 – Personal and Community Health
> HLT 141 – Introduction to Medical Terminology
> HLT 230 – Principles of Nutrition and Human Development
> SDV 101 – Orientation to Healthcare
> PHI 227 – Bio-Medical Ethics
> PSY 230 – Developmental Psychology
> SOC 200 – Principles of Sociology

At the end of 2020, I did clinical rotations at a nursing home in Central Virginia at night and on weekends. For the rotations, the shifts were only four hours, and they consisted mostly of taking vital signs, changing bed sheets, wiping butts, and bringing patients meals (not in that order though). There was also usually a little bit of downtime where I'd just wait for the patients to press the button asking for help with something. Sometimes patients would press the button just to get someone to come talk to them. I imagine patients in nursing homes are always lonely, but the pandemic was a particularly hard time for the elderly, because they didn't see their family and friends as much.

Once I had finished my nurse aide training, I applied to work at a regional healthcare system, and got a job as a full-time overnight nurse aide, while keeping my day job. This was idiotic on my part, which I would soon find out. The shift schedule for nurse aides is roughly the same as for nurses, usually three 12-hour shifts per week, one of which is on a weekend. I asked for Thursday, Friday, and Saturday shifts to attempt to not let the second job impact my main job. I was so foolish to think this would work. Instead of maximizing my enjoyment, learning, and growing at one job, I sacrificed quality of life and risked losing my high-paying job.

I eventually came to understand the 12-hour shifts in three four-hour sections, and I had a different perspective on each. The first four hours of every 12-hour shift, I was well rested, happy, and eager to learn. The second four hours of every 12-hour shift, I was a little tired and just wanted to get through all of my tasks for the night. The last four hours of every 12-hour shift was brutal, and I would often find myself questioning my life decisions. Then at the end of every 12-hour shift, I'd go home and crash, sleeping for as long as I could. Needless to say, I am not a fan of the 12-hour shift, and I did not continue down the 80-hour workweek path for very long.

During that short stretch of time where I was working two jobs, I saw the contrast of the pandemic experience of blue-collar workers versus white-collar workers. During the day, I was the stereotypical government contractor working remotely in the safety of my apartment. At night and on weekends, I was seeing a different reality. There were patients experiencing the worst days of their lives with an added layer of uncertainty and risk associated with the pandemic. Early on in the pandemic, there was also a shortage of ventilators. There were nurses and technicians that I worked with that had gotten COVID early on in the pandemic, and had experienced turmoil and confusion around protocol, time off, and pay. There was a significant amount of turnover and more demand for travel nurses and technicians. Nurses and technicians were being told they were required to do shifts on the COVID unit, and many were simply not willing to accept the additional risk. They were already working in a hospital during a pandemic. I completely understand why nurses and technicians would adopt a certain threshold for risk.

Before I left that nurse aide job, I was among the first wave to receive vaccinations. This process also illuminated a very different experience between my blue collar nursing co-workers and my white-collar remote co-workers. My remote co-workers were eager to get the vaccine, while some of my nursing co-workers at the hospital wanted to wait to make sure it was safe. I worked with some smart medical professionals, so I also wasn't sure if getting the vaccine in the first wave was a good choice on my part. Were we serving as guinea pigs in the first wave of vaccinations? Ultimately, I decided to trust the vaccine development process and our institutions even though the process had been accelerated.

The hospital of course wanted as much of their staff vaccinated as quickly as possible, presumably so that scheduling would become less of a nightmare. With more staff vaccinated, there would be less staff taking required time off because of being diagnosed with COVID, and there would be more nurses and technicians willing to staff the COVID units, because they would be less at risk having been vaccinated.

For most working class lower-income Americans, the pandemic was a prolonged nightmare that resulted in a major reduction in quality of life. But there were also many young, single middle class higher-income office workers for which the pandemic had some significant benefits. At the beginning of the pandemic, I loved that my hours of commuting had been eliminated. I had more free time for hobbies, for learning, and for additional work. I saved on transportation costs and used that money to pay down debt, invest in more education, and seek out a better quality of life. It reminded me of the opening of *A Tale of Two Cities* by Charles Dickens.

> *"It was the best of times, it was the worst of times, it was the age of wisdom, it was the age of foolishness, it was the epoch of belief, it was the epoch of incredulity, it was the season of Light, it was the season of Darkness, it was the spring of hope, it was the winter of despair, we had everything before us, we had nothing before us, we were all going direct to Heaven, we were all going direct the other way—in short, the period was so far like the present period, that some of its noisiest authorities insisted on its being received, for good or for evil, in the superlative degree of comparison only."*

This phenomenon of diverging qualities of life is what some economists termed "the K-shaped recovery". While some people were able to thrive during a global emergency, many people were faced with numerous challenges that negatively impacted livelihood and caused a significant reduction in quality of life. A K-shaped recovery is a sign of growing income inequality, which means that social unrest was likely to continue even after the pandemic. What is frustrating to me is that leading up to 2020 there was no shortage of warnings from public health researchers and leaders about the potential of a pandemic in the near term. In fact, many public health researchers and leaders expect that there will likely be another pandemic in the next 10 to 20 years. As a society that just experienced a global pandemic, are we ready to navigate another?

> ***Rainy Day Economics Design Prompt 17:*** *Imagine you are in charge of preparing your small town for the next pandemic. Develop a plan for maintaining and improving the quality of life for everyone in your community while the pandemic is happening. How might we prepare for and navigate the next pandemic?*

## *Semper Paratus – Always Ready*

The United States Coast Guard's motto is *semper paratus*, which means **"Always Ready"**. Does it feel like the United States was ready for the Coronavirus? No. We, as a society, had not planned for this, though many public health and emergency management professionals were prepared. And, if we're being honest with ourselves, things could get much worse with the next outbreak. Winston Churchill had a saying that is still used today — *"America will always do the right thing, only after they've exhausted every other possibility."* As a country, we should strive to prove Winston Churchill wrong. We should aspire to be *always ready* to lead the world through a crisis. Here are five learnings from the pandemic. These societal learnings should be committed to memory for generations so that we are prepared for the worst the future has to offer.

1. **We need rainy day funds.** The coronavirus has made it abundantly obvious that every individual, company, nonprofit, municipality, state, and country needs a sizeable rainy day fund that is only used for natural disasters, pandemics, and the like.

2. **We need more and better public healthcare.** Unfortunately, healthcare has become an absurdly politicized topic. We need to implement a Medicare For All type federal program while at the same time empowering local communities to increase the capacity of their own public health programs. We also need to focus deeply

on personal and community health in our public schools and community centers.

3. **We must consider Universal Basic Income.** Until the pandemic, Universal Basic Income had been talked about as a solution to wide spread automation and artificial intelligence. Those rapidly developing technologies are predicted to continue to eliminate and transform jobs performed by humans. What the coronavirus showed us is that Universal Basic Income has a second use case. When there is an outbreak, the economy slows significantly. More people are not able or allowed to work. Social distancing impacts the flow of money. Savings depletes. Debt increases. Poverty spikes. A Universal Basic Income would mitigate the negative economic impacts of an outbreak. Andrew Yang's advocacy for Universal Basic Income during his Presidential campaign from 2017 to 2020 undoubtedly accelerated conversations about cash relief payments during the pandemic. We should keep this conversation going at minimum for future pandemics.

4. **We must acknowledge that *productive and creative* remote work is possible.** We as a society have to acknowledge and/or make possible productive remote work arrangements. Emphasis on productive. For people that think the pandemic was an opportunity to relax while working from home, instead consider making it abundantly clear to your employer that you can be equally or even more creative and productive while working from home.

5. **We must rethink the national debt.** We need to shift the way we think about monetary economics. We need a reset moment that doesn't include laying off hundreds of thousands of federal workers. As our national debt grows, more and more money will be siphoned away from public health, infrastructure, sustainability, security, and education to national debt payments. Does it have

to be that way? We need to adopt a system dynamics approach to monetary economics.

There will undoubtedly be many more learnings that need to be committed to societal memory. There will also be many cracks revealed in the system of systems we have created in our country's short history. In any case, we should view the pandemic as an opportunity to evolve and get stronger as a society. We should strive to be a nation that is ***always ready*** to lead through crisis and uncertainty. In order to achieve sustainability and resilience, the 2$^{nd}$ and 4$^{th}$ pillars of Rainy Day Economics, our approach to and understanding of monetary theory is essential.

## *The Problem or Not-so Problem with Modern Monetary Theory*

There exists a theory in economics called the "Modern Monetary Theory" that may prove to be an important part of the five pillars of Rainy Day Economics. If we look at this theory with a scientific frame, Modern Monetary Theory is more of an observation at a moment in time. There aren't many dependable laws in economics the way there are in physics and chemistry. For example, Newton's laws in physics are pretty reliable out in the real world, but in economics even the most widely accepted theories don't always hold up in the real world. Economics is also different from physics and chemistry, because in many cases we as a society decide the rules of economics. As a society, we decide what is true and not true for our societal architecture. We do this through policies, laws, and institutions that we design. This is to say that if we want Modern Monetary Theory to hold true in our economy, we can make it so to some extent. Remember the first pillar of Rainy Day Economics is design. If we intentionally design our economy, then Modern Monetary Theory can be both true and vital if we decide it to be.

Modern Monetary Theory (MMT) suggests that governments that

issue their own currency can pay for whatever they need to pay for without having first collected taxes or revenue. In other words, MMT says that deficit spending is generally acceptable, so long as we are capable of printing money. It is also worth noting that deficit spending is acceptable to some extent at the state level in the United States. While most states are required to maintain balanced budgets, they are also able to take on debt. Every state has limits associated with debt, but they are able to take on debt, which is effectively deficit spending. States also use rainy day funds to address potential economic shortfalls.

In the case of virtually every societal problem set and also any catastrophic event, we would of course be better off with either a rainy day fund or deficit spending than without. And it is obvious that we need to be intentional about how we design and utilize these tools. Our states have developed rainy day funds and constraints around deficit spending, and the federal government can model future approaches after the states.

The commonly perceived problem with MMT, at least at this current moment in time, is that there are seemingly no bounds associated with federal government spending. While we have debt ceilings, they are usually raised fairly quickly after some compromises are made in Congress. Some might also argue that is encouraging the continuation of short-term thinking rather than adopting a long-term view in our federal budget conversations. However, Modern Monetary Theory is actually the key to unlocking an important conversation about how we go from the current state of our economy to a future state of our economy. We need to ask and answer this question – *how much money should exist?*

In 1949 New Zealand economist Bill Phillips took a mental model of the workings of the economy and made it into a physical representation, which he called a Monetary National Income Analog Computer, or MONIAC. The machine was used to demonstrate and predict the flow of money through an economy at a high level. The MONIAC was a hydro-mechanical computer built out of plastic and wood. Water flowed through the tanks at specified rates as set by Phillips to represent investment and tax rates. The resulting output was the national income. Phillips was able to calibrate this machine to predict national income accurately. The original intent was to use this as a teaching aid, but it also turned into a powerful economic simulator. Imagine if we could optimize our economy by mapping the flow of money, adjusting the levers accordingly, and determining how much money should exist in the system based on a multitude of factors.

We need a new MONIAC. Obviously, we are capable of building a more sophisticated computer today than Bill Phillips was able to build in the 1940's and 1950's. And, the field of design has advanced as much as the field of supercomputing. We need to be able to visualize our economy with a great deal of precision. If we are able to do this, then we can more thoroughly research and develop long-term funding solutions for all of our societal architecture.

> *"When you change the way you look at things, the things you look at change."*
>
> — *Max Planck, German quantum theorist, Nobel Prize winner*

There is also the Will McAvoy "column inches" reason for not talking about MMT. I'm referring to the epic opening monologue of Aaron Sorkin's show "The Newsroom" where the lead character, played by Jeff Daniels, suggests to a Democratic pundit that the reason she shouldn't advocate for the National Endowment for the Arts (NEA) is because *"He gets to hit you with it anytime he wants. It doesn't cost money. It costs votes. It costs airtime and column inches."* Can you imagine if we stopped advocating for ideas because we knew the opponents of our ideas would get more time to talk about why they are opposed? I think it is worth taking the time to talk about Modern Monetary Theory, even if it gives opponents more opportunities to refute the tenants of the theory.

For the record, the National Endowment for the Arts is a good idea in my opinion. Rainy Day Economics strives to help people and communities thrive even in the worst of times. What if artists weren't always starving? What if there was a self-sustaining national endowment that funded the arts in communities across the United States especially in the worst of times. I think that is something worth discussing, committing to, and working towards. This would be consistent with the 5$^{th}$ pillar of Rainy Day Economics – investing in the arts, especially during hard times and in the wake of disasters and tragedies.

In my humble and accurate opinion, a conversation about Modern Monetary Theory and the MONIAC is essential to our ability to reset our national debt while not disrupting the rest of our societal architecture. We should not shy away from talking about Modern Monetary Theory. The current Administration in 2025 is effectively creating massive shocks, uncertainty, and chaos in the name of government efficiency. It is obvious that these shocks to the system will cause more rainy days at least at the individual and community level in the Mid-Atlantic, but it is also conceivable that these shocks will incite a Global Great Depression.

# Chapter 15

## A GREEN NEW DEAL BY ANOTHER NAME
### November 15, 2021

*"The universe looks more and more like a great thought*
*rather than a great machine."*

*- Sir James Jeans*

---

In 2021, my girlfriend at the time lived just outside of Charlottesville on a little plot of land. She had renovated a small house that was tucked away from the city and perfectly located near some hidden trails that only locals knew about. She was an excellent designer. Her home was modern, elegant, and warm. She had a vegetable garden in the back and a flower garden on the side of the house. Her screened in porch had a cozy couch with a view of the Blue Ridge Mountains to the west where we would watch the sunset after dinners we made together.

The first snowstorm Buddy and I experienced together was at my girlfriend's house. We spent the night as if we were a new family. When we awoke, Buddy was like a kid on Christmas morning. He peered out the windows at the snow. He had never seen snow before. We bundled up with multiple layers of clothes, and ventured out with Buddy off leash. He was ecstatic, bouncing and prancing and dancing through the snow.

We brought a sled to a nearby hill, and my girlfriend and I went down the hill together while Buddy barked at us and chased us. In between sled runs, we threw Buddy his frisbee and he made epic catches with the picturesque landscape in the background. My girlfriend took a picture of

Buddy looking heroic in the snow, which she later turned into a watercolor painting of him. She was enamored with Buddy. I joked that she was only dating me to hang out with Buddy. She always gave me a lighthearted hard time, and so of course she agreed that Buddy was a large part of why she was dating me.

What my girlfriend didn't know at the time was that I had decided to get a second dog. I had made the decision just before we met, and so I wasn't sure how to approach the conversation with her. We were only weeks into dating, and while it was going well, I didn't think it made sense to make a decision like that together. I figured it would just be one of those "ask forgiveness rather than permission" kind of things. And given how much she loved Buddy, it seemed unlikely that she would take issue with Buddy's brother being added to our wolf pack.

A friend of mine had a family member that bred chocolate labs on a farm on Maryland's Eastern Shore. Buddy had been the best decision of my life, and so I figured deciding to get Buddy a brother would be the second best decision of my life. A few weeks after the snowstorm, I set course for the farm on Maryland's Eastern Shore. This was the longest trip I had ever attempted in my new electric vehicle.

Imagine for a moment the user experience associated with a typical gas station. We don't really think about it anymore. People that use gas stations have done so since they started driving, and the experience is essentially ubiquitous. When drivers refuel at a gas station, they are on autopilot. There is little thought involved.

Now imagine a driver arriving at an electric vehicle charging station. First they bought the electric vehicle, which was a thoughtful and intentional decision. Then when they need to charge, they use an app to find a charging station, and then when they arrive at the charging station, they are greeted with an underwhelming experience. An experience that is at best forgettable and at worst day-ruining. The last thing you want in society is infrastructure that causes rainy days.

The trek to Maryland's Eastern Shore turned out to be quite a learning experience to say the least, and I was teeming with ideas for how to make charging stations better. The trip also seeded a number of ideas related to Rainy Day Economics and how new infrastructure has the potential to improve quality of life and reduce economic hardship at the individual and community level.

When I arrived home from Maryland's Eastern Shore, Buddy was confused at first as I introduced him to his new brother, Grizzly. Buddy investigated Grizzly and decided he was alright. I told Buddy to show Grizzly a toy. Buddy brought a toy out and put it in front of Grizzly. Grizzly had sharp puppy teeth and began to tear the toy. Buddy didn't like that. Grizzly loved playing with Buddy. He'd crawl up to Buddy and wrestle with him. Buddy would allow it as long as Grizzly didn't use his sharp puppy teeth.

Buddy was easy to train when he was a puppy. I had him potty trained and doing a dozen different tricks in a matter of weeks. Grizzly was different. Grizzly was a much slower learner, and got into a lot more trouble. I couldn't leave Grizzly alone, nor did he want to be left alone. In a few short weeks, the nice apartment that Buddy and I had spent months nesting in was destroyed by Grizzly's sharp puppy teeth. He tore up the carpet, ripped the couch cushions to shreds, chewed on all of the wood furniture, and peed everywhere. Over time, Grizzly would slowly learn how to behave, mostly, and Buddy and I learned to tolerate him when he wasn't behaving.

In the summer of 2021, our little wolf pack went on a vacation to Michigan for a family reunion. This was going to be the first time my boys were meeting everyone. Heading out on our first long electric vehicle road trip from Virginia to Michigan, I knew it was going to be different. But

I thought it would be a little easier. I was optimistic about the future of America's charging network because of the infrastructure plan that was being discussed at the time that included 500,000 new electric vehicle chargers. But the charging network as it existed in the summer of 2021 was worse than I thought it would be.

After two long days of travel in my little electric spaceship, our wolf pack arrived at the family reunion in northern Michigan. The boys got to meet their cousins for the first time in person. It was on this trip that I learned how much of a water dog Grizzly was, and how much Buddy really just preferred to stay on land. I attempted to take both of them out on a paddleboard. Grizzly loved it. Buddy did not.

On our way back from Michigan, we noticed that there was a charging station at the Toledo Museum of Art. It would've been easy enough to simply stay on the interstate and use the Electrify America charging stations for the remainder of our travels. Having experienced the boredom that comes with waiting for your car to be charged numerous times on a long road trip, we decided the Toledo Museum of Art was the exact change of scenery we wanted.

Imagine millions of drivers making that decision every year. There will of course still have to be many charging stations close to the interstates across the country. But just think of the amount of traffic that we could drive to America's art museums and parks and small businesses simply by placing charging stations at or nearby those places. There is a real probability that charging networks will simply double down on their current locations to get their numbers up, which would just mean more chargers at every gas station and big box store in the United States.

America's **public** charging network shouldn't be built for the benefit of large corporations. America's **public** charging network should supercharge the American experience and American wanderlust. In a post-pandemic era when small businesses and art communities across the country were hurting more than ever, a vision for how we build new infrastructure could revitalize America's creative, entrepreneurial, and thoughtful identity. Intentional design of new infrastructure can help individuals, communities, cities, and regions recover from rainy days.

At the Toledo Museum of Art, I walked the dogs around the outside of the museum and laughed as they did the confused dog head tilt whenever they saw sculptures that they didn't understand. I'd explain to the boys that the sculptures were meant to make them think differently. If all of the sculptures looked the same, then art would be boring. Buddy understood this concept. Grizzly did not.

I loved discovering the chargers at the Toledo Museum of Art. I had never been to Toledo. And this visit was enabled only because there were charging stations at the Toledo Museum of Art. Installing electric vehicle charging stations at art museums across the United States could drive massive amounts of new traffic to art museums.

Think about this moment in time. Art museums, like most businesses and institutions, suffered from a lack of traffic in recent years due to the pandemic, and now electric vehicles are on the rise. And those electric vehicles need to charge somewhere. And those electric vehicle owners want to get out and see the world again. Art museums need to have electric vehicle charging stations, and they need to have a lot of them. Any art museum that isn't trying to install electric vehicle charging stations right now isn't trying to attract more visitors.

> **Rainy Day Economics Design Prompt 18:** *Imagine you are in charge of economic development in a small city in America. Develop a way to drive traffic to your city and bring in new businesses and also bring new people to those new businesses and to your cultural institutions in the wake of a pandemic or natural disaster.*

We completed our circle around the outside of the museum and found a bench in a courtyard with the museum and sculptures in view. I sat down on the bench and soaked in the view and the moment. The dogs sat down next to the bench and waited patiently. It was a rare undisturbed moment. The dogs were calm, and there was no noise coming from an interstate near by. There was no sound of shopping carts rolling through a parking lot. There was no bright gas station lighting or litter or smell of gasoline. We were sitting in a place that was designed for us to be at peace. That bench was there for us to reflect and be present in the moment with the people we were with. It was serene. There was stillness to the universe in that moment.

## Gravity versus creativity

Sir James Jeans was a physicist, astronomer, and mathematician. But, his work is relevant to economics today. Jeans suggested that clouds of interstellar dust have a critical radius where gravity overcomes outward pressure, which is the point at which the cloud collapses. At first glance, you might be thinking that this means we need to keep growing our economy forever to counteract the "gravitational pull" of a collapse. But, in the context of the economy, the "outward pressure" is not production. Rather, it is anti-deterioration (sustainability), maturity, and creativity.

If you've been brought up to think all growth is good, this may be a tough concept to wrap your head around. My response to the mentality that all growth is good is simply to say that physics and natural laws present hard limits to the economy that are non-negotiable constraints. The economy is a subsystem of the planet, and society must come to terms with that.

The question is — if not growth, then what should we focus on? The answer is simple — ***creativity, maturity, and sustainability***. All plants and animals stop growing in size at some point in their lives, but they don't stop creating, maturing, living, and iterating. In that same way, our economy can operate within the constraints of the size and scope of our planet while continuing to create, iterate, mature, and improve quality of life for more people for more time.

What does this look like? To start, we can shift our thinking away from productivity and towards creativity, maturity, and sustainability. An economy that focuses on production will inherently be more constrained by planetary limits than an economy that focuses on creativity, maturity, and sustainability. If the name of the game is production, then society will constantly extract from the natural environment and over-exploit humans and animals. But, if we focus on creativity, maturity, and sustainability, then society will shift to more regenerative practices.

The result of a production-focused economy is more useless stuff. Likewise, production worship breeds profiteering and greed. If we want to sustain our cloud of interstellar dust, then we need to understand the constraints of our planet and shift away from a production-focused economy to an economy focused on creativity, maturity, and sustainability.

Without a focus on sustainability and long-term thinking, society is destined to continue repeating history. And at this moment in time, it is looking more and more like we will have a repeat of the Great Depression, which lasted from roughly 1929 to 1939. Except this time it is happening more insidiously. Looking back, there was a recipe for disaster that led to the Great Depression. That recipe included the Stock Market Crash of 1929, the Smoot-Hawley Tariff Act, bank failures, and some missteps by the Federal Reserve. The money supply had increased significantly in the decade before 1929, and then after the stock market crashed, the Federal Reserve cut the money supply by about a third, which created liquidity problems for banks and extended the economy's recovery time.

The President at the time was Herbert Hoover. There are quite a few similarities with the current Administration today. Hoover scapegoated

Mexican Americans, and he also led a major deportation initiative. Hoover advocated against intervening in the Russian Civil War in the name of saving lives. Hoover also appointed a Cabinet of largely wealthy businessmen, including Andrew Mellon, an industrialist that owned multiple energy and transportation related businesses. Mellon was also focused on reducing the national debt. And then there was the Smoot-Hawley Tariff Act that was intended to protect the American economy from foreign competition, which is obviously similar to what the Administration is trying to do at present in 2025. Most economists and economic historians, however, have continuously asserted that tariffs have the opposite impact and actually don't protect the American economy in the way they are intended to.

The turning point in the Great Depression, according to most economists and economic historians, was the beginning of Franklin Roosevelt's tenure in 1933 and the implementation of The New Deal. In the Presidential election of 1936, Franklin Roosevelt was re-elected and received over 60% of the popular vote and over 98% of the electoral vote. Pause for a moment and think about where we might be on a potentially similar or repeating timeline. I can't imagine the current Administration in 2025 changing course anytime soon. I would love to see a Presidential election where over 60% of Americans are on the same page.

During the pandemic, I thought we were on the verge of sliding into a Great Depression, but it also felt like there were enough elected leaders working together and rowing in the same direction so to speak that we might bounce back quicker than the country did after the Stock Market Crash of 1929. There had been conversations for at least a couple years about a Green New Deal, thanks to Congresswoman Alexandria Ocasio-Cortez and other young sustainability-minded leaders. I loved the idea of a Green New Deal, but until the pandemic, I never thought it would come to fruition.

## *A Tipping Point for Sustainability and Resilience*

Do you remember that "Tipping Point" book that was published decades ago? It was a mildly successful book by Malcolm Gladwell that describes how ideas, products, and messages eventually reach a moment of critical mass and then spread like viruses. In the wake of a global pandemic, I started to think society had reached a tipping point where we were all on the same page about investing in sustainability and resilience. For the longest time, it had seemed like conversations related to sustainability and resilience were limited to just a small group of thoughtful and committed citizens. But then, on November 15th, 2021, President Joe Biden signed into law the Infrastructure Investment and Jobs Act, also known as the Bipartisan Infrastructure Law.

The legislation included about $1.2 trillion in spending focused on sustainable infrastructure. It included $110 billion for roads and bridges, $11 billion for transportation safety, $39 billion to modernize urban transit, $66 billion for passenger and freight rail, $7.5 billion for a national electric vehicle charging network, $73 billion for power infrastructure, and $65 billion for broadband development. It also included over $25 billion for water infrastructure programs and $8 billion for Western states dealing with extreme drought. The Infrastructure Investment and Jobs Act represented the largest investment in sustainability and resilience ever in our history.

Imagine for a moment everyone in society rowing in the same direction towards an exciting, thriving, and sustainable future. What does that look like? Maybe we should back up and define sustainability. Here is my favorite definition:

*"Sustainability is living within the regenerative capacity of the Earth, so that the essential needs of present generations can be met without compromising the ability of future generations to meet their essential needs"*

—*Miriam Nielsen*

This is obviously a macro level definition of sustainability. People can also use the word sustainability to describe things at a micro level. For example, at the micro level, we could discuss the sustainability of a product, a business, a career, or an initiative. When talking about sustainability in the context of society, there are really three types of sustainability we are talking about.

*Environmental Sustainability* — This is probably the most important as it relates primarily to the habitability of the planet. When we talk about environmental sustainability, we are generally talking about things like emissions, O-zone depletion, ecosystem collapse, and ocean acidification. On the solution side, we are generally talking about things like renewables, utility-scale batteries, electric vehicles, reducing pollution and waste, maintaining biodiversity, and reforestation.

*Social Sustainability* — When we think about our long-term vision for society, there are certain social pillars that must be addressed like healthcare, shelter, and education. These pillars are vital to maintain quality of life for humanity across the globe.

*Financial Sustainability* — It is also important to think about sustainability through a financial systems lens. At a macro level, it is essential to consider the fragility and stability of markets and supply chains, the impact of massive unemployment on the whole system, and the consequences associated with a culture of extraction and exploitation. The economy is a subsidiary of the environment, and so if the environment collapses, so does the economy.

What the Bipartisan Infrastructure Law enabled was a once in a generation opportunity for states and local communities to think about sustainability in all of its dimensions. Most local communities don't have large sums of discretionary funds to invest in sustainability. An injection of capital from the federal government would allow local communities and states to adopt their own place-based visions of what an exciting, thriving, and sustainable future would look like. This is how we could get society rowing in the same direction, by giving state governments and local communities the money to invest in sustainable infrastructure.

The other massive benefit of the Bipartisan Infrastructure Law was that it would supercharge the *Purpose Economy*. In Aaron Hurst's book *The Purpose Economy*, he talks about the progression of the human economy over time. As we have evolved, so has our economy. We have gone from the Agrarian Economy to the Industrial Economy to the Information Economy. Aaron proposed in his 2014 treatise, our economy is evolving into the Purpose Economy where doing well and doing good are deeply interconnected. Aaron Hurst's Purpose Economy is fundamental to the third pillar of the Rainy Day Economics framework – human-centered capitalism.

In the Information Economy, work for most people had very little meaning. People in the Information Economy worked so that they could live. But this is changing in the Purpose Economy. In the Purpose Economy, people find meaning in their work, and they are committed to their work for reasons that go far beyond collecting a paycheck. People seek out work-life balance and work that allows them to not burnout. Likewise, in the Purpose Economy, people are navigating away from boring jobs and seeking out work that aligns with their values.

*"Burnout is being overwhelmed by work. Boreout is being underwhelmed by work. Having too much responsibility is exhausting. Having too little is deflating. Idle time and pointless tasks undermine energy. Motivation depends on balancing what's meaningful with what's manageable."*

*— Adam Grant*

So, what happens when the Purpose Economy changes from being a trend among Millennials to being a new operating condition for our entire economy? After the pandemic, there was a confluence of trends that was effectively supercharging the Purpose Economy. The pandemic may have caused a Great Resignation, where people en masse decided that their happiness was more important than a stable career trajectory. And heading into 2022, with the passage of a major infrastructure bill at the federal level in the United States, there was an opportunity for millions of Americans to plug into the Purpose Economy through sustainability-related jobs.

*"**Autonomy:** the urge to direct our own lives. **Mastery:** the desire to get better and better at something that matters. **Purpose:** the yearning to do what we do in the service of something larger than ourselves. These are the building blocks of an entirely new operating system for our businesses."*

*— Daniel H. Pink*

The Bipartisan Infrastructure Law wasn't the only source of purpose-driven money. Major corporations, cities, and large philanthropic foundations were all putting significant resources into creating a socially and environmentally sustainable economy that works for everyone. The new Purpose Economy was being designed to add value by doing good in the world. The focus on sustainability, including environmental, social and financial, was driving this transformation. Over the next few decades, the Purpose Economy was going to grow significantly in large part due to our collective action on issues related to sustainability.

Carbon Leaf is my favorite band, and they have a song called *"Life Less Ordinary"* that came out in 2004. The opening to the song starts with lyrics that seem relevant – *"Live a life less ordinary. Live a life extraordinary with me. Live a life less sedentary. Live a life evolutionary with me."*

This chapter was written on Valentine's Day (February 14th) 2025 as approximately 200,000 federal government employees were laid off before they were able to complete their first year of public service. It is difficult for me to imagine all of those 200,000 federal government employees finding meaningful purpose-driven work immediately after being abruptly fired.

# Chapter 16

## MEASURING WHAT MATTERS

### August 16, 2022

*"Distinctions must be kept in mind between quantity and
quality of growth, between costs and returns, and between
the short and long run. Goals for more growth should
specify more growth of what and for what."*

*- Simon Kuznets (considered by many economists to be the father of GDP)*

---

In March 2022, Buddy, Grizzly, and I left Virginia and headed west to live in Colorado for a short while. The 2020 Nissan LEAF, or my little electric spaceship as I affectionately refer to it, was not designed to traverse the American Heartland. It was designed for short daily commutes in suburbia. The modest 150-mile range is really more like 100–120 miles of range when you account for wind, hills, weight, air conditioning, the heat of the battery, and a number of other little things that add up. If you're smart though, you can stretch every mile of range out of your electric vehicle to make sure you make it to your next fast charging station as you travel across the country.

In the few very long days of travel from Charlottesville, the national charging network had failed me twice, which had added days to my trip, because if a fast charger doesn't work and you are in the middle of the country, your options are to slow charge your vehicle or get it towed.

I remember one particular leg of that long trip vividly. I had started off the day somewhere in between St. Louis and Kansas City. I stopped for lunch at the intersection of 47th and Mission at the famous Joe's Kansas City Bar-B-Que (I think it was once called Oklahoma Joe's), where there is always a long line, but of course there is no electric vehicle charger there. I made my way into Kansas and stopped at a charging station at Rock Chalk Park in Lawrence, Kansas. This was a great charging location, because there were extensive hiking trails at the park, and I was traveling with my dogs, so there was something to do to fill the time as I waited for my car to charge. We need more of this — more charging stations near trails, art museums, and local food hubs.

After charging in Lawrence, Kansas, I proceeded to charge in Topeka, Kansas, which is not that far, but the next leg after Topeka I knew was going to be a stretch. The stretch from Topeka to Salina, Kansas was just far enough to make me nervous with no backup charging spots in between. I turned off the air conditioning. I unplugged my phone. I turned on the e-brake. I basically tried to save as much power as I could, so that I could make sure I got to the next charging station in Salina, Kansas. It kind of felt like powering down the Lunar Excursion Module in Apollo 13. If you've seen the movie, you may remember Ed Harris and his team of NASA engineers problem solving to get the astronauts home. Power is everything.

### *"We gotta turn everything off, now!"*

Sure enough, I arrived at the Salina, Kansas fast charging station with eight miles of range to spare… and then the charger didn't work. My heart sank. This one broken charging station in the middle of the country embodied the sentiment of every person that wasn't ready to buy an electric vehicle. This was the argument for not buying an electric vehicle. You can't reliably venture out on a great American roadtrip without range anxiety and a high risk of a derailed journey.

So now what?

The fast charger was at a gas station. I had my portable charging cable with me, so I plugged into the 110-volt outlet on the outside of the building without asking permission. I got a few extra miles of range while I assessed the situation. There was another fast charger 30 miles south of Salina, but that would've just meant I'd be stranded 30 miles south of Salina instead, because the next closest fast charging stations would either be out of range of my little electric spaceship or they would've put me on a path to Texas instead of Colorado.

So, I had a choice. I could have my little electric spaceship towed to the next fast charging station two hours west of Salina in Hays, Kansas. Or, I could slow charge at a motel until my little electric spaceship could stand on its own two feet. It would take forever, but I'd still have my dignity… maybe. Hopefully someday there will be so many fast chargers in Kansas and the rest of the American Heartland that any yuppie in an electric golf cart or little electric spaceship will be able to make it across the country without any hiccups. Until then, slow charging at motels will have to do.

> ***Rainy Day Economics Design Prompt 19:*** *Develop a plan to build a reliable national charging network for a new wave of electric vehicle drivers. Make it so that anyone from anywhere in the country can traverse the American Heartland. How do we design and build new reliable and sustainable infrastructure systems?*

You may be wondering why I'm telling silly stories about traveling across the American Heartland in my little electric spaceship. How does this relate to Rainy Day Economics? I think it is a useful metaphor for how society travels through time relying on infrastructure, energy, and human ingenuity to complete a long journey while maintaining a quality of life that is enjoyable. We design our little electric spaceship to carry us through time, and we also design it to make the journey fun and sustainable.

## *A game of "Would you rather…"*

Have you heard of this game "would you rather…"? It is a simple game that some people like to play on road trips to spark interesting conversation and share a good laugh. It starts with one person coming up with a ridiculous "would you rather…" question. The idea is to make the question at least a little bit absurd. Pause for a moment and come up with a ridiculous "would you rather…" question, and then save it for your next conversation.

Comparing alternatives is something that we all do every day, sometimes without even thinking about it. And when it comes to policymaking, thoughtfully comparing alternatives is particularly important. And it seems like right now politicians are playing the "Would you rather…" game with us. Would you rather have high inflation and jobs or lower inflation and significantly less jobs? Would you rather have a large federal government that is imperfect or a smaller federal government that is less and less effective? Would you rather have a lower national debt or employ millions of people through the federal government? This is how the alternatives are being framed for society right now, but we shouldn't be playing this would you rather game. Instead we should be designing our economy with long-term human-centered goals in mind.

In this current moment in February 2025, it is as if the Administration is powering down the Lunar Excursion Module saying to Americans that this is the only way we survive. In this metaphor, the Lunar Excursion Module is the federal government, and "powering down" is firing millions or at least hundreds of thousands of federal government workers. The problem with this approach is that it could incite a Great Depression.

Objectively, this is a realistic outcome of the efforts of the Department of Government Efficiency. There are now very few checks and balances to the legacy party in power, which means that quick actions can be taken to cut federal spending and the size of the federal government. They have also committed to complete this work by July 4th, 2026, which should at least give us some sense for how quickly all of this will happen.

If the current Administration is successful in cutting over 30% of federal spending (in less than two years), that would result in the complete decimation of the regional economy of the Washington, D.C. metropolitan area. Virginia, Maryland, and the District of Columbia would face major shortfalls in tax revenue, and there would be an exodus from those states causing an economic free fall, at least regionally. The Washington metropolitan region would face unemployment rates exceeding 20%, and the regional real estate market would implode. And there is no guarantee or reason to believe that people will be able to just absorb the losses on their homes and go buy a home in another market, especially considering many of these people relocating won't have jobs right away.

Wouldn't cutting government spending help the United States as a whole? No. In the short run, there are no positive impacts to taxpayers associated with this effort. Any surplus created would go straight to paying down the national debt. Taxpayers would not receive any immediate financial benefit. The services that the federal government provides would decline in funding and therefore quality, and trust in our institutions would erode even quicker, which would then justify more cuts according to the Administration's thinking.

The private sector would not hire more with a sudden influx of recently fired government employees. The private sector would not suddenly have more spending power. There would be hundreds of thousands of customers that no longer have incomes due to recent layoffs. Consumer spending would decline significantly, and most corporations would feel the hurt and eventually layoff more workers as a result. This would be the beginning of a vicious cycle downwards.

Ironically, many states led by the legacy party in power will suffer the most from decimating the federal government. For example, over 50% of

Louisiana's state revenue in fiscal year 2022 was from federal government grants. In 2022, most of the southern states received federal grants that made up 30–40% of their state revenue. Do we honestly think that will be possible after the current Administration is done making deep cuts to federal government spending and the federal government workforce? Instead of causing rainy days for individuals, communities, and entire regions of the country, we need to focus on the third pillar of Rainy Day Economics, human-centered capitalism, and designing our economy with human-centered goals in mind.

## An alternative approach

Simple math tells us that we can't cut our way out of the national debt in any reasonable amount of time. What we need to do is focus on maximizing purpose-driven employment, optimizing our tax structure to help the poor and the middle class, and investing in entrepreneurial ecosystems and technological moonshot initiatives across the country while adopting a long-term approach to monetary policy.

Have you ever seen the movie *"Ford v Ferrari,"* starring Matt Damon and Christian Bale? On the surface, the movie is all about Ford's effort to build a fast car that beats Ferrari's fast car. But if we read deeper into the story, it was really about how Ford Motor Company was in a rut and trying to grow their company by innovating. There is no doubt that car companies have been the instigators of many wave layoffs, but in this particular story the project was focused on innovating.

In the movie, there is a scene where Matt Damon's character, Carroll Shelby, is waiting to see if he is getting fired. Shelby watches as a folder is passed through four pairs of hands before it is ultimately brought to Henry Ford II for consideration, which didn't include the "22 or so other Ford employees that probably poked at it before it made its way up to the

19th floor". Shelby then pointed out how inefficient and bureaucratic the Ford Motor Company was. He goes on to assert — "You can't win a race by committee."

At first glance, this scene is a good illustration of inefficient bureaucracy. The notion of 26 employees contributing to a relatively straightforward investment decision seems like a waste of resources, especially the last few hand-offs of the folder in the waiting room. But how wasteful was including 26 people in that decision and process? In the story, Carroll Shelby has been tasked with building the fastest car ever. This is something that the Ford Motor Company undoubtedly had the staff and knowledge capital to do internally, right? So, why even outsource the project to Carroll Shelby's team? And then after outsourcing it, why involve 26 employees in decisions related to the project? Does any of this make sense when you are trying to run an efficient, market-leading company?

Yes. It makes sense, and it was smart for Ford Motor Company to approach the project the way they did and involve as many people as they did. The Ford Motor Company at that time had over 150,000 employees. I think having 26 people involved in an ambitious, highly visible project makes total sense. You want smart people inside the company engaged in the process. You want to develop and maintain institutional memory. You want to start to think about longer-term plans, implication to other projects in the company, and new opportunities that are developing. And you want people to contribute to understanding lessons learned. So, then you might ask, why outsource the project to Carroll Shelby?

Carroll Shelby's qualifications were likely unmatched at the time, and he had been a part of a winning team at the 24 Hours of Le Mans in 1959. But there are other reasons to outsource for a project like this. In the movie, Henry Ford II asks (I'm paraphrasing) — "Do you think the United States federal government beat the Nazis in World War II?" The answer is of course "no." But the federal government did fund the Ford

Motor Company and others to build all of the capabilities needed to win. Outsourcing makes sense for a number of reasons including tapping into specialized capabilities, reducing costs, mitigating risks, and maintaining communities of practice.

The federal government's role in society is *not* to run a profitable business. It makes no sense to have business leaders decide what government programs, employees, agencies, departments, and initiatives should exist. They are instantly assuming the role of the bureaucrats they claim to despise, and making decisions that will undo decades of work and institutional memory. **The role of the federal government is not to make a profit.**

You cannot and should not approach federal government budgeting like a business. We are trying to do more than balance a budget. And there are people that were elected that are responsible for leading, compromising, and budgeting. And, all of the people that are being fired by the current Administration— they are taxpayers, they are members of local communities, they are Americans. The third pillar of Rainy Day Economics, human-centered capitalism, acknowledges that government is a force for good and plays a critical role in making sure that capitalism works for all of society not just the people at the top.

## *Inflation and the National Debt*

Did you know it costs more than a penny to make a penny? It also costs more than a nickel to make a nickel. What does this mean and why does it matter? This is one of many examples where government investment in societal architecture doesn't align with how businesses think about return on investment. The function of a penny is to represent the level of granularity of our currency and our prices in the market. If we eliminate the penny, our currency and prices become less granular, at least when we use cash. If something has a price of $0.99 now, then removing the penny from circulation would either cause the price to increase to $1.00 or would result in an imprecise transaction. A person paying $1.00 for a $0.99 product would not get a penny in return anymore.

At scale, this would translate to inflated prices and/or millions of imprecise transactions every year, which would also inherently be inflationary. And if the business minded return on investment analysis leads to eliminating the penny, then it would also lead to the elimination of the nickel. If you eliminate the nickel, then that is an even more significant inflation and/or even less precise transactions. There may be a path to keeping the same granularity in our currency and prices while getting rid of physical coins and shifting to digital currency. However, that transition would disproportionately hurt small businesses that are currently able to avoid certain digital processing fees by dealing in cash. Also, there are and would still be costs to maintaining and tracking digital currency. For now, we need pennies and nickels to continue being made.

There are many systems in society that are not meant to or are simply unable to generate a profit. A functioning society is an expensive endeavor. And governments of, by, and for the people are responsible for making sure we have a functioning society that works for everyone, not just the wealthy. Costs should not only be measured in dollars. We should also consider opportunity costs and how different actions will impact our way of life and our quality of life in the long term, and particularly on rainy days.

Eliminating pennies isn't the only way to cause inflation, obviously. Inflation is simply the general increase in prices of goods and services over time. Many people will point to monetary policy as the reason prices have gone up so much. However, there are many other causes of inflation that must be considered, including:

- Supply chain shocks
- Increased labor costs
- Increased demand

- Higher cost of inputs
- Changes in consumer expectations
- Increased import costs
- Increases in energy prices
- Higher risk profiles
- Uncertainty in the market
- Corporations increasing profit margins

We can ask a place-based question to dig deeper – *"Why is everything so much more expensive in this region compared to ten years ago?"* Well, consider each of the points above before blaming the Federal Reserve. Did the businesses in your region experience supply chain shocks during the pandemic? Did the minimum wage go up in your state? Have more people moved into the region where you live? Did your electric utility raise prices on energy? Are people less certain about the future than they were ten years ago? These are all questions that lead us to the conclusion that the Federal Reserve can only do so much to control inflation. The rest is up to fiscal policy at the federal, state, and local level.

President Biden signed the Inflation Reduction Act into law on August 16th, 2022. As the name would suggest, this legislation had a number of provisions that were intended to help reduce inflation. The legislation was designed with long-term sustainability in mind and included $891 billion in investments in sustainability and healthcare for communities across the country.

Some people right now are saying that to fight inflation, we need to increase supply. No. The answer to inflation is not to arbitrarily increase production and supply of everything that has ever been invented. The answer to inflation is to focus on long-term sustainability. Increasing supply is such a nearsighted solution. The systems we've built to run our economy are allowing inflation to happen. And it is conceivable that increasing supply just to fight inflation is going to exacerbate problems related to environmental sustainability, water scarcity, global trade, and poverty.

Instead of trying to manipulate the market in unnatural ways, why don't we design an economy that is inflation proof or at least more inflation resistant? This would be a likely outcome of utilizing Rainy Day Economics – an inflation resistant society, or perhaps a hyperinflation proof society.

Imagine for a moment you were starting at the beginning of the economy. Not the beginning of time, but the beginning of the economy. Is that too abstract? Ok, pretend thousands of people just landed on Mars, and they now want to jump start an economy. How would they design the economy to be inflation proof? How much money should exist on Mars?

This is the prompt we should be considering. We shouldn't be trying to wrestle inflation in the moment. We should instead just design a system that accounts for all of the global dynamics that can occur in society. We as humans with our great minds should be able to design an inflation-proof society even though we have a complex supply chain, numerous nation-state actors, constrained resources, and an ever-changing mix of companies providing products and services to the world.

You've probably heard of Ernest Rutherford. He won the Nobel Prize in Chemistry in 1908 "for his investigations into the disintegration of the elements, and the chemistry of radioactive substances." You are probably less familiar with Frederick Soddy who worked with Ernest Rutherford on those investigations and later proved the existence of isotopes of radioactive elements. Frederick Soddy also won the Nobel Prize in Chemistry, but not until 1921.

After winning the Nobel Prize in Chemistry, Frederick Soddy decided to take on the field of economics. His economic theories are more relevant today than ever before. Congress faces yet another cycle of deciding what to do about the debt ceiling, which seems like something that is going to continue to perpetuate uncertainty until we change the way we approach our national debt.

Frederick Soddy suggested that national debt had the potential to eat away at a nation's wealth, because of the exponential growth of debt. This makes sense. As our nation's debt grows, the payments on that debt become a larger and larger portion of the federal budget, which inherently means that money isn't going to things like infrastructure, education, and public health.

Soddy's economics are rooted in physics and have become the basis for the field of ecological economics, which is slowly seeping into mainstream economics by way of concerns related to environmental, social, and financial sustainability – the second pillar of Rainy Day Economics.

It should come as no surprise that financing multiple wars, a housing market crash, and a pandemic response will ultimately result in a ballooning and uncontrollable national debt. This spike in debt has really only become unsustainable over the course of a couple decades, which is a relatively short span of time. A number of questions arise from this massive debt problem.

Is it reasonable to expect a nation's annual budget to pay for a war? For many of us, the notion of true peacetime is a little bit foreign as the United States has been involved in the Middle East in different ways for so long. But, if a nation is to adopt the 'World Police' identity (or 'World First Responder' identity), then perhaps it is reasonable that we have such a large defense (or emergency response) budget. However, is it reasonable to allow war to undermine a country's financial well being? Probably not. So, how should countries financially prepare for the potential of war? Would it make sense to have a rainy day fund for the specific purpose of potential armed conflicts? Should wars be funded through taxes and debt, or should they be funded in new ways that don't bankrupt the country or rob future generations?

How do we plan for environmental and public health disasters (hurricanes and pandemics)? We are now keenly aware of the fragility of our economy. Disease and environmental sustainability are undoubtedly top of mind for intelligent policy makers. How do those risks translate to our approach to our national debt? We can't be beholden to a massive national debt in times of great crisis. We need to be able to respond effectively to pandemics and natural disasters without worry of financial ruin.

This also relates to how we think about society's capital investments versus operations and maintenance. Like many debts, it seems most of the national debt was incurred for line items that are not associated with operating and maintaining our society, but rather the national debt was largely incurred because of disruptive events like wars, a market crash, and a pandemic – rainy days. So, what does that say about our approach to debt? It says our approach is to not be prepared for anything and to simply finance the necessary reaction to whatever the world throws at us. This is shortsighted thinking and it will undoubtedly result in the deterioration of our country's wealth.

We obviously need a longer-term view of budgeting that includes paying for disruptive rainy day events like wars, market crashes, pandemics, and natural disasters. Perhaps a 100-year budget would be more effective than an annual budget. Long-term budgeting would be another likely outcome if we adopt Rainy Day Economics.

## *Gross Domestic Product vs. the American Scorecard*

Part of the reason that our national debt has ballooned is that we have prioritized the growth of Gross Domestic Product (GDP) over other measures of growth and performance. We use GDP as the singular measure of our economy's success, and that has only served to lead our society away from sustainability, human-centered capitalism, and resilience.

How do we measure the growth and performance of humans? Is it by how much we eat? Is it by how much we poop? Is it by how fast we run or how much weight we can lift? Is it by how well we perform on a cognitive test? The growth and performance of a human has thousands of different dimensions, everything from size to health to maturity to speed and strength. The growth and performance of humans is also contextual and dynamic. A human could grow in size while declining in athletic performance and improving in cognitive ability. We don't measure the growth and performance of humans using a singular measure, so why would we use a singular measure to articulate the growth and performance of our economy?

You've probably heard politicians and pundits talk about growing the economy. They might say something like "the economy grew by two percent last year." What does that mean? They are referring only to the Gross Domestic Product (GDP). They are not referring to anything else. GDP is the market value of all the final goods and services produced in a specific time period by a country. And the formula is the sum of consumption, investment, government expenditures, and net exports.

$$GDP = C + I + G + NE$$

It is important to note that all of these inputs have limits. In other words, in any given year, all of the elements of GDP have maximums. Consumption can't exceed certain levels based on income and debt tolerances. Investment can't exceed certain levels of available capital. Government expenditures can't exceed tax revenue and deficit tolerances. Net exports can't exceed total international demand for products and services. So, the notion of GDP increasing forever is limited by the maximum levels of the elements that make up GDP.

GDP is also not all good to begin with. Imagine all of the goods and services you pay for in a given year. Are they all goods and services that you are excited to pay for? For example, replacing broken windows, fixing broken bones, car maintenance, and medicine. In at least those examples, we know that decreasing the need for those goods and services would be good for society. In other words, if cars required less maintenance, because they were made better to last longer, society would be better off. Likewise, if a population is healthier and requires less medicine, society is better off, but wouldn't contribute as much to GDP. GDP also doesn't speak to negative externalities.

Consider the words of Simon Kuznets (father of GDP), one of the most influential economists of the 20th century. His work developing some of the first measures of national income eventually resulted in a Nobel Prize. Kuznets knew that any simplified measure of an economy could be abused and misused. As he put it:

> *"Distinctions must be kept in mind between quantity and quality of growth, between costs and returns, and between the short and long run. Goals for more growth should specify more growth of what and for what."*

There is this narrative that because GDP has historically grown at the same time as increases to quality of life, it is therefore the single most important measure of a country's economic health. Just because countries produced more goods and services while simultaneously improving the quality of life, does not mean that simply producing more goods and services will improve quality of life in the future. And in fact, this mindset has undoubtedly misguided policymakers and caused entire legislatures to put GDP on a pedestal and tout it as the purest distillation of economic performance. But nothing could be further from the truth.

People often describe a growth in GDP as a growth in the size of the economy, but that is perpetuating the wrong units. GDP can't be a measure of a size, because it doesn't have the appropriate units. The units of GDP are dollars per year, which indicates that it is a rate of activity. Therefore, a "rise" or "growth" in GDP is actually acceleration or a rate increase. This should make everyone wonder what we are accelerating toward. Are we accelerating toward a better tomorrow? An iceberg? A cliff?

Another way to think about GDP is to consider what would happen if the economy were to do the exact same thing from one time period to the next. Imagine that the economy goes through two time periods where it produces the exact same set of goods and services. If the market value (GDP) remains the same for the exact same set of goods and services, then this is a signal that the economy has not innovated or created any efficiencies over that time period. If the economy were to innovate and create efficiencies, then producing the exact same set of goods and services would have a lower market value (GDP) than the year before. If we hold everything else equal *(ceteris paribus)*, then we should expect that the market value of everything we produce (GDP) — associated with all of the goods and services that make up a quality life — will decline. *Moving forward, a maturing economy will be defined by a declining GDP as quality of life continues to improve for a population.*

In an increasingly complex society, we are using a single measure of economic success that was developed before we landed on the moon, before we understood our environment, before we built our interstate highway system, and before the Information Age. GDP doesn't measure anything related to the health of a population, the national debt, access to clean water, the poverty rate, environmental degradation, or access to high-quality education. And, we are seeing that GDP can grow while more and more Americans get left behind.

So, what is the solution? **An American Scorecard.** This solution would capture the multidimensional nature of economic success and societal wellbeing in America, and it would help redefine and build up human value. Andrew Yang introduced this concept in his 2020 Presidential campaign and identified a handful of metrics that could be used as a starting point for this conversation.

- Quality of life and health-adjusted life expectancy
- Happiness/Well-Being and Mental Health
- Environmental quality
- Affordability
- Childhood success rates
- Underemployment
- Income Inequality
- Consumer and Student Debt
- Work and civic engagement levels
- Volunteerism
- Infant mortality
- Quality of infrastructure
- Access to education
- Marriage and divorce rates
- Substance abuse and related deaths
- National optimism
- Personal dynamism/economic mobility

We could also add to this measures of effectiveness related to natural disaster response and recovery. If we prioritize and measure these things, then we will be more likely to see progress on multiple fronts. GDP has been dominating society's attention for decades. The era of the myopic pursuit of GDP growth must end. We need to focus on measuring what matters, especially on rainy days.

> ***Rainy Day Economics Design Prompt 20:*** *Develop an American Scorecard that includes all of the metrics you think necessary to measure the performance of our economy. How might we set and pursue societal goals to improve quality of life, particularly on rainy days?*

# Conclusion

## IT MIGHT BE THE RAINY DAY ECONOMY.
### November 5, 2024

*"Let us never forget that government is ourselves and not an alien power over us. The ultimate rulers of our democracy are not a President and Senators and Congressmen and government officials, but the voters of this country."*

— *Franklin D. Roosevelt*

---

My grandfather was born in 1921 in Indiana, and he grew up there during the Great Depression. He was a preacher's kid and a talented basketball player in high school and college. After serving in the Army Air Force during World War II, he spent the rest of his life as an educator, first as a teacher and basketball coach, then as a school principal and eventually as a professor at Indiana University. I spent a lot of time with him when he was in his 80s and 90s. In the last few years of his life, I noticed he would say this one phrase almost every time we would hang out. He would say, *"Just keep loving each other."* I think he started saying it so often because of who he was - a preacher's kid, a teacher, a coach, a principal, a professor, and a grandfather, and if people were going to remember one thing he said, then he wanted it to be a message of love. I think he also felt the need to say it more because the world was becoming more hateful. He passed away in 2017 a couple months after the tragedy in Charlottesville.

There are always going to be people that want to see the world burn, people that seek to do harm, people that are intent on tearing down society. And, there will always be rainy days. This book was written in the months immediately following the 2024 Presidential election in the United States. This particular paragraph that you are reading right now was drafted starting at 8:11 pm Eastern Standard Time on January 9th, 2025 as wildfires were devastating Los Angeles and the surrounding area in California. Los Angeles is the second most populated metropolitan region in the United States with over 12.5 million people living there. Anderson Cooper was again reporting on a disaster standing in front of homes that had burned to the ground with a smoke filled sky as he helped people tell their stories of survival and resilience. President Jimmy Carter's funeral service was held earlier in the day. President Carter was known for being honest, well meaning, and service-oriented.

> *"A fundamentalist can't bring himself or herself to negotiate with people who disagree with them because the negotiating process itself is an indication of implied equality."*
>
> *– President Jimmy Carter*

Just weeks before the fires in Los Angeles, there was an all too familiar threat of a federal government shutdown due to some political standoff. American politics is a broken record stuck on repeat. I've heard countless political pundits conclude that the results of the 2024 President election were directly related to the condition of the economy. I imagine the results of the 2028 Presidential election will also be directly related to the condition of the economy. I wonder what our elections would be about if the economy was in good condition for decades. What would it look like to have as our basic resting pulse an exciting, thriving, sustainable, and resilient economy that works for everyone?

Rainy Day Economics is about learning to thrive in hard times as individuals, communities, and as a society. The five pillars of Rainy Day Economics are just a starting point for a conversation.

1. **Design**
2. **Sustainability**
3. **Human-centered Capitalism**
4. **Resilience**
5. **The Arts**

It is my hope that this Rainy Day Economics framework will advance societal architecture, the systems we design, build, and iterate on together to improve quality of life for everyone, especially in the worst of times.

There will always be some form of rainy days in life, but we have the power to influence the scale and impact of those rainy days. We can stop some rainy days from happening. For other rainy days, there is no prevention mechanism. For all rainy days, we can design systems that make it more likely for people to recover quickly and thrive. However, it is difficult to design a system that helps people through tragedy and economic hardship when the current Administration is actively causing more economic hardship for millions of Americans, including farmers, teachers, students, nurses, the elderly, federal workers and of course the families of all of those people.

## *Friendly neighborhood government workers*

A few months before the Presidential election in 2024, I was out walking my dogs in the Washington, D.C. area. As you can imagine, walking two young dogs is sometimes an ordeal. As I was negotiating with and wrangling my dogs, a former Congresswoman that I knew I disagreed with politically walked by and said hi while clearly being amused by the sight of a grown man having a conversation with his dogs. My dogs and I had crossed paths with this Congresswoman before, and every time she was as friendly as any other neighbor, simply saying hello the same way every other neighbor does when I'm out walking my dogs.

Over the course of the second half of 2024 and into early 2025, the Congresswoman was in the news quite a bit. I've since reflected on how normal it was to cross paths with her in the Washington, D.C. area, and yet, for the over 98% of Americans that don't live in the Washington, D.C. area, crossing paths with a former Congresswoman from one of the most remote states would definitely be considered abnormal. Likewise, most Americans don't interact with and cross paths with federal government employees on a regular basis.

I think it is important for us to understand this dynamic. Many Americans will look at the Washington, D.C. metropolitan area and see a region that is more recession-proof than any other part of the country because of federal government spending. And I honestly think that is a point of extreme tension and resentment felt by the people in the Heartland of America that have been devastated by automation and globalization. However, I thought we were heading in the right direction after the pandemic when we had unprecedented investments in states and communities across the country for infrastructure, sustainability, public health, resilience, and economic development. And those programs were being implemented by public servants in the federal government for the benefit of people in the Heartland of America.

*Public Servant Oath of Office*

*"I will support and defend the Constitution of the United States against all enemies, foreign and domestic; that I will bear true faith and allegiance to the same; that I take this obligation freely, without any mental reservation or purpose of evasion; and that I will well and faithfully discharge the duties of the office on which I am about to enter. So help me God."*

By the time I finish writing this book, the President will have had significant time in his second Administration to do what he thinks is right for America. But I think he has already failed because of his inability to build consensus, or even attempt to build consensus. We need a consensus-driven leader now more than ever. We need to be rowing in the same direction on a lot of issues to make our society sustainable and resilient. We need to settle the political pendulum and move the ball forward.

## Finding the right frequency

They say our country has never been more divided. Perhaps it is because we've lost interest in consensus and working together. We've forgotten that government workers are out neighbors, our fellow Americans. We've become so focused on winning that we've forgotten what it means to be in community with each other. Our operating condition shouldn't be about winning elections. Rather, it should be about driving consensus. In order to move forward as a society, we can't keep debating issues the way we have been. Think of the Thanksgiving statements that come from your family.

> *"Let's just agree to disagree."*
> *"Well, I guess I'm just stupid."*
> *"You're just parroting Fox News or MSNBC garbage."*

All of these statements represent mentalities that generate stalemates in our one-on-one conversations and our national debates. These mentalities don't optimize the number of people that could potentially support ideas, policies, and the like. Instead of trying to simply win the conversation of the day, we should be trying to create ways of understanding each other. It is only through understanding each other that we will be able to change minds effectively.

My mother has had a hearing disability for as long as I can remember.

The challenge has always been finding the right frequency to communicate with her without raising our voices so much that it overwhelms her. I think this is the same challenge in political conversations. We are simply trying to find the right frequency that resonates with as many individuals as possible. Some frequencies will be common among large portions of the population. Other times, it will take deep exploration to find the right words that will resonate with particular portions of the population. Encouraging storytelling at the local level across the country is one way for us to understand our national mosaic and the tapestry of our country and how we weave together.

If we as individuals and society develop the skill of changing hearts and minds, then creating the changes we want to see in the world will become easier. Below are 10 strategies to help us build consensus.

1. ***Don't give up on the conversation before it starts.*** So often we find ourselves thinking there is no common ground. We need to put in the time and effort to wade through the nuance of an issue and discuss it at length.

2. ***Understand why it is important to have the debate.*** The "why" is about both the issue at hand and the reasons we should debate each other. We need to debate, because other people are the lenses through which we read our own minds. No matter how far apart or close together we are on an issue, it makes sense to debate and discuss to further understand how we as individuals and as a society think.

3. ***Define and unpack words and ideas as much as possible.*** So often we talk past each other, because we don't truly understand the concepts being talked about or how the person we are talking to understands those concepts. If we take the time to find common understanding of the foundational concepts related to any given

issue, then we are much more likely to at least understand each other.

4. ***Keep issues separate whenever possible.*** Most, if not all, issues are connected to other issues. It is easy for us to yell at each other about 10 different issues at once, but the more difficult task is to be intentional about which issue we want to talk about, and then spend the time focusing in on just that one issue.

5. ***Identify your own biases and assumptions. Distrust your own reason.*** This is often very hard to do. If we start from a position of righteousness, we will never find common ground.

6. ***Be intentional about having a debate.*** Don't argue for the sake of arguing. For some, arguing can be entertaining. Some people love to play "devil's advocate". And, some people, particularly in the media, get paid to argue. In our communities and our families, we need to have time away from television sets to debate in a meaningful way.

7. ***Stay calm, cool, and collected.*** The things we debate are important. So, it makes sense that people debating will debate passionately. But, sometimes the passion and emotion can make the debate personal when it doesn't need to be. Don't forfeit the passion, but understand the emotional nature of some of the issues we debate, and practice staying calm, cool, and collected as you seek to understand the points of view of others.

8. ***Don't try to win. Instead, try to find common ground.*** If our only goal is to make people agree with precisely what we believe the answer to be, then we will never actually change the way people think. If we approach our debates with the intention of finding common ground, then it is more likely that the people we are debating will understand the inner workings of our own minds. It is conceivable that someday some of the issues we debate over

and over again, could have a societal calculus. We could simply run the numbers on different policy ideas, and have logic and math prevail, but that will never be possible if it is always about one side winning and one side losing.

9. **Lead by example, and don't belittle the way someone else argues.** Everyone is different, and everyone thinks differently. So, if someone isn't making any sense to you, try to structure your arguments in a way that they might try to emulate. There are always better ways to explain things, and leading by example is the best way to debate. Belittling the way someone is arguing only makes them less likely to want to find common ground with you.

10. **Don't give up on the conversation when it ends, and tell the story of the debate to the next generation.** The world changes over time. Circumstances change. People change. So the result of any given debate is never final, and we should never sit back and act as if an issue is resolved permanently. History often repeats itself in no small part because we as a society forget things.

*"The great secret of succeeding in conversation is to admire little, to hear much; always to distrust our own reason, and sometimes that of our friends; never to pretend to wit, but to make that of others appear as much as possibly we can; to hearken to what is said and to answer to the purpose."*

— *Benjamin Franklin*

I know there are a lot of people in America that are hurting. And I know the federal government isn't perfect. But I really believe the federal government has a unique ability to make rainy days less bad. Individuals, local and state governments, nonprofits and businesses, they all have a role to play too. But the federal government is where we come together to address large complex societal problem sets and where we are able to develop unique capabilities at scale designed to address even the worst rainy days. The federal government is necessary for Rainy Day Economics to operate at the scale of societal problem sets, and at the scale of tragedies that impact our communities and our country. Focusing on the five pillars of Rainy Day Economics – design, sustainability, human-centered capitalism, resilience and the arts – will result in a better and more united America.

Whether it is a terrorist attack, a natural disaster, or any other kind of bad day – individuals, communities, states, regions and even other countries should be able to say with confidence – *"Don't worry. Help is on the way. The **United** States of America has our back. We're going to get through this. It's just another rainy day."*

~~The end.~~

…the middle…

# ACKNOWLEDGEMENTS

To my parents, thank you for connecting me with nature at an early age. Thank you for raising me in a community of public servants. Thank you for sending me to good public schools. Thank you for providing me with food, shelter, and healthcare growing up. Thank you for always being a safe haven. Thank you for enabling me to take risks. Your love has allowed me to live a meaningful life.

To my long time mentor, Jesús de la Garza, thank you for the numerous occasions when you've helped me navigate to the next phase of my career. You've been supportive of so many of my varied career and academic trajectories that undoubtedly inspired and informed much of the content of this book, as well as, the work I do today.

To my editor, Jeff Raderstrong, thank you for working with me on this project. From the early stages of developing this book, the opportunity to collaborate with you inspired me to get into a creative rhythm that was absolutely necessary to move this project forward. The accountability and thought partnership that you provided was vital.

To my cover designer, Katarina Naskovski, thank you for your creativity and patience. The cover art design served as motivation throughout the process of writing this book. Your ability to take an idea and translate it into something beautiful is truly inspiring.

To my friends, family, and colleagues that served as first readers on this project, thank you for taking the time to both read my work and challenge me to think differently. Your feedback continues to shape my perspective everyday.

To the readers, thank you for taking the time to read this book. Your willingness to entertain these stories, ideas, and opinions is a testament to your curiosity, compassion, and humanity.

# NOTES

## Chapter 0


1. Ellis, Carolyn, et al. "Autoethnography: An Overview." *Forum Qualitative Sozialforschung / Forum: Qualitative Social Research*, vol. 12, no. 1, 2011. *www.qualitative-research.net*, https://doi.org/10.17169/fqs-12.1.1589.

2. McDonough, William. *Cradle to Cradle Design. TED Talks. www.ted.com*, https://www.ted.com/talks/william_mcdonough_cradle_to_cradle_design.

3. Yang, Andrew. *The War on Normal People: The Truth about America's Disappearing Jobs and Why Universal Basic Income Is Our Future*. Hachette Books, 2019.

4. Bruneau, Michel. *The Blessings of Disaster: The Lessons That Catastrophes Teach Us and Why Our Future Depends on It*. Prometheus Books, 2022.

5. *Dead Poets Society*. Directed by Peter Weir, Touchstone Pictures, Silver Screen Partners IV, A Steven Haft Production, 1989.

6. *Fiscal Data Explains the National Deficit*. https://fiscaldata.treasury.gov/americas-finance-guide/national-deficit/. Accessed 17 May 2025.

7. "Homeland Security Budget | Costs of War." *The Costs of War*, https://watson.brown.edu/costsofwar/costs/economic/budget/dhs. Accessed 17 May 2025.

8. Wright, Robert E. *One Nation under Debt: Hamilton, Jefferson, and the History of What We Owe*. McGraw-Hill, 2008.

9. Lioy, Paul J., et al. "Characterization of the Dust/Smoke Aerosol That Settled East of the World Trade Center (WTC) in Lower Manhattan after the Collapse of the WTC 11 September

2001." *Environmental Health Perspectives*, vol. 110, no. 7, July 2002, pp. 703–14. *DOI.org (Crossref)*, https://doi.org/10.1289/ehp.02110703.

10. Carter, Brandon. "Jon Stewart Blasts Lawmakers In Hearing For Sept. 11 Victim Compensation Fund." *NPR*, 11 June 2019. *NPR*, https://www.npr.org/2019/06/11/731706492/jon-stewart-blasts-lawmakers-in-hearing-for-sept-11-victim-compensation.

11. *Measuring the Effects of the September 11 Attack on New York City - FEDERAL RESERVE BANK of NEW YORK*. https://www.newyorkfed.org/research/epr/02v08n2/0211rapa/0211rapa.html. Accessed 17 May 2025.

12. "Human Costs of U.S. Post-9/11 Wars: Direct War Deaths in Major War Zones | Figures | Costs of War." *The Costs of War*, https://watson.brown.edu/costsofwar/figures/2021/WarDeathToll. Accessed 17 May 2025.

# Chapter 1

1. Hazlitt, Henry. *Economics in One Lesson*. Arlington House Publishers, 1979.

2. U.S. Department of Defense. "Remembering Hurricane Katrina a Decade Later." *U.S. Department of Defense*, www.defense.gov/News/News-Stories/Article/Article/615149/remembering-hurricane-katrina-a-decade-later.

3. Bruneau, Michel. *The Blessings of Disaster: The Lessons That Catastrophes Teach Us and Why Our Future Depends on It*. Prometheus Books, 2022.

4. "AmeriCorps on the Front Lines of Disaster Recovery."

*AmeriCorps*, americorps.gov/newsroom/press-releases/2010/
americorps-front-lines-disaster-recovery.

5. Brinkley, Douglas. *The Great Deluge: Hurricane Katrina, New Orleans, and the Mississippi Gulf Coast.* 1. ed, Morrow, 2006.

6. National Association of Home Builders Research Center, Inc., et al. "A Case Study of the Mississippi Alternative Housing Program." *Executive Summary*, 2011, www.fema.gov/pdf/about/ programs/ahpp/ahpp_ms_cs_summary.pdf.

7. Center for Public Integrity. "FEMA Trailers Filled With Formaldehyde." *Center for Public Integrity*, 8 Jan. 2022, publicintegrity.org/politics/ fema-trailers-filled-with-formaldehyde.

8. "Building Back Better: New Orleans Public Schools" *USGBC* www.usgbc.org/resources/ building-back-better-new-orleans-public-schools.

9. NASA Earth Observatory. *New Orleans and Lake Pontchartrain* earthobservatory.nasa.gov/images/7311/ new-orleans-and-lake-pontchartrain

10. Roth, Lawrence H., P. E. ,. G. E. ,. F. ASCE and USACE IPET and ASCE's ERP. *The New Orleans Levees: The Worst Engineering Catastrophe in U.S. History – What Went Wrong and Why.* biotech.law.lsu.edu/climate/ocean-rise/against-the-deluge/01-new_orleans_levees.pdf.

## Chapter 2

1. Giovanni, Nikki, *Virginia Tech Magazine Memorial Issue.* www.archive.vtmag.vt.edu/memorial07/VTMagazinePDF/ convocation.8.pdf.

2. Hawke, Ethan. "Give Yourself Permission to

Be Creative." *TED Talks*, www.ted.com/talks/
ethan_hawke_give_yourself_permission_to_be_creative

3.  "Yankees Visit Va. Tech Memorial, Play Exhibition - ESPN."
    *ESPN.com*, 18 Mar. 2008, www.espn.com/mlb/spring2008/
    news/story?id=3299946.

# Chapter 3

1.  Dixson, Bob. "Sustainable Rebuilding Post Disaster | Bob
    Dixson | TEDxHerndon." *TEDx Talks*, 4 Aug. 2016, www.
    youtube.com/watch?v=9_gp1PM8yjQ.

2.  NOAA's National Weather Service. *Historical Kansas Tornado
    Statistics*. www.weather.gov/ict/kstorfacts.

3.  NOAA's National Weather Service, *Storm Report From the Udall
    Tornado*

4.  Smith, Michael R. "The Greensburg Miracle – Where there
    is life, there is hope." 20th Annual Lightning Detection
    Conference. 2008

5.  Taleb, Nassim Nicholas. *The Black Swan: The Impact of the
    Highly Improbable*. Random House, 2007.

6.  Hines, Andy, and Peter Bishop. *Thinking about the Future:
    Guidelines for Strategic Foresight*. Social Technologies, 2006.

7.  Pesner, Jeremy. "How to Predict the Future(s) | Jeremy Pesner
    | TEDxHerndon." *TEDx Talks*, 16 June 2017, www.youtube.
    com/watch?v=Yhlcj9rS_34.

8.  National Association of State Budget Officers (NASBO).
    "Budget Processes in the States." 2021.

9.  *Greensburg Sustainable Comprehensive Plan, May 2008*

## Chapter 4

1. De la Garza, J.M. "America's Lifelines | Jesus de la Garza | TEDxHerndon." *TEDx Talks*, 21 May 2016, www.youtube.com/watch?v=7hXy4W9PZrY.

2. Frost, Robert. "The Road Not Taken." Complete Poems of Robert Frost, edited by Edward Connery Lathem, Holt, Rinehart and Winston, 1969, pp. 105-106.

3. Gervásio, H., Jr., et al. "Guidelines to Perform Life Cycle Analysis of Bridges." *University of Coimbra*, 2000.

4. U.S. Department of Transportation and Federal Highway Administration. "2021 INFRASTRUCTURE REPORT CARD." *2021 INFRASTRUCTURE REPORT CARD*, infrastructurereportcard.org/wp-content/uploads/2020/12/Bridges-2021.pdf.

5. Minnesota Legislative Reference Library. *Economic Impacts of the I-35W Bridge Collapse*. 2008, www.leg.mn.gov/docs/2010/other/100687.pdf.

6. Bruneau, Michel. *The Blessings of Disaster: The Lessons That Catastrophes Teach Us and Why Our Future Depends on It.* Prometheus Books, 2022.

7. *Economy in Freefall, City Pages*. 5 Sept. 2007.

8. Scheck, Tom. "Rebuild May Begin in September." *MPR News*, 7 Aug. 2007, www.mprnews.org/story/2007/08/07/capitol.

9. *Governor Scott Authorizes Temporary Regulatory Relief to Expedite Emergency Response and Infrastructure Rebuild | Office of Governor Phil Scott.* governor.vermont.gov/press-release/governor-scott-authorizes-temporary-regulatory-relief-expedite-emergency-response-and.

10. National Governors Association. "Strategies to Address

Engineering Workforce Challenges." *National Governors Association*, 24 Aug. 2023, www.nga.org/publications/ strategies-to-address-engineering-workforce-challenges.

## Chapter 5

1. Associated Press. "'Joe the Plumber' Becomes Focus of Debate." *YouTube*, 16 Oct. 2008, www.youtube.com/ watch?v=PUvwKVvp3-o.

2. *Swing Vote.* Costner, Kevin., et al. Walt Disney Studios Home Entertainment, 2009.

3. McDonough, William, and Michael Braungart. *Cradle to Cradle: Remaking the Way We Make Things.* North Point Press, 2002.

4. McDonough, William. *Cradle to Cradle Design. TED Talks. www.ted.com*, https://www.ted.com/talks/ william_mcdonough_cradle_to_cradle_design

## Chapter 6

1. "Our Story." *Preservation Hall,* https://www.preservationhall. com/about/. Accessed 18 May 2025.

2. *Anderson Cooper | Tulane Commencement*, 2010. commencement.tulane.edu/archives/anderson-cooper.

3. CNN. "CNN: Survivors of Oil Rig Explosion Speak." *YouTube*, 5 June 2010, www.youtube.com/watch?v=70GhJqAazx0.

4. *Largest Oil Spills Affecting U.S. Waters Since 1969 | response. restoration.noaa.gov.* response.restoration.noaa.gov/oil- and-chemical-spills/oil-spills/largest-oil-spills-affecting-us- waters-1969.html.

5. "We Just Decided To." *The Newsroom.* Created by Aaron Sorkin, Season 1, Episode 1, HBO, 2012.

## Chapter 7

1. Aoki-Alcerro, Sayaka. "The Actual Meaning of Wabi-Sabi." *Nakamoto Forestry*, 30 Apr. 2024, nakamotoforestry.com/japanese-culture-the-actual-meaning-of-wabi-sabi.

2. *A Beautiful Mind*. Directed by Ron Howard, Universal Pictures, 2001.

3. McDonough, William. *Cradle to Cradle Design. TED Talks. www.ted.com*, https://www.ted.com/talks/william_mcdonough_cradle_to_cradle_design

4. NASA. "Asteroids, Comets & Meteors." *NASA Science*, 9 May 2025, science.nasa.gov/asteroids-comets-meteors.

## Chapter 8

1. MSNBC. "Chris Christie on Post-Sandy Obama Meet: 'I Would Do It Again' | Morning Joe | MSNBC." *YouTube*, 30 Aug. 2017, www.youtube.com/watch?v=YvCtA-8nf2k.

2. *Gun Ownership in America: 1973 to 2021*. Violence Policy Center, Nov. 2022, www.vpc.org/studies/ownership.pdf.

3. *Senator Robert F. Kennedy. Kansas State University, March 18, 1968*.

## Chapter 9

1. The Fund for Peace, et al. "Fragile States Index Annual Report 2023." The Fund for Peace, 2023, fragilestatesindex.org/wp-content/uploads/2023/06/FSI-2023-Report_final.pdf.

2. United Nations. "Ending Poverty | United Nations." *United Nations*, www.un.org/en/global-issues/ending-poverty.

3. Tut, Buey Ray. "Don't Just Teach a Man to Fish, Create a

Market For Him | Buey Ray Tut | TEDxOmaha." *TEDx Talks*, 17 Nov. 2014, www.youtube.com/watch?v=0hZm6iPi45w.

4. Gettleman, Jeffrey. *Love, Africa: A Memoir of Romance, War, and Survival.* Harper, 2017.

5. O'Regan, Catherine, et al. *Towards a Safer Khayelitsha.* 2014, www.masiphephe.org.za/wp-content/uploads/2021/08/ Khayelitsha_Commission_Report_WEB_FULL_TEXT_C.pdf.

6. Mansuri, Ghazala, et al. *Localizing Development: Does Participation Work?* The World Bank, 2013, https://doi. org/10.1596/978-0-8213-8256-1.

7. Gerardo Berthin, et al. *A Practical Guide to Social Audit as a Participatory Tool to Strengthen Democratic Governance, Transparency, and Accountability.* 2011, www.undp.org/sites/g/ files/zskgke326/files/migration/latinamerica/Practical-Guide-to- Social-Audit.pdf.

8. Fadell, Tony. "The First Secret of Design Is ... Noticing." *TED Talks*, www.ted.com/talks/ tony_fadell_the_first_secret_of_design_is_noticing.

## Chapter 10

1. Stevenson, Bryan. "We Need to Talk About an Injustice." *TED Talks*, www.ted.com/talks/ bryan_stevenson_we_need_to_talk_about_an_injustice.

2. Zacarías, Karen. *Native Gardens.* Concord Theatricals, 2019.

3. Mitchell, Tom. "Stillbrave: One Father's Journey to Accept the Unacceptable | Tattoo Tom Mitchell | TEDxHerndon." *TEDx Talks*, 3 Apr. 2015, www.youtube.com/watch?v=5wyXEDuau14.

4. Mitchell, Tom. "Redefining What Life Is About in

America." *Carbon Radio*, 9 Jan. 2019, www.youtube.com/
watch?v=N-Riiq-cm6U.

5. Buxhoeveden, Stephanie. "Thriving in the Face of Adversity |
Stephanie Buxhoeveden | TEDxHerndon." *TEDx Talks*, 3 Apr.
2015, www.youtube.com/watch?v=zuLOT6GsAxw.

6. Giridharadas, Anand. "A Tale of Two Americas. And the Mini-
mart Where They Collided." *TED Talks*, www.ted.com/talks/
anand_giridharadas_a_tale_of_two_americas_and_the_mini_
mart_where_they_collided.

7. Driver, Adam. "My Journey From Marine
to Actor." *TED Talks*, www.ted.com/talks/
adam_driver_my_journey_from_marine_to_actor.

8. Guterres, António. "Refugees Have the Right to
Be Protected." *TED Talks*, www.ted.com/talks/
antonio_guterres_refugees_have_the_right_to_be_protected.

9. Lazarus, Emma. *The New Colossus*.

# Chapter 11

1. Carroll, Antionette. "Designing for Justice." *TED Talks*, www.
ted.com/talks/antionette_carroll_designing_for_justice.

2. Roy, Elise. "When We Design for Disability, We
All Benefit." *TED Talks*, www.ted.com/talks/
elise_roy_when_we_design_for_disability_we_all_benefit

3. "The Iron Throne." *Game of Thrones*. Created by David Benioff
and D.B. Weiss, Season 8, Episode 6, HBO, 2019.

4. "U.S. History: How Teaching America's Past Varies Across The
Country." *CBS News*, 19 Feb. 2020, www.cbsnews.com/news/
us-history-how-teaching-americas-past-varies-across-the-country.

5. Matthews, Crys. "Sing, Don't Shout — an Alternative Approach

| Crys Matthews | TEDxHerndon." *TEDx Talks*, 13 June 2017, www.youtube.com/watch?v=s5Sb1dZq2gk.

## Chapter 12

1. Allen, Greg. "In Puerto Rico's Debt Crisis, There Are No Easy Solutions." *NPR*, 5 May 2015, www.npr.org/2015/05/05/403290738/ in-puerto-ricos-debt-crisis-there-are-no-easy-solutions.

2. "Puerto Rico Lawmakers Approve Sales Tax Increase; Gov Expected to Sign Bill." *US News & World Report*, 26 May 2015, www.usnews.com/news/business/articles/2015/05/26/ puerto-rico-lawmakers-give-final-nod-to-sales-tax-increase.

3. Attanasio, Cedar. "Puerto Rican Students Protest Gov. Alejandro Garcia Padilla's Education Cuts Amid Debt Crisis." *Latin Times*, 14 May 2015, www.latintimes.com/puerto-rican-students-protest-gov-alejandro-garcia-padillas-education-cuts-amid-debt-316593.

4. "Puerto Rico Sees Historic Population Drop as More Come to U.S." *NBC News*, 11 June 2015, www.nbcnews.com/news/ latino/puerto-rico-sees-historic-population-drop-more-come-u-s-n177501.

5. "Governor's Office of Foundation Liaison." *Council of Michigan Foundations*, 6 May 2025, www.michiganfoundations.org/ policy/governors-office-foundation-liaison.

6. Andrés, José. "How We Fed an Island After Hurricane Maria Hit Puerto Rico." *TED Talks*, www.ted.com/talks/jose_andres_ how_we_fed_an_island_after_hurricane_maria_hit_puerto_ rico.

7. Bruneau, Michel. *The Blessings of Disaster: The Lessons That*

*Catastrophes Teach Us and Why Our Future Depends on It.* Prometheus Books, 2022.

## Chapter 13


1. Hugo, Victor. *Les Miserables.* Penguin UK, 1982.

2. Simon, Robert E., Jr. "Reston Founder Robert Simon Shares His Inspiration Behind Building the Town Centers - Washingtonian." *Washingtonian - The website that Washington lives by.*, 21 Sept. 2015, www.washingtonian.com/2015/09/21/reston-founder-robert-simon-shares-his-inspiration-behind-building-the-town-centers.

3. Yang, Andrew. *The War on Normal People: The Truth about America's Disappearing Jobs and Why Universal Basic Income Is Our Future.* Hachette Books, 2019.


## Chapter 14


1. Dalton, Michael, et al. "The K-Shaped Recovery: Examining the Diverging Fortunes of Workers in the Recovery From the COVID-19 Pandemic Using Business and Household Survey Microdata." *BLS WORKING PAPERS*, 536, July 2021, www.bls.gov/osmr/research-papers/2021/pdf/ec210020.pdf.

2. Dickens, Charles. *A Tale of Two Cities.* Omni Publishing, 2019.

3. Kelton, Stephanie. *The Deficit Myth: Modern Monetary Theory and the Birth of the People's Economy.* PublicAffairs, 2020.

4. "MONIAC and Bill Phillips." *Engineering NZ*, www.engineeringnz.org/programmes/heritage/heritage-records/moniac-and-bill-phillips.

5. "We Just Decided To." *The Newsroom.* Created by Aaron Sorkin, Season 1, Episode 1, HBO, 2012.

## Chapter 15

1.  "Infrastructure Investment and Jobs Act." *US Department of Transportation*, www.transportation.gov/infrastructure-investment-and-jobs-act.
2.  Hurst, Aaron. *The Purpose Economy: How Your Desire for Impact, Personal Growth and Community Is Changing the World*. Elevate Publishing, 2014.

## Chapter 16

1.  Howard, Ron, dir. Apollo 13. Perf. Tom Hanks, Kevin Bacon, Bill Paxton, and Ed Harris. Universal, 1995.
2.  Thiess, Rebecca, et al. "Record Federal Grants to States Keep Federal Share of State Budgets High." *The Pew Charitable Trusts*, 10 Sept. 2024, www.pewtrusts.org/en/research-and-analysis/articles/2024/09/10/record-federal-grants-to-states-keep-federal-share-of-state-budgets-high.
3.  *Inflation Reduction Act of 2022 | Internal Revenue Service*. www.irs.gov/inflation-reduction-act-of-2022.
4.  James, Mangold et al., Ford v Ferrari. 20th Century Fox Home Entertainment, 2020.
5.  Yang, Andrew. *The War on Normal People: The Truth about America's Disappearing Jobs and Why Universal Basic Income Is Our Future*. Hachette Books, 2019.